China's Belt and Road Initiative

Understanding the Dynamics of a Global Transformation

Series on China's Belt and Road Initiative

Print ISSN: 2591-7730
Online ISSN: 2591-7749

This book series showcases the most up-to-date and significant research on China's Belt and Road Initiative (BRI) by leading scholars from inside and outside China. It presents a panoramic view on the BRI, from the perspectives of China's domestic policy, China's foreign investment, international relations, cultural cooperation and historical inheritance. As the first English book series on the BRI, this series offers a valuable English-language resource for researchers, policymakers, professionals and students to better understand the challenges and opportunities brought by the BRI.

Published:

Vol. 7 *China's Belt and Road Initiative: Understanding the Dynamics of a Global Transformation*
edited by CHAY Yue Wah, Thomas MENKHOFF and Linda LOW

Vol. 6 *The Belt and Road Initiative in the Global Context*
edited by WANG Linggui and ZHAO Jianglin

Vol. 5 *China's Belt and Road Initiative and Building the Community of Common Destiny*
edited by WANG Linggui and ZHAO Jianglin

Vol. 4 *Belt and Road Initiative: Chinese Version of "Marshall Plan"?*
by FENG Da Hsuan and LIANG Hai Ming

Vol. 3 *Silk Road: The Study of Drama Culture*
by LI Qiang
translated by GAO Fen

For the complete list of volumes in this series, please visit
www.worldscientific.com/series/scbri

Series on China's Belt and Road Initiative – Vol. 7

China's Belt and Road Initiative
Understanding the Dynamics of a Global Transformation

Edited by

CHAY Yue Wah
Singapore University of Social Sciences, Singapore

Thomas MENKHOFF
Singapore Management University, Singapore

Linda LOW
Singapore University of Social Sciences, Singapore

World Scientific

NEW JERSEY · LONDON · SINGAPORE · BEIJING · SHANGHAI · HONG KONG · TAIPEI · CHENNAI · TOKYO

Published by

World Scientific Publishing Co. Pte. Ltd.
5 Toh Tuck Link, Singapore 596224
USA office: 27 Warren Street, Suite 401-402, Hackensack, NJ 07601
UK office: 57 Shelton Street, Covent Garden, London WC2H 9HE

Library of Congress Cataloging-in-Publication Data
Names: Chay, Yue Wah, editor. | Menkhoff, Thomas, editor. | Low, Linda, editor.
Title: China's belt and road initiative : understanding the dynamics of a global transformation / [edited by] Yue Wah Chay (Singapore University of Social Sciences, Singapore), Thomas Menkhoff (Singapore Management University, Singapore), Linda Low (Singapore University of Social Sciences, Singapore).
Description: New Jersey : World Scientific, [2019] | Series: Series on China's Belt and Road Initiative ; vol. 7 | Includes bibliographical references.
Identifiers: LCCN 2019006782 | ISBN 9789811203268 (hardcover)
Subjects: LCSH: China--Commercial policy. | China--Commerce. | China--Foreign economic relations. | Economic development--China. | Economic development--Developing countries.
Classification: LCC HF1604 .C45255 2019 | DDC 382/.30951--dc23
LC record available at https://lccn.loc.gov/2019006782

British Library Cataloguing-in-Publication Data
A catalogue record for this book is available from the British Library.

For any available supplementary material, please visit
https://www.worldscientific.com/worldscibooks/10.1142/11354#t=suppl

Desk Editor: Jiang Yulin

Typeset by Stallion Press
Email: enquiries@stallionpress.com

Printed in Singapore

List of Contributors

Batzhan Akmoldina is the Director of the Center of Social-demographic Development Research at JSC Economic Research Institute, Ministry of Economy, Republic of Kazakhstan. Her Ph.D. dissertation topic is entitled *The Mechanism of Increasing Household Welfare of Small Towns in the Republic of Kazakhstan* (2009). She has participated in scientific research on numerous projects including "Assessment of the Impact of Measures and Decisions taken by Local Executive Bodies on the Social Well-being of the Population" (2017), "Expert and Analytical Support for the Development of a Program to Stimulate the Export Potential of the Republic of Kazakhstan" (2017), "Improving Migration Policy in the Republic of Kazakhstan" (2014–2015), "Prospects for the Development of the Labor Market and the Formation of an Effective Employment Policy of the Republic of Kazakhstan" (2014), "Analysis of the Feasibility of Introducing a Progressive IIT in Conditions of Kazakhstan and the Possible Effect on the Economy" (2010), "Analysis of the Factors of Economic Development and Macroeconomic Forecast for 2010–2014 Years" (2009). She was a member of the UNDP Project (2016) studying regional differences and non-equality in Kazakhstan. Dr. Batzhan was country consultant in 2015–2017 for the ADB and contributed an article, "Employment Policy and Labor Market in Kazakhstan". Her email: akmbat@mail.ru.

Sara Alpysbayeva is the Director of the Center for Macroeconomic and Applied Quantitative Economic Research at the Economic Research Institute JSC, a think tank under the Ministry of National Economy of Kazakhstan. Professor Alpysbayeva is a Member of the Council under the Prime Minister and has been a consultant for the ADB, OECD and World Bank. She has published extensively and received numerous grants from the Ministry of Education and Science for projects related to economic growth determinants, macroeconomic forecasting, multiplier effects of the integration processes within the CIS countries, human capital formation and development of research methods to tackle social modernisation of Kazakhstan including education, health, labour, employment and social protection. Her email: zhanna.kapsalyamova@nu.edu.kz.

Chay Yue Wah, Singapore University of Social Sciences, has held various faculty and administrative appointments at the National University of Singapore, Singapore Management University (SMU), Nanyang Technological University and SIM University. A psychologist by training, he has published in the areas of entrepreneurship, work commitment, citizenship behaviour, expatriation and technology. His current research interests are focused on innovation and the historical development of maritime ports. His email: ywchay@suss.edu.sg.

Dai Shiyan is the Deputy Director of the Nanyang Centre for Public Administration (NCPA), Nanyang Technological University, Singapore. He holds a Ph.D. in Management and Organisation and a Master's degree in Business Administration (MBA) from National University of Singapore. His 40 years of work experience in China, the United States, and Singapore spans academia, journalism, executive training and consultancy. Over the past two decades, he has, apart from his current capacity as a senior administrator, been engaged in the training and consultancy sector. His professional expertise comprises fields of talent assessment and development, strategic human resource development and management, organisational change management, crisis management and communications. His email: sydai@ntu.edu.sg.

Christopher M. Dent is a Senior Lecturer in Economics and International Business at Edge Hill University, which he joined in 2018 after having previously held positions at the Universities of Leeds, Hull and Lincoln. For most of his professional career, he has studied the impact of the East Asia region (China, Japan, Korea and Southeast Asia) on the global economic system, especially with regards to trade and trade diplomacy, energy, climate change, sustainable development, regional integration and international business. He has conducted scholarly work in over 40 countries and has acted as a consultant advisor to the governments of numerous European and Asian countries (including the USA), as well as the Asian Development Bank (ADB), European Commission, ASEAN Secretariat, Asia-Pacific Economic Cooperation (APEC) Secretariat, Secretariat for Central American Economic Integration and Nike Incorporated. He has been an invited speaker at numerous international conferences and is widely published, with 14 books (seven single-author monographs) and over 100 papers, reports and other publications. He has been on the editorial board of four journals, an external examiner for undergraduate and postgraduate programmes at five universities and has supervised a number of Ph.D. students. His email: christopher.dent@edgehill.ac.uk.

Andrew Elek is a Visiting Research Fellow of the Crawford School of Economics and Government at the Australian National University (ANU). He has worked extensively in development economics in South Asia and the South Pacific, and as a Senior Economist with the World Bank. He worked for the Australian Government from 1985 to 1990. In 1989, he was the Inaugural Chairman of APEC Senior Officials, with a central role in the establishment of the APEC process. From 1990 to 1994, he was a Senior Research Fellow at the ANU. Since then, Andrew has been a self-employed economic policy researcher and part-time consultant. He has published many papers on international economics and economic cooperation, including APEC, the G20 and the Belt and Road Initiative. Dr. Elek was appointed a Member of the Order of Australia in 1991, for service to international relations. His email: elek@netspace.net.au.

Abdul Rahman Embong, Ph.D., is Emeritus Professor in Sociology of Development at the Institute of Malaysian and International Studies (IKMAS), Universiti Kebangsaan Malaysia (UKM), where he served as a Principal Research Fellow for more than two decades until his retirement in January 2018. From 2000 to 2010, he was President of the Malaysian Social Science Association (PSSM) and has since served as the Association's Special Adviser. His research focus is on development, middle class, ethnicity, corruption and integrity and globalisation. He has written many books, journal articles and chapters in books. Some of his important works include: *State-led Modernization and the New Middle Class in Malaysia* (Palgrave, 2002), *Globalisation, Culture and Inequalities: In Honour of the Late Ishak Shari* (ed. Penerbit UKM, 2004), *Transforming Malaysia: Dominant and Competing Paradigms* (ed. with Anthony Milner & Tham Siew Yean, ISEAS, 2014), *Connecting Oceans: Malaysia as a Maritime Civilization* (ed. with Hans-Dieter Evers & Rashila Ramli, Penerbit UKM, 2019). His email: rahmanhe@ukm.edu.my.

Hans-Dieter Evers is an Emeritus Professor of development planning, University of Bielefeld, Senior Fellow, Center for Development Research (ZEF), University of Bonn, and 2015–2018 Pok Rafeah Distinguished Chair Professor, IKMAS, UKM. He was formerly Professor and Head, Department of Sociology, University of Singapore, Associate Professor of Sociology and Director of Southeast Asian Studies, Yale University, and held Visiting Appointments (among others) at Universitas Indonesia, Universitas Gajah Mada, Chulalongkorn University, National University of Singapore, SMU, University of Hawaii and Oxford University. He specialises in urban and maritime sociology, development studies and knowledge management. He is the author of *Sosiologi Perkotaan* (Jakarta: LP3ES, 1982), *Strategische Gruppen* (Berlin, 1988) and several other books. Among his recent co-edited books are: *The Straits of Malacca: Knowledge and Diversity* (Berlin, 2008), *Living in Smart Cities: Innovation and Sustainability* (London, Singapore, Beijing, 2018), *Governing and Managing Knowledge in Asia* (Singapore, 2010, 3rd edn., 2019), *Catalyst for Change. Chinese Business in Asia* (London, Singapore, Beijing, 2014) and *Connecting Oceans: Malaysia as a Nusantara Civilization* (Bangi, 2018). He is also the author of many articles on social theory, urban sociology, Southeast Asia and the South China Sea. His email: hdevers@gmail.com.

Shintaro Hamanaka is currently Overseas Fellow of the Institute of Developing Economies of Japan External Trade Organization (IDE-JETRO), based in Washington, D.C. He holds a Visiting Fellowship at Reischauer Center for East Asian Studies at the School of Advanced International Studies (SAIS), Johns Hopkins University. Before joining the IDE-JETRO in 2016, he worked for the ADB for eight years. Between 2006 and 2008, he was involved in the Doha Round services trade negotiations at the Japanese Mission to the World Trade Organization (WTO) in Geneva. He also worked for Bank of Japan for eight years and was involved in economic research and policy-making on regional financial cooperation in Asia soon after the Asian financial crisis. He is the author of *Asian Regionalism and Japan: The Politics of Membership in Regional Diplomatic, Financial and Trade Groups* (Routledge, 2009), and *Asian Free Trade Agreements and WTO Compatibility* (World Scientific, 2014). Shintaro has a Ph.D. from the University of Sheffield. His email: Shintaro_Hamanaka@ide.go.jp.

Gary Hawke was the Head of the School of Government and Professor of Economic History at Victoria University of Wellington. He held visiting appointments at Stanford University, All Souls' College, Oxford, the ANU, and a number of institutions in Japan. He is a Fellow of the Royal Society of New Zealand, Distinguished Fellow of the NZ Association of Economists and Fellow of the Institute of Public Administration of New Zealand. He is a Companion of the New Zealand Order of Merit. He consults for government on education policy. Gary is a member of the board of the New Zealand Committee of the Pacific Economic Co-operation Council, NZPECC, and a member of the Academic Advisory Council of the Economic Research Institute for ASEAN and East Asia, and represents NZ Institute for Economic Research on its Research Institutes Network. He is now Emeritus Professor, Victoria University of Wellington, and Senior Fellow, NZ Institute of Economic Research. His email: gary.hawke@vuw.ac.nz.

Zhanna Kapsalyamova is an Assistant Professor of Economics at Nazarbayev University. During her past career she worked as a Deputy Director of the Center for Macroeconomic Research and Quantitative Economic Modeling at the Economic Research Institute under the Ministry of National Economy of Kazakhstan. She was a Fulbright Visiting Scholar at Massachusetts Institute of Technology and post-doctoral research associate at the Masdar Institute of Science and Technology in the United Arab Emirates. In the past she worked as part-time consultant for the DIW ECON, OECD and World Bank. She holds her Doctoral degree in Economics from Christian Albrechts University of Kiel. Her research interests lie in Energy Economics, Environmental Economics, and Computable General Equilibrium Modeling. Her email: zhanna.kapsalyamova@nu.edu.kz.

Li Mingjiang is an Associate Professor at the S. Rajaratnam School of International Studies (RSIS), Nanyang Technological University, Singapore. He is also the Coordinator of the China Program at RSIS. He received his Ph.D. in Political Science from Boston University. His main research interests include Chinese foreign policy, Chinese politics, China–ASEAN relations, Sino–US relations and Asia-Pacific security. He is the author (including editor and co-editor) of 13 books. His recent books are: *China's Economic Statecraft* (World Scientific, 2017) and *New Dynamics in US–China Relations: Contending for the Asia Pacific* (lead editor, Routledge, 2014). He has published papers in various peer-reviewed outlets including *Asian Security*, *Oxford Bibliographies*, *Journal of Asian Security and International Affairs*, *Journal of Strategic Studies*, *Global Governance*,

Cold War History, *Journal of Contemporary China*, *Chinese Journal of International Politics*, *Chinese Journal of Political Science*, *China: An International Journal*, *China Security*, *Harvard Asia Quarterly*, *Security Challenges* and *International Spectator*. Dr. Li frequently participates in various track-two events on East Asian regional security. His email: ismjli@ntu.edu.sg.

Deborah Lim is a student at UCLA. She has interned in various investment banks and asset management firms where she worked on private equity and M&A transactions. Her email: deborahlim@g.ucla.edu.

Joseph Lim is an Associate Professor at the Singapore University of Social Sciences where he teaches Finance. He has also taught at the National University of Singapore and the SMU. Joseph spent several years in the finance industry working for a Fortune 500 company and advisory firms, advising on private equity, valuation and public investments. Joseph, who is a CFA charter holder, is a past president of CFA Singapore. He has served in various committees at the CFA Institute, the Investment Management Association of Singapore (IMAS) and the Securities Investors Association of Singapore (SIAS). He was on the board of the National University of Singapore Academic Staff Provident Fund and was board member of two Singapore National Eye Centre endowment funds. His email: josephlimys@suss.edu.sg.

Linda Low, Associate Professor, Singapore University of Social Sciences, started in the Ministry of Finance, Singapore doing tax research before joining the National University of Singapore, then became a Senior Research Fellow at the Institute of Southeast Asian Studies (now Yusof Ishak Institute, Singapore). For eight years, she was the Head of Strategic Planning in Abu Dhabi Government (United Arab Emirates, UAE) and Senior Economic Adviser for Abu Dhabi Council for Economic Development as well as Adjunct Professor at UAE University and UAE Higher Colleges for Technology. Her research includes public sector economics and public policy, public enterprises and privatisation, social security and retirement, ageing, health economics, human resources development and manpower policies, international trade and regionalism, international political economy and development economics, with publications in Asia-Pacific, Association of Southeast Asian Nations (ASEAN) and Gulf Cooperation Council (GCC). She works with the Asia-Pacific Economic Cooperation (APEC) and Asia-Pacific Economic Cooperation Council (PECC). She also collaborates with National Trades Union Congress (NTUC) and Singapore Civil Service College for skills training. Her email: lindalowls@suss.edu.sg.

Thomas Menkhoff is a Professor of Organisational Behavior & Human Resources (Education) at the Lee Kong Chian School of Business, SMU. Between 2013 and 2018, he served as the Academic Director of SMU's Master of Science in Innovation Programme. Three of his edited publications are *Catalyst for Change — Chinese Business in Asia* with Chay Yue Wah, Hans-Dieter Evers and Hoon Chang Yau (World Scientific, Singapore, 2014); *Governing and Managing Knowledge in Asia* with Hans-Dieter Evers and Chay Yue Wah (3rd revised edition, 2019, forthcoming) and *Living in Smart Cities: Innovation and Sustainability* with Kan Siew Ning, Chay Yue Wah and Hans-Dieter Evers (World Scientific, Singapore, 2018). His email: thomasm@smu.edu.sg.

Pan Zhengqi is a Lecturer in the School of Business, Singapore University of Social Sciences. He earned his Ph.D. from the University of North Carolina at Chapel Hill and received his post-doctoral training at the National University of Singapore's Global Production Networks Center. His broad research agenda relates to the politics of international trade. In particular, he is interested in the institutional governance of trade and global production networks by major political actors such as the state and intergovernmental organisations. Moreover, he bases most of his work on the regions of Northeast and Southeast Asia, given the regions' strategic state-led developmentalism and meteoric rise as a global manufacturing hub. Together, his research offers insights to both the dynamics of Asian state–business relations and the role that international organisations play in an increasingly complex and interconnected world. He has published research on international trade, international organisations and strategic innovation partnerships. His email: zqpan@suss.edu.sg.

Rashila Ramli is a Principal Fellow, Professor of Political Science and former Director at the IKMAS, UKM. Her areas of specialization are Political Development, Gender and Politics and Human Security. Her current research focus centres on the Governance of the South China Sea and its implication on ASEAN, Promoting Social Inclusion through Public Policies and Global ASEAN. Three selected publications are: *Towards a Region of Peace: Dynamics of Southeast Asia and the South China Sea* (2018), *Human Security in Archipelagic Southeast Asia*, 2015 (with Sity Daud and Zarina Othman) and *Social Constructivism and Malaysia's International Relations*, *Akademika*, Vol. 8, No. 1: 39–51, 2011. Her professional appointments and engagement include, among others, PSSM, member of the Council of Security Cooperation in Asia-Pacific (CSCAP) Malaysia, and Assistant Sec-General of the National Council for Women's Organizations (NCWO), Malaysia. Her email: rashila@ukm.edu.my.

Wang Xiangquan is an Associate Professor of Jilin University Sports Institute and Master Instructor. His main research interests are in population and health. Dr. Wang hosted the Jilin Provincial Social Science Fund Project, participated in the National Social Science Fund Project and the Ministry of Education Humanities and Social Science Fund Project. He has published numerous papers in various Chinese journals including *Journal of Beijing Sport University* and *Population Journal.* His email: xiangquan@jlu.edu.cn.

Xue Gong is a Research Fellow with the China Programme at the RSIS, Singapore. Her current research interests include China's economic diplomacy, China's overseas investment activities and China–Southeast Asian economic relations. She has published in peer-reviewed journals like *Contemporary Southeast Asia*, *Harvard Asia Quarterly*,

International Public Policy Studies (Japan). Her recent publications include book chapters in *China's Economic Inducement towards Vietnam: What Lies ahead in China's Economic Statecraft* (World Scientific, 2017), *Securing the Belt and Road Initiative: Risk Assessment, Private Security and Special Insurances along the New Wave of Chinese Outbound Investment* (Palgrave Macmillan, 2018). Her recent journal paper entitled *The Role of Chinese Corporate Players in China's South China Sea Policy* has been covered by Reuters exclusively. Xue Gong's work is also published regularly in the *South China Morning Post* and *The Diplomat*, among other current media. Her email: isgongxue@ntu.edu.sg.

Yang Yang graduated from Xiamen University with a Master's Degree in World Economics. Upon completing his studies in 1996, Yang Yang went on to join Xiamen University where he is mainly engaged in Chinese higher education and policy research, cooperation with domestic schools and social services. He has published extensively in journals and was Nanyang Technological University Visiting Scholar in 2017. His email: yyxx@xmu.edu.cn.

List of Figures

Chapter 10

Chapter 11

List of Tables

Contents

Introduction: Understanding the Transformational Power of China's Belt and Road Initiative

Chay Yue Wah and Thomas Menkhoff

This book features several introductory readings about the "Belt and Road Initiative" (BRI), a strategic development initiative launched by the Chinese Government under the leadership of President Xi Jinping in 2013 to jointly build an economic belt along the Silk Road. Some of the key objectives of BRI, previously known as One Belt, One Road (OBOR) or Silk Road Economic Belt, include promoting infrastructure development, trade and investments in Asia, Europe and Africa. BRI is a gigantic development initiative whose key components include the creation of several interconnected economic land corridors (=belts): China–Mongolia–Russia; China–Central Asia–West Asia, China–Pakistan, the China–Indochina peninsula and Bangladesh–China–India–Myanmar.

BRI's evolving overland infrastructure network includes the "New Eurasian Land Bridge" (see Figure 1) which consists of several

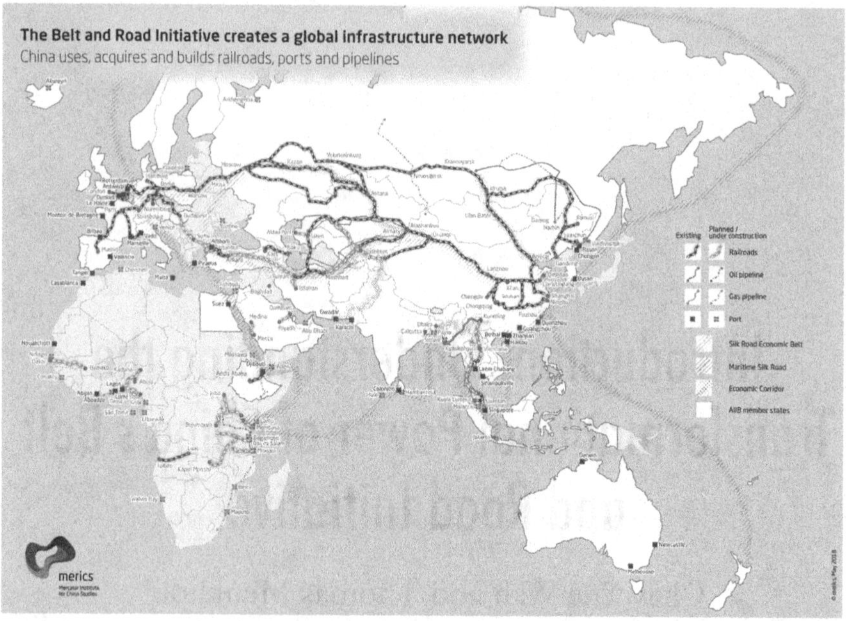

Figure 1. A map of the BRI

Source: Reproduced with the kind permission from Mercator Institute for China Studies (MERICS), Berlin, Germany.

rail corridors linking Yiwu in eastern China with European destinations such as Duisburg (Germany), Madrid (Spain) or London (UK).

A noteworthy case is the Belgrade–Budapest Railway project that will eventually link the Greek ports of Piraeus and Thessaloniki with the economic and trade partners in Eastern Europe. Once construction is completed by the end of 2023, planners envisage that the Budapest–Belgrade railway line will be the fastest transport route between Greece and the interior of Europe. Stakeholders see in the Budapest–Belgrade line a grand flagship project, which shows that China is capable of working according to EU construction standards and legal requirements with regard to fair competition and prevention of dishonest or fraudulent conduct. While the European Union (EU) and China have built a deep, strategic partnership over the years, there are also critics who have cautioned that a new eastern entryway to markets in Western Europe (WE) will carry a significant economic price for many European countries, for instance, China's increasing diplomatic and commercial influence as well as greater control (e.g. over resources) through sheer physical connectivity.

The "21st Century Maritime Silk Road" is a complementary initiative to promote maritime-related development in countries adjoining the South China Sea, the South Pacific Ocean and the Indian Ocean. It envisions the development of key seaports along traditional and new sea routes to Southeast Asia, Africa and the Mediterranean region with good connectivity to land-based transportation routes. Port development with "Chinese engagement" from Port Klang in Malaysia to Sri Lanka, to Gwadar in Pakistan, to gulf state ports in the Middle East, to Piraeus in Greece and beyond, provide a string of valuable pearls in the form of harbours from which adjoining areas can be serviced through feeder vessels or railway lines by Chinese government-linked companies.

BRI is a gigantic regional integration project that involves more than 60 countries in Asia, Oceania, East Africa and Europe. Funding and support is available from new financial institutions established by the Chinese Government such as the Silk Road Fund (US$40 billion) founded in 2014 (http://www.silkroadfund.com.cn/enweb/23773/index.html) and the Asian Infrastructure Investment Bank (AIIB) formed in 2016. AIIB is "a multilateral development bank with a mission to improve social and economic outcomes in Asia and beyond" (https://www.aiib.org/en/about-aiib/index.html). Its headquarters is located in Beijing. AIIB has 80 approved members from various parts of the world: "By investing in sustainable infrastructure and other productive sectors today, we will better connect people, services and markets that over time will impact the lives of billions and build a better future" (https://www.aiib.org/en/about-aiib/index.html).

The "Central belt" is aimed at integrating countries in Central and West Asia with linkages to the Persian Gulf and the Mediterranean Sea. Central Asian countries such as Kazakhstan, Kyrgyzstan, Uzbekistan and Turkmenistan urgently require large-scale infrastructure investments, and the BRI is seen as a welcome source of funds and support. One of the completed projects in Kazakhstan is the Khorgos dry port that connects China and Kazakhstan (see Figure 2).

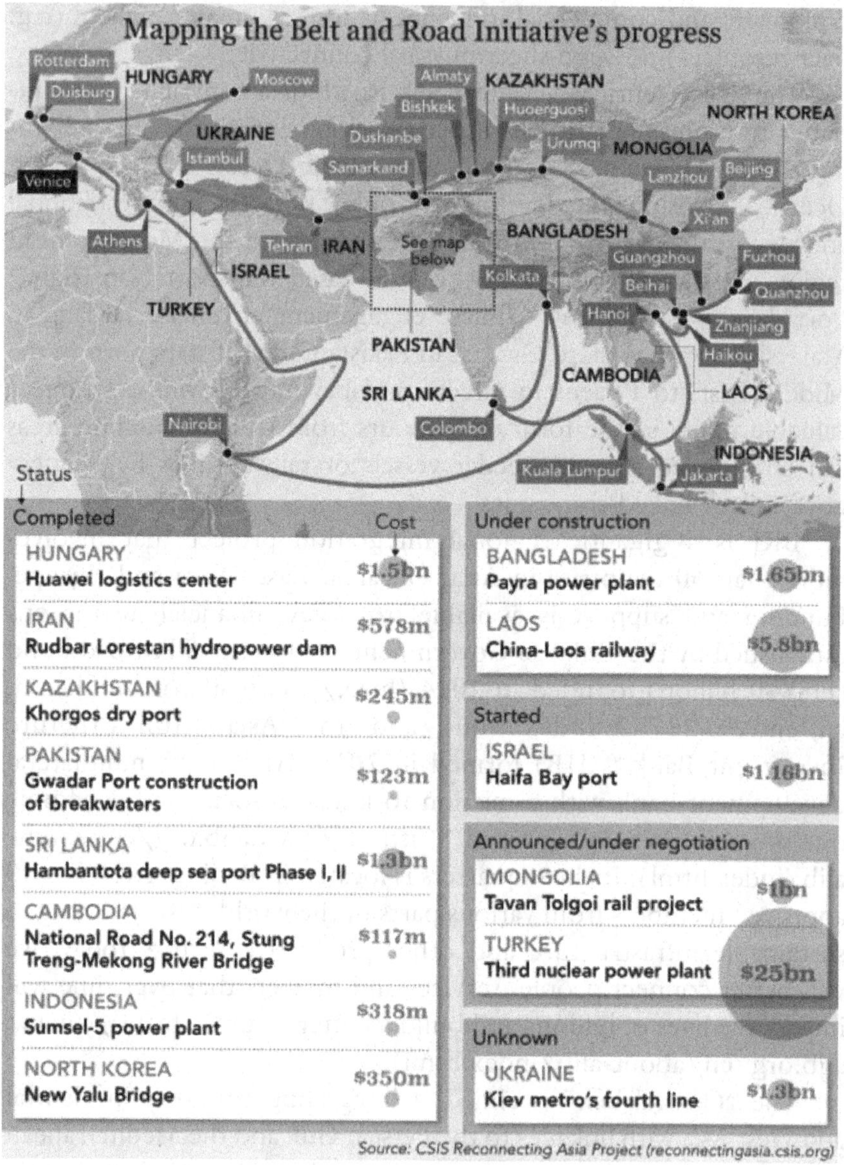

Figure 2. Examples of BRI projects

Source: *Nikkei Asian Review* 28/3/2018, https://asia.nikkei.com/Spotlight/Cover-Story/Is-China-s-Belt-and-Road-working-A-progress-report-from-eight-countries.

A key cooperative project between Kazakhstan and China is the emerging Western Europe–Western China (WE–WC) Expressway, which will connect the port of Lianyungang, on the Yellow Sea in China, to the port at St. Petersburg, on the Baltic Sea in Russia. WE–WC is mainly funded by The World Bank's IBRD (International Bank for Reconstruction and Development), Japan International Cooperation Agency (JICA), Asian Development Bank (ADB), the Inter-American Development Bank (IADB) and the European Bank for Reconstruction and Development (EBRD). The WE–WC Expressway is positioned as a core element of a newly emerging multimodal transport system that will comprise other highways, railway lines and transport hubs, interlacing China, the Commonwealth of Independent States (CIS), Eastern Europe, South Asia and the Middle East with Kazakhstan as Eurasia's logistical heart. Economic benefits include reduced travel time, industrial development, job creation, domestic tourism and increasing tax revenues.

Besides further extending the belt to countries in South Asia and Southeast Asia (=South belt) via new rail lines such as the high-speed railway project linking China to Thailand's ports, the strategy is to create a "North belt", connecting Central Asia, Russia and Europe. China's President Xi Jinping has promoted a plan to create a Northern Sea Route (NSR) (="Ice Silk Road") in collaboration with Russia, with emphasis on oil and gas exploration in the Arctic region, including shipping, infrastructure construction, tourism and science (see Figure 3).

As a country with massive expertise in building roads, tunnels, bridges, high-speed trains for rail projects, etc., China's BRI seems to be a logical outcome of the country's domestic development approach with its emphasis on infrastructure development. Besides its forte as a massive transformational development force directed at the underdeveloped Eurasian landmass, BRI can also be seen as a strategy to address China's uneven development of inland western regions and the prosperous eastern seaboard states. Instead of investing more state funds on underdeveloped provinces within China, regional economic integration is seen as a more effective approach towards poverty alleviation and sustainable development.

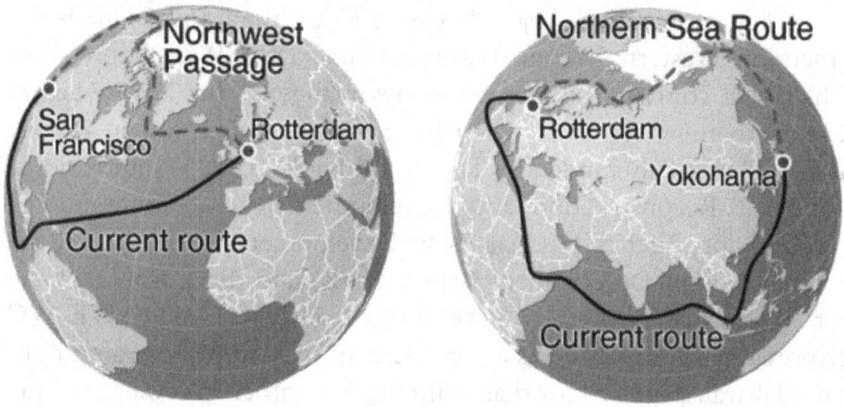

Figure 3. Northern sea route

Source: http://www.grida.no/resources/7150; Maps by Hugo Ahlenius, UNEP/GRID-Arendal.

A related case of interest in the overall scheme of the BRI is the China–Pakistan Economic Corridor, which connects Kashgar in the landlocked Xinjiang with the Port of Gwadar in Pakistan (where the China Overseas Ports Holding Company has an operating lease). The development of corridor-related road upgrading works have angered India because they are conducted in Gilgit–Baltistan which is a part of the greater Kashmir region, a disputed territory that is the subject of a long-standing conflict between Pakistan and India. Eventually, the China–Pakistan Economic Corridor is expected to entail highways, pipelines, power plants, optical connections and railways. Analysts expect that greater linkages between the restive province of Xinjiang and Central Asia will lead to significant economic and national security dividends.

At the sea port of Gwadar, the China–Pakistan Economic Corridor meets the Maritime Silk Road (see Figure 4) which gives China access to the Indian Ocean with its important sea routes, including oil and gas from the Middle East.

For many collaborating provinces and external countries, the BRI is a welcome source of much needed infrastructure investments to tackle infrastructural gaps and to stimulate more trade. For others, the potential BRI threats outweigh the benefits (Table 1). BRI has been interpreted as an attempt to create a new world order with China as

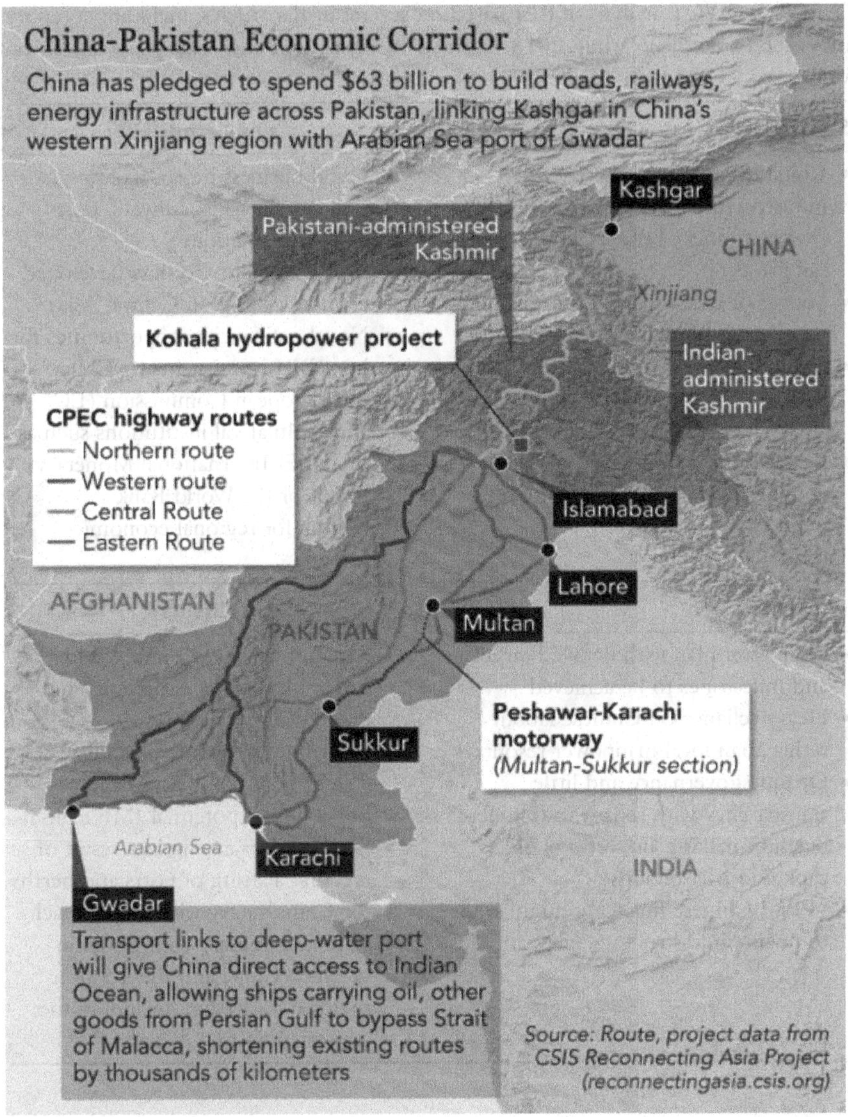

Figure 4. China–Pakistan economic corridor

Source: *Nikkei Asian Review* 28/3/2018, https://asia.nikkei.com/Spotlight/Cover-Story/Is-China-s-Belt-and-Road-working-A-progress-report-from-eight-countries.

Table 1. SWOT analysis of BRI based on several media articles, including a report in *The Economist*, 26th July 2018, entitled "China's belt-and-road plans are to be welcomed — and worried about"

Strengths	Opportunities
• China has massive expertise in infrastructure development know how (roads, tunnels, bridges, high-speed rail projects) • Source of much needed infrastructure investment to stimulate more trade • Creation of new funding institutions by China (e.g. Silk Road Fund, Asian Infrastructure Investment Bank) • Better local, regional and global connectivity as well as novel trading networks	• Good business prospects for builders of roads, railways, ports and power stations • More prosperity for less-developed economies (e.g. in Central Asia) • Novel cofinancing opportunities for joint BRI investments by China, the European Commission (EC) and multilateral institutions such as the IMF (International Monetary Fund) or the World Bank • Stimuli for regional economic growth
Weaknesses	**Threats**
• No master plan with detailed targets and milestones to be achieved • Heavy reliance on Chinese labour rather than local manpower resources • Opaque governance and little transparency with regard to (Chinese) decision-making and returns on capital in BRI regions • "Easy" Chinese financing might lead to "white infrastructural elephants"	• Attempt to create a new world order with China as preeminent power (new hegemony) • Debt burden cum dependency ("debt trap diplomacy") and possibility of potential IMF bailouts • Security risks arising as a result of creating a string of ports and berths for China's navy with global reach • Potential military confrontation between China and the US over regional leadership, including the contested South China Sea

preeminent power. There is concern that China's new partnerships in (Eastern) Europe could have a negative effect on the integration project of the EU (with its emphasis on "good" governance, democracy and human rights), which overlaps with Russia's Eurasian Economic Union (EAEU) project. Another worry is the potential debt burden cum dependency ("debt trap diplomacy") of mega infrastructure projects funded by China. Sceptics have pointed to security risks which may arise as a result of creating a string of ports and berths for China's navy extending its global reach.

In Sri Lanka, for example, China financed the construction of a new sea port in Hambantota with state-owned China Merchants eventually holding a majority stake after Sri Lanka encountered difficulties in the loan repayment. Additionally, a small group of China watchers have stressed the potential of a military confrontation between China and the US over regional leadership, including the contested South China Sea.

BRI's track record since it was unveiled in late 2013 suggests that China has become a champion of globalisation and an advocate of inclusive growth, filling a gap left by the more protectionist stance of the USA. In many Southeast Asian nations, BRI is regarded as a new force for regional economic integration — filling a vacuum created by the cessation of the Trans-Pacific Pact (TPP).

Structure of the Reader and Contributors

The book's contents are aimed at discussing the following broad questions:

- What is the programmatic focus of BRI (beyond infrastructure investments or power grids) and its impact on selected partner countries who are involved in it?
- What explains China's growing proactivism in international affairs?
- How will BRI modify the geopolitical order in Asia and how do Asian countries respond?
- What is the role of the China-led AIIB vis-à-vis traditional development banks such as the ADB?
- What motivates China to finance these infrastructure-driven economic growth strategies in selected regional land corridors/belts and what are potential development outcomes?
- What is the impact of Chinese capital and infrastructure investments on Sino–Southeast Asian economic relations in general and Southeast Asia's maritime trade routes in particular?

- How do Southeast Asian nations such as Malaysia view China-financed BRI projects and what long-term geopolitical scenario is likely to arise with regard to the contested South China Sea?
- Why and how do countries in Central Asia like Kazakhstan participate in the Eurasian transcontinental corridor "Economic belt of the Silk Road"?
- How and under what conditions is economic power captured by China through the BRI?
- How will China's increasing geoeconomic power translate into geopolitical power?

In Chapter 1, Dai Shiyan, Wang Xiangquan and Yang Yang ("External Challenges Arising from BRI Development and Approaches for Solutions") provide insights into the increasing number of BRI projects worldwide in areas such as transport infrastructure, energy development and industrial park construction. External challenges include concerns that the further development of BRI will lead to an over-reliance on China, socio-cultural cum language barriers between BRI-involved nations and China, weak regulatory systems (e.g. finance), disputes over borderlines, investment risks and so forth. As the authors argue, effective communication can help BRI stakeholders achieve a good mutual understanding of the objectives and significance of BRI, "which could be more important than the hardware facilities of connectivity among the countries along the Belt and Road routes". They conclude that China is well advised to further enhance the external communication and publicity about BRI as there have been growing concerns about this gigantic blueprint.

Gary Hawke sheds light on the complex issue of how to absorb the new BRI (which he views as a vision, not a plan) into an international economic architecture in Chapter 2, "Economic Historical Development and Leadership Underlying the BRI Strategy". He discusses how the BRI can accommodate the various economic systems in a synergetic, positive and peaceful fashion vis-à-vis the narrative of China's past humiliation and the historical primacy of the USA in Asia-Pacific. As he concludes his wide-ranging politico-economic analysis of BRI, which also sheds new light on its multiple security dimensions vis-à-vis Washington's strategic competition consensus, he notes that "... it takes time for the new to become familiar. In a situation where one economy is gaining a leadership position while another's is declining, the novel is especially threatening." The development of the 21st century BRI will test China's peaceful rising, especially by those affected outside of China.

In Chapter 3 ("Frontier Infrastructure: OBOR and Northern Sea Route (NSR) in Comparative Perspective"), Christopher M. Dent introduces the concept of "frontier infrastructure" as an analytical device to explain both the nature and historic significance of the BRI and the NSR. He discusses how this discourse plays out in current debates about the governance and promotion of international trade in the 21st century. As illustrated in Figure 3, the NSR connects the Barents Sea near Russia's border with Norway with the Bering Strait between Siberia and Alaska. Melting ice sheets as a consequence of climate change suggest that the NSR might become an alternative maritime route by 2040, making the Suez Canal less important in the long run.

How the BRI impacts Central Asia in general and Kazakhstan in particular is discussed in Chapter 4, "The Belt and Road Initiative: Case of Kazakhstan" by Batzhan Akmoldina, Sara Alpysbayeva and Zhanna Kapsalyamova. Kazakhstan is landlocked and the biggest of the Central Asian countries by land mass. With vast oil and natural gas reserves, it is strategically positioned as a trade and logistics hub between China, Europe and South Asia to become the logistical heart of Eurasia. Kazakhstan participates in three directions of the Eurasian transcontinental corridor "Economic belt of the Silk Road": (i) China–Kazakhstan–Russia–Europe, with access to the Baltic Sea; (ii) China–Kazakhstan–Turkmenistan–Iran–Pakistan, with access to the Persian Gulf and the Indian Ocean and (iii) China–Kazakhstan–Azerbaijan–Georgia–Turkey–Europe, within the framework of the international Transport Corridor Europe Caucasus Asia (TRACECA) program, with access to the Black and Mediterranean Seas. The TRACECA program was launched at a conference in Brussels in 1993 to create a transport corridor on a West–East axis from Europe, across the Black Sea, through the Caucasus and the Caspian Sea to Central

Asia. TRACECA members include Armenia, Azerbaijan, Bulgaria, Georgia, Kazakhstan, Kyrgyz Republic, Moldova, Romania, Tajikistan, Turkey, Turkmenistan, Ukraine and Uzbekistan. How the country will continue to manage its relations with China, Russia, the EU and the US will be an interesting lesson in statecraft. Common ground entails promoting domestic and regional economic growth, strengthening regional security, mastering digitization and enhancing institutional efficiency.

In Chapter 5 ("Financing the OBOR Initiative"), Joseph Lim and Deborah Lim take a closer look at the gigantic BRI financing needs. While China has sponsored and financed many BRI projects like those in Pakistan, Sri Lanka or Laos, they argue that it cannot shoulder the financing burden alone. Without private capital and national governments serving as equity holders, the BRI is unlikely to succeed. Many BRI projects are located in developing countries whose political leaders struggle with their national finances. Particular challenges include the management of sovereign risk, systemic investment risks and exchange risks. What is needed are new mechanisms for redistributing the risks that debt holders are facing in conjunction with other risk amelioration measures such as tranching, investing through a special purpose vehicle (which is an entity incorporated for the purpose of investing in the bonds of a BRI project), contingent convertible bonds or special infrastructure funds. According to their analysis, there can be no doubt that the nodes along the "belt and road" will see a parallel development of the (much-needed) financial infrastructure.

The (arguably) "irreconcilable rivalry" between China and Japan in regional cooperation in the areas of finance and trade forms the core subject of Chapter 6 by Shintaro Hamanaka ("Explaining Irreconcilable Sino–Japan Rivalry"). There are fundamental differences with regard to policy preferences between both countries. While China prefers goods-centric free trade agreements (FTAs) and supports international financial institutions (IFIs) to finance infrastructure development measures in support of trade facilitation such as transport infrastructure, Japan places emphasis on more comprehensive development approaches "beyond just lending money", including regulatory reforms and the establishment of regulatory standards (e.g. environmental standards) of partner countries. The "irreconcilable rivalry" argument is further developed with reference to the trade-related Regional Comprehensive Economic Partnership (RCEP) and Trans-Pacific Partnership (TPP) as well as the workings and rationale of finance-related institutions such as the AIIB and the ADB. Whether the stated rivalry will eventually lead to more harmony amongst regional powers like China/Japan (and the US) and constructive negotiations for mutual benefits as a result of ever-evolving geopolitical dynamics remains to be seen.

A Southeast Asian perspective of BRI is provided by Xue Gong and Li Mingjiang in Chapter 7, "The Belt and Road Initiative: Progress and Prospect in Southeast Asia". The authors contrast the different responses of three groups of countries vis-à-vis the prospects of BRI in order to assess how it may make progress in the region: (i) Cambodia, Brunei, Thailand and Singapore; (ii) Malaysia, Indonesia and the Philippines and (iii) Vietnam and Myanmar. A case in point is Malaysia under the leadership of Prime Minister Mahathir Mohamad which has suspended work on multibillion infrastructure projects such as the US$20 billion East Coast Rail Link project (agreed upon during the Najib administration) due to concerns about affordability and debt servicing. There are also strategic concerns with regard to the free movement of ships through the South China Sea and the Strait of Malacca.

In Chapter 8, Hans-Dieter Evers, Abdul Rahman Embong and Rashila Ramli examine "The Impact of Chinese Maritime Policy on Malaysia: A Long-term Geopolitical Scenario". Their paper concentrates on the maritime part of this development policy, which entails heavy infrastructure investments in ports and railroads, and real-estate property developments, for instance, satellite cities and/or condominiums, offered for sale mainly to Chinese citizens. According to their analysis, there will be obvious commercial benefits to economies along the Southern Silk Road, but also geopolitical effects like increasing political dependency due to Chinese capital investments and acquisition of property rights in ports and condominiums. Regarding these developments, a Malaysian maritime policy is called for to match BRI and the Indonesian Maritime Fulcrum, as well as

ASEAN integration. Indonesia's "Global Maritime Fulcrum" refers to the country's grand maritime vision to turn Indonesia into a "fulcrum" of Indo-Pacific maritime activity. Strategic goals include the development of Indonesia's Navy into a regional maritime power and to create a more interconnected Indonesia with modern ports, fisheries and shipping. This includes the upgrading of Indonesia's naval base at Natuna Island. As China and Indonesia have overlapping claims on maritime rights in the South China Sea, the future maritime security environment is set to become more challenging.

Chapter 9 ("China's Belt and Road Initiative and ASEAN's Maritime Clusters") by Hans-Dieter Evers and Thomas Menkhoff deals with the potential impact of BRI on maritime clusters in Southeast Asia. It makes a case for further examining the possible effects of the complementary "Maritime Silk Road" on maritime clusters involving Singapore, Malaysia and Indonesia. Whether China's heavy investments in land and maritime infrastructure in Indonesia and Malaysia will lead to the development of strong and dense maritime clusters with deep connectivity and complementary (maritime) subclusters for mutual socio-economic development benefits remains to be seen. Academic research to better understand these trends, as well as the creation of a comprehensive maritime policy, is advocated for ASEAN nations.

In Chapter 10 ("Strategic Linkages: China's Belt and Road Initiative and Power Capture through Global Value Chains"), Pan Zhengqi examines an important aspect of the BRI: the development of international relations networks of countries economically and politically linked by the BRI that in turn make them increasingly dependent on one another (with China as the strategic core in the network of geoeconomic and geopolitical relations). The author argues that dense GVC linkages formed by the BRI with China as the hub will not only result in disproportionately large trade and investment benefits for China, but also considerable financial gains through the greater use and internationalization of the renminbi (RMB). Importantly, increasing trade and financial connections between China and the rest of the BRI countries will lead to a more comprehensive diplomacy, albeit the effects of China's direct political influence being constrained by scepticism regarding debt trap diplomacy. However, the overall geopolitical ramifications of the BRI remain salient: China's BRI can be seen as a grand strategy to decrease dependence on and influence of the American-led liberal world order.

In Chapter 11 "Sustaining the Momentum of the Belt and Road Initiative", Andrew Elek discusses some of the key enablers of BRI's long-term viability and sustainability such as efficient infrastructure maintenance and operationality, objective project monitoring, high and sustained level of policy coordination as well as the generation of sound economic rates of return. As he argues, all this will require huge improvements in the skills, institutional capacity and policy environment of most of the countries involved: "A system with one dominant leader — China — will be a massive aid program rather than any new model of cooperation." The main pillars of building BRI include: (i) the generation of mutual trust and mutual respect among a very diverse group of countries, (ii) shared leadership of the process, (iii) reaching win-win agreements on priorities and targets, (iv) sharing responsibility for efficient project design, construction, operation and maintenance and (v) mobilization of the massive funds that are required. He concludes that the future of the BRI remains uncertain as several of the challenges above have yet to be tackled effectively.

In the concluding chapter, Linda Low writes that China is forging ahead with globalising the BRI, albeit with Chinese characteristics; "doing by its own way". China has arrived in a more challenging bipolar world with the USA's more domestically focused "to be great again" somewhat eclipsed as China's BRI continues to transform its domestic economy and the destiny of some of the participating nations. The novel BRI is China's approach to becoming a powerful global leader by building new investment links and trading networks regionally and internationally along the old Silk Road. The "21st Century Maritime Silk Road" initiative is yet another approach to capitalise on geopolitical and geoeconomic advantages amid the current global and regional uncertainty. This initiative is planned to promote maritime-related development in countries adjoining the South China Sea, the South Pacific Ocean and the Indian Ocean. Creating maritime clusters around port cities will help to satisfy

Chinese geopolitical needs for secure trade routes. The creation of these maritime clusters will further fulfil the participating states' need for vibrant port cities and effective maritime economies, provided project implementation efforts with cluster effects are viable, sustainable and confidence-building.

Chapter 1

External Challenges Arising from BRI Development and Approaches for Solutions

Dai Shiyan, Wang Xiangquan and Yang Yang

1. Overview and Development of China's Belt and Road Initiative (BRI)

It has been more than five years since Chinese President Xi Jinping announced the launch of the initiative of jointly building the Silk Road Economic Belt and the 21st century Maritime Silk Road (hereafter referred to as the "Belt and Road Initiative" or BRI) in October 2013. BRI has indicated an ambitious goal to link up China and the rest of Asian countries, as well as Europe and Africa. This unprecedented gigantic strategic initiative, once accomplished, will engage around 65 countries in the world with a total population of 4.4 billion and will be capable of generating approximately 40% of the world's economic output (Si 2017, Wu 2015). In pursuit of the historic strategic undertaking, China appears dedicated to developing "a community of shared interests, shared responsibilities, and shared future" in the world (National Development and Reform Commission, Ministry of Foreign Affairs and Ministry of Commerce 2015).

Since it was put forward, the BRI has received wide attention and active response from across the world; China has been doing quite well to garner from the world community an increasing understanding and support of this ambitious strategy, the total investment in association of which boasts to surpass US$1 trillion (Ferdinand 2016), and Beijing has so far managed to achieve substantial progress with this far-reaching project.

Over the past five years, an increasing number of projects have been launched in those BRI-involved countries and regions, and more and more countries have respectively engaged themselves in the BRI projects and collaborations. Specifically, the Chinese official website indicates there are as many as 103 countries or international organisations which were reported to have signed a total of 118 agreements with China for the BRI-related collaboration projects (Yu 2018). Many countries have already established institutional arrangements for collaboration with China.

Rapid progress was reported by the media from time to time about China's collaboration with some countries along the Belt and Road routes in terms of the major connectivity and infrastructure projects. Some major prominent projects include Mombasa–Nairobi Standard Gauge Railway, Jakarta–Bandung High Speed Rail, China–Laos Railway, Addis Ababa–Djibouti Railway, Belgrade–Budapest Railway, as well as the construction of Gwadar Port in Pakistan and Port of Piraeus.[1]

Meanwhile, Chinese enterprises are reported to have opened up a total of 82 zones of economic and trade collaboration in more than 20 countries along the BRI-involved countries, pumping in a total of US$28.9 billion, contributing a total of US$1.1 billion tax revenue for the host countries and creating as many as 241,000 job opportunities for the BRI-related countries.[2]

Media reports also showed that as of May 2017, 47 out of 98 Chinese central government-led enterprises had directly participated,

---

[1] Details can be found at the website: www.yidaiyilu.gov.cn.

[2] Details can be found at the website: www.yidaiyilu.gov.cn.

partnered or invested in a total of 1,676 projects in the host countries along the BRI-involved regions. The projects are mostly concentrated in the fields of transport infrastructure, energy development and industrial park or hi-tech zone construction (Hu 2018). One example reported was that China Communication Construction Company Limited had built more than 10,000-kilometre-long quality highways, 2,000-kilometre-long railway, more than 150 bridges, 95 deep-water ports and 10 airports throughout the BRI-related countries.

The world has witnessed that a multiple-functioned infrastructure network led by China–Pakistan, China–Mongolia–Russia and New Eurasian Continental Bridge is forming up to perform their significant functions.

Apart from the rapid development of infrastructure connectivity, economic and trade exchanges and cooperation, significant progress has also been made in terms of cultural, information and knowledge, and people exchanges over the past five years. For example, China has formulated plans for specialised collaboration with some BRI-involved countries in many fields related to education, science and technology, finance, energy, agriculture, inspection and quarantine, and standard connectivity. In 2017, there were as many as over 320,000 exchange students sent by those countries along the BRI route, and more than 60,000 received by those countries along the BRI route (Qi 2018).

All these evidences have indicated a stark fact that the BRI has over the past five years made a tremendous development, gradually transforming the BRI from concept to action, and from vision to reality.

2. External Challenges Encountered

Despite the rapid development and accomplishment of the BRI, however, the BRI's implementation has encountered various difficulties and challenges amid the changing situation of the world economy and political landscaping. Though countries along the BRI routes are abundant with various natural resources and energy reserves, there exist remarkable differences among those countries in terms of their social, political, religious and economic systems and also their cultural, religious and infrastructural conditions. Moreover, the changing world economy and changing political landscapes have often affected those BRI countries, resulting in a series of conflicts and disputes. These situations can in turn give rise to tough hurdles and challenges for the BRI development and implementation. In the rest of this chapter, the authors will list some major factors which are categorised as external challenging factors and analyse them closely. Moreover, the authors will make an attempt to explore and discuss possible approaches of solution for tackling these challenges.

2.1. *Differences in Strategic Interest and Intentions from Different Countries*

Along with China's rapid rise over the last few decades, there appears a widespread concern in the world that the existing world order will be affected. Based on this concern, the launch of BRI and its subsequent construction will in turn increase the doubt about China's rise among some of the countries along the BRI routes. We have seen some countries have even compared China's BRI to "the Marshall Plan" or "the European Recovery Plan".

The proposed routes of BRI cover a large number of countries, many of which enjoy a status of geographical strategic importance and advantage, and have long become locations for big countries to compete for. Therefore, the geopolitics in those countries or regions have long remained complex and sensitive. Specifically, be it Central Asia, Middle East, or Southeast Asia or South Asia, they have traditionally remained the place for big countries to compete for and influence. Although the Chinese government has entered those regions by means of economic and trade cooperation, it has still alerted the relevant big countries in the region with suspicion and vigilance. Some countries have even been politicising the economic issues, as they appear to be worried that the BRI construction will eventually jeopardise their influence and presence in the region. Thus, they have not only repelled or resisted the BRI, they have also made effort to resist or contain it. For example, the collaboration project of China–Pakistan Economic Corridor covers Kashmir, which has long been a disputed area between Pakistan and India, has been strongly opposed by India. During his official visit to China in April 2018, Indian Prime Minister Narendra Modi clearly indicated the project was "unacceptable". For China's Belt and Road Forum for International Cooperation held in May 2017 and attended by representatives from over 130 countries and 70 international organisations, India did not send any representative, either.

In addition, some developing countries along the BRI routes have good potential for further developing their economy; however, they have yet to show their determination or take action to promote reform and rapid economic development probably due to the limited aspirations or actual means to rely on. Some countries may also have the fear that the further development of BRI may invariably lead to their overreliance on the Chinese government. Consequently, these countries are not only reluctant to undertake the BRI collaboration projects, but also want to keep them outside their countries.

2.2. *Cultural Differences between Countries*

At present, the BRI implementation has involved several regions including Asia, Europe and Africa. Cultural exchanges along the Belt and Road routes between countries and regions have become constant and frequent. Along with the expansion of collaboration scopes and scales, the cultural conflicts are reported from time to time. This kind of outcome will increase the cost of transactions and exchanges, and the cultural differences will in turn bring about the unpredictable and unprecedented challenges for the collaboration among countries along the BRI routes.

In general, the cultural differences between China and those BRI-involved countries are usually demonstrated in the three major areas. First, China has long designated English as the first foreign language for students across the country to learn from primary schools to universities. As a result, people have long neglected the need of learning those official languages widely used in those BRI countries or regions. This language barrier has directly constrained the smooth cultural exchanges and collaborations between China and those BRI-involved countries. Second, it is found that in China about 52% of population have no established religious belief (Liu and Huang 2017), and the religious concentration is relatively low throughout the country. In contrast, most of those countries covered by Belt and Road routes are densely populated with a prevailing one particular religion. For instance, Saudi Arabia is a country in which 100% of the people believe in Islam. Lack of a good understanding of the relevant religion may give rise to a range of potential risks when it comes to economic and trade collaboration. Third, part of the BRI-involved countries have long kept a close relationship with a big western country and have been deeply influenced by that big country. Specifically, most of the countries along the Maritime Silk Road have long maintained a close relation with the United States through the economic or military ties, and the United States' strategies of Asia-Pacific rebalancing and India–Asia-Pacific rebalancing have produced a substantial impact on these countries in their political and economic dimensions. The differences between China and the United States including the cultural and now trade fields will result in additional risks to the development of China's BRI implementation in these regions.

2.3. *Unconventional Security Problems*

The development of BRI has involved many countries, where there exist a wide range of complicated problems pertaining to terrorism, financial crises, environment security and energy safety. All these problems take on a great variety of forms and are often intertwined. In some countries, the forces of terrorist organisations, ethnic separatists and religious extremists have remained rampant, bringing substantial threats to the lives and assets of local people in those countries. The situation in Central Asia and Middle East regions has been far more complex, with ethnic and religious cultures being complex, series of historical grievances difficult to reconcile, and terrorism and religious extremism long remaining rampant.

Meanwhile, countries along the Belt and Road routes mostly belong to the category of developing nations, with their financial market and infrastructure still weak and fragile and their regulatory system far from being established or efficient. Therefore, they are vulnerable to the volatility on account of adjustment and change of monetary policies by some countries in or outside the region. In addition, many countries along the Belt and Road routes are situated in a poor ecological environment, and their ability of environmental recovery and resistance is rather weak. All these factors will result in the fact that it will produce a prolonged and devastating consequence once a substantial damage or disruption occurs in their environments.

In addition, along the BRI route, there are quite a number of countries which have often been involved in the disputes over the marine areas or borderlines. As a result of western countries' intervention, these disputes are likely to be misinterpreted or taken advantage of by some countries involved. This could possibly place China's strategies of utilising relevant energies in the situation of unconventional security threat, and this kind of unconventional security threats has also gradually affected or altered the methods of international security collaboration. Therefore, this kind of situation has produced a high level of expectation and request for China's BRI implementation.

2.4. *Risks of Investment along the BRI Routes*

Despite the fact that many countries along the Belt and Road routes have a relatively good macro-environment with some having abundant resources and some having strategically important geographic locations, many of them are developing countries and their infrastructure is still relatively inferior.

Among those countries, there exist remarkable differences in terms of their economic development standards, in part on account of their historical affiliation with the old developed economies and/or with the emerging newly industrialised economies. Some countries have traditionally practised a single model for their economic development, and the markets in these countries are imperfect and their connectivity and communication systems are inferior and the development of them is slow.

Meanwhile, there are also prominent differences in terms of the investment environment in those regions and countries covered by the Belt and Road routes. The changes in some host countries in terms of their political landscaping, fiscal and financial policies, and economic environment will invariably create difficulties for predicting a reasonable return rate for the investment. Moreover, the increasing amount of cross-border trade and investment in those BRI-involved countries, which have practised different trade barriers and entry requirements, could also bring about more potential risks resulting from currency settlement, cross-border capital transaction and financing as well as the development of cross-border businesses. For example, most countries in Southeast Asia and Central Asia adopt the continental laws, and their domestic legal system is still below the ideal and efficient standard. They are often found to introduce or amend their laws and regulations frequently, or frequently adjust their guidelines for foreign investment by means of presidential decrees or government regulations, which are often found to be somewhat arbitrary or unpredictable. All these could in turn create considerable risks for investment in the BRI-involved countries or regions.

3. Approaches of Solution

The implementation of BRI will cover vast areas, involve a wide range of sectors and fields and take a very long time to accomplish. Quite a number of countries along the land route of BRI are undergoing an unstable domestic situation, with their domestic political systems vulnerable and incidents of religious extremists and terrorists occurring from time to time. Concurrently, many countries along the Maritime Silk Route are also faced with territorial disputes in the East China Sea and South China Sea, the transportation security along the life passage through Europe and Asia and Africa and Asia. It is reasonable to say that the factors such as each country's strategic agenda and intention, geopolitics, unconventional security issues, conflicts of cultures and religions as well as financial risks for investment among the BRI-involved countries will all pose tough hurdles and challenges.

Therefore, from the beginning of BRI implementation, it is necessary to take precautions for all kinds of risks, make a comprehensive and thorough analysis of every collaboration with those BRI countries and rationally handle the balance of "development" and "safety" in the progress of BRI implementation with an aim to achieve a steady and long-term progress of BRI.

3.1. *Strengthen the Exchanges and Communication for the Collaborative Construction of BRI*

3.1.1. *Expand the Publicity on BRI*

With regard to China's BRI, there have been diverse reactions and interpretations from different countries across the world. Think tanks from the United States hold that China's BRI is meant to serve as a countermeasure against the United States' strategic intention of returning to Asia. They think the BRI has disrupted the existing relations between the big countries, with an intention to pursue a mechanism for power balance between China and the United States in the strategic space over land and sea in the regions (Chu and Gao 2015). India has also held its own suspicious views about China's genuine strategic intention in the region and has demonstrated a deep concern over China's rising influence in the region. As India has long taken South Asia and Indian Ocean as its own traditional power zone and has attempted to seek a dominant status in the Indian Ocean, China's BRI has been regarded by India as a containment strategy against its strategic intention in the areas (Duan 2016). In the face of speculations and concerns from countries including the United States, India, Japan, etc., it may be necessary and advisable for China to step up its external communication and publicity about the BRI's strategic goals and pragmatic significance, so as to win a good understanding and consensus from the relevant countries in the world.

Since the BRI implementation actually involves vast areas and many sectors in different regions and it is not possible to develop and complete in just a few years, China may find it necessary to make a steadfast and continuous effort for the external communication and publicity with the following characteristics. First, the external communication and publicity should be grounded by the theory of jointly developing a sustainable harmonious world, guided by a shared value highlighting peaceful development, and propelled by a mindset to pursue a mutual benefit and win-win outcome of economic cooperation and multiple cultural exchanges, and to promote dialogues of civilisations with inclusive and mutual respect features. The ultimate objective of all these is to achieve the peaceful and harmonious development among different countries and civilisations. Second, along with the development of the BRI implementation, it may be of great help to secure a widespread understanding and support by highlighting the prominent benefits for those BRI-involved countries as an outcome from the accomplishments of the BRI development. It is advisable to always adhere to a special set of diplomatic philosophy in properly tackling the relationship with those collaborating countries. This set of diplomatic philosophy should comprise such guidelines as upholding the principles of maintaining good neighbour relations and neighbourhood watch, treating cooperating partners or countries with empathy, inclusiveness and sincerity, adhering to mutual benefits with justice and friendship prevailing over interests. By ways of doing so, China's BRI will gradually produce expected positive influence among those countries along the Belt and Road routes.

Last but not the least, China may find it a priority to step up promoting the good neighbourhood policy with major objectives such as amity, security and common prosperity with neighbouring countries, and further strengthen the two-way exchanges with those collaborating countries. There may be several ways of publicity which could be experimented and adopted. They include the joint preparation and production of feature documentaries, which can be broadcast in the countries along the Belt and Road routes after the special documentaries are translated into the major official languages used in those countries, and also the setting up of special newspapers or television channels. All these attempts may want to highlight how the countries along the Belt and Road routes and their people can benefit from the BRI implementation and development, thus achieving common prosperity in the long run.

By those effective external publicity means and channels, it will hopefully help China secure a good understanding of its BRI objectives among those BRI-involved countries and in turn convince the world that China has no intention to use the BRI to achieve the alleged ambition of expansion, or to politicise the economic collaboration issues. Instead, the BRI is actually meant to pursue common prosperity as its ultimate goal, as reiterated by the Chinese leaders.

3.1.2. *Broaden the Communication Channels between Collaborating Countries*

It was in the contemporary world with several prevailing trends featuring globalisation, multipolar world, information society and cultural diversity that China brought forward the BRI in an attempt to explore a new model of global governance, and the primary objectives of the BRI, China has reiterated, is to maintain an open world economy and free global trade system, promote orderly and free flow of economic factors, as well as increase the efficiency of resources allocation and integration of markets. Therefore, it is extremely important to acquire a consensus among all partners or countries involved as it is an indispensable foundation for advancing the BRI implementation in a steady and sustainable way, a critical nexus for passing through generations the BRI spirit of friendly cooperation and an essential assurance for joint construction through consultation to meet the interests of all. It is therefore a prerequisite to have effective communication channels or platforms in order to reach an expected consensus.

Specifically, there are a few thrusts to make particular efforts for achieving the consensus. First, it is imperative to build an efficient platform of exchange and communication. In addition to relying on the current cooperation forms by means of regional or subregional cooperation organisations, free trade zones, economic corridors, forums and exhibitions, etc., it is necessary to strengthen the bilateral dialogues and exchanges between relevant cities, enterprises, and carry out multichannel and multilevel consultation and exchanges by ways of setting up joint committees, consultation committees, management committees and guiding committees so as to coordinate the cooperation planning and jointly explore the feasible roadmap for specific actions. Second, it is necessary to adopt a flexible way to build a partnership network for strategic cooperation, and a good one can be achieved by means of visiting and exchanges, joint research, personnel/officials training, and conferences and exhibitions. The purpose for doing so is to enable the relevant parties and partners to have a better understanding and consensus about the BRI's significance, principles, targets and tasks and strategic deployment. Last, it is helpful to promote the historical and cultural heritages in those BRI-involved countries by jointly organising exclusive summits or forums pertaining to the special trade, investment and cultural exchange.

3.2. *Deepen the Foundation of Cooperation*

3.2.1. *Enhance the Sharing of Information*

With regard to the BRI implementation, as Chinese President Xi put forward, at the Sixth Ministerial Conference of China–Arab States Cooperation Forum held on 5th June 2014, the guiding principle of jointly building the Belt and Road is through consultation to meet interests of all parties involved.[3] China may have reiterated that the general concept behind the BRI is to adhere to the principles of peace and cooperation, openness and inclusiveness, mutual learning and mutual benefit, and develop all-round cooperation, and promote policy coordination, facilities connectivity, unimpeded trade, financial integration and people-to-people bonds as the five major goals. To accomplish all these targets, it is critical to strengthen the information flow, and enhance the sharing of information.

To attain a satisfactory standard of information exchange and sharing, there may be several approaches. One very important task is to build a multilateral data alliance and a modern data processing centre for the BRI development, which should prioritise the standardisation of all document contents and formats within each region,

[3] The details could be found at the website: /www.mfa.gov.cn/chn//gxh/tyb/gdxw/t1162491.htm.

provide efficient data support to the countries along the BRI routes and promote good cooperation and mutual benefit by means of information convenience. Another important task is to engage collaborating countries in each region to share information by means of holding regular meetings, and organising different kinds of symposiums, forums or conferences. All these activities can be formed into an effective exchange system, and many information exchanged can be turned into written materials and made available to the general public through Internet or websites, which have become increasingly important channels of information flow and sharing. There is still another way for information sharing. That is to promote academic research exchanges and sharing of science and technology among the BRI-involved countries by means of building joint laboratories, research centres and international technology transfer centres.

3.2.2. *Develop Connectivity Network*

Unlike China's past national strategies which appeared to emphasise the self-centred features, China has stated the building of the Belt and Road is actually meant to be a global initiative to enhance regional economic cooperation. At the dialogue entitled *Developing Connectivity Partnership* during the APEC conference in November 2014, Chinese President Xi pointed out that the BRI and connectivity network could be integrated and complementary (Zhang and Lan 2016). Obviously, efficient connectivity is of special importance to the BRI development. To date, China has achieved considerable progress in terms of connectivity of the infrastructure systems with many of the BRI-involved countries. China has built the world's largest high-speed rail network covering a total distance of 7,547 kilometres, with nine countries connected with the railway, 45 countries or cities connected with direct flights and 58 countries connected with maritime transports (Li 2016).

Good connectivity can be attained in several ways and by multi-approaches including both "hardware" and "software" dimensions. By "hardware", it refers to the connectivity of infrastructure development between the BRI-involved countries in terms of communication and transport, energy and power and telecommunication. However, "software" connectivity has become increasingly vital to the smooth development of the BRI in the contemporary world, as it has a special power to help with conflict mitigation and mutual trust between collaborating countries. To achieve good connectivity, close attention should be paid to the following four areas. The first area is policy exchange and communication between the collaborating countries, which could be done by means of visit exchanges by top-level government officials and multilevel government policy exchange mechanisms and interactive mechanisms. These can help to proceed with policy dialogue and consultation, join efforts to formulate planning and measures for promoting regional cooperation, and collaborate to properly handle problems arising from the collaborative projects. Consequently, they will help create a favourable environment for good connectivity. Second, it may be helpful for the BRI-involved countries to strive for an effective compatibility in their cooperation planning for foundation industries as well as for technology standardisation. By means of effective information exchange and building of compatibility standard, they will be able to gradually remove the cooperation barriers and also identify the critical nexus, which will in turn promote a better connectivity. Third, it is advisable to promote a free flow and reasonable allocation of innovation factors including talents, information, technology, capital, etc. in each country or within a region. Fourth, it may be helpful to study and evaluate problems and risks rising from the collaboration and prepare an effective emergency response plan in advance. It is necessary to evaluate relevant parties and members based on the previous projects and their performance, and set up a credibility and reputation archives, and those with records of agreement breach should have their credibility downgraded, thus increasing their cost for contract breach and prompting the relevant collaborating parties to observe the agreements.

3.3. *Develop the Mechanism of Legal Protection*

3.3.1. *Improve the Inter-countries Cooperation Agreements*

The BRI advocates those BRI-involved countries to leverage on the bilateral or multilateral mechanism of cooperation, strengthen the connectivity between the collaborating countries and to join hands to develop the land economic corridors and maritime nexus of cooperation along the Belt and Road routes. Due to the defects of BRI cooperation mechanism, however, the BRI development is often confronted with an insecure situation resulting from various problems related to the rivalry of complex geopolitics, religious strife, different law and legal systems, and so on and so forth. To react properly to various and complex situations which often erupt beyond control, it is important for collaborating countries to establish the forward-looking contracts, and make good efforts to construct a good contractual relation with such features as being open and equal and in compliance of order and rule.

Good cooperation contracts should be built with an aim to promote a new and equal order for international economic development. They must take into account a wide range of factors which may possibly affect the collaborating countries, and the factors should include national standard of development, tradition and religion, legal and law system, market orientation, characteristics of industries and markets, enterprises and their ownerships and operation patterns, as well as the principles, rules and systems of the contract, etc. And good contracts can help form up a flexible and effective relation with several forms such as alliance, network, bilateral and multilateral types. Successful implementation of BRI cannot be made possible without the consensus and support from the governments of countries involved, mutual trust between the countries with different cultures, social and political systems, religions and different levels of economic development. Good contractual relations between collaborating countries will enable all parties involved to develop a trust in each other and share the benefits from their collaboration.

3.3.2. *Enhance the Rule of Law Mechanisms among the BRI Countries*

As we know, the BRI implementation will involve different countries' national interest and economic interest, and meanwhile, it may be likely to trigger disputes over the historical, cultural and religious issues. This is to a large extent on account of that the bilateral relations or multilateral relations arising from the BRI implementation could be complicated and keep changing. Therefore, it is far from being sufficient to emphasise only the proper formality or settlement of collaboration contract plans, since there always exist the constraints and limitations in each of the collaborative methods. When there is a lack of constraint mechanism for promoting international cooperation, or lack of the spirit of rule of law for equality and mutual benefit or common interest, the international economic and trade relations will become unstable. Once a dispute erupts, it will invariably result in an increase of the construction cost for the Belt and Road implementation. A professor from the Department of Economics, National University of Kazakhstan was quoted as saying that the new energy collaboration between China and Kazakhstan needed not only the input of relevant factors including equipment, technology and capital, but also relevant system mechanisms to safeguard the rights and interests of both parties in the collaboration (Jiang 2017). As an important way or means to pursue the civilised order or achieve good social governance in a peaceful time, rule of law can be regarded and adopted as a relatively ideal way to guide or regulate the various acts in the BRI implementation. Therefore, it is highly necessary to build and enhance the safeguard mechanism of rule of law along with the BRI implementation.

There are two major ways of building a mechanism of rule of law from a macro point of view. One is to build a sound coordination mechanism for the BRI action planning and relevant negotiation and decision-making activities. The other is to establish a set of rule of conducts to be observed by the BRI-involved countries. A good set of rule of conducts should be established in such a way that they are acceptable to and will be observed by the collaborating countries before it can play a good role for those countries in their collaborative activities. And it can be established by ways of negotiation and consultation between the collaborating countries based on the specific national conditions, with an ultimate aim to address a wide range of various issues including political, economic, legal as well as the formality specification of bilateral or multilateral contracts. In order to promote the construction of rule of law, it may be helpful and necessary to set up relevant enforcement organizations, which can be directly engaged to coordinate or assist the relevant parties involved to tackle some particular problems arising from their collaborative projects. It may also be helpful to set up a supervisory organisation to oversee how those collaborating parties perform their obligations.

There could possibly be a few other alternatives of prevention and solution to address all those external difficulties and challenges arising from the process of BRI implementation, which require the joint endeavours by China and those hosting countries in future. And arbitration could be one of them. Arbitration could be adopted to resolve those disputes arising between the collaborating partners when their differences get out of their hand.

In conclusion, effective communication can help people in those BRI-involved countries to achieve a good understanding of the objective and significance of the BRI, which could be more important than the hardware facilities of connectivity among the countries along the Belt and Road routes. Effective communication will help the people as well as the countries involved to reach a consensus which will in turn help the BRI to progress steadily and smoothly, and China may have yet to further step up its efforts to strengthen the external communication and publicity about its BRI before the gigantic blueprint develops into great reality.

References

Chu, Y. and Gao, Y. (2015). Three questions with the strategic position of China's "One Belt One Road". *International Economic Review* (3), 92.

Duan, K. (2016). "Yidai Yilu" Zhanlueshishi Mianlindetiaozhanyuduice. [Implementing the "Belt and Road Initiative": Challenges and Countermeasures]. Master Dissertation, Xiangtan University.

Ferdinand, P. (2016). Westward Ho — the China Dream and 'One Belt, One Road': Chinese foreign policy under Xi Jinping. *International Affairs* 92(4), 941–957.

Hu, B. (2018). Prospects for the Belt and Road Initiative implementation. *Chinese Journal of Population Science* (1), 2–18.

Jiang, X. (2017). Green energy light up the China pavilion. *Yazhou Weekly*. 30 July.

Li, H. (2016). Three major problems in need of urgent solution in the infrastructure connectivity amid "One Belt One Road" development. *China Economic Times*, 23 June.

Liu, W. and Huang, X. (2017). Actively reacting to cultural differences to help promote "One Belt One Road" regional cooperation. *Chinese Social Sciences Net*. Available at: www.cssn.cn (Last accessed: 14 May 2017).

National Development and Reform Commission, Ministry of Foreign Affairs and Ministry of Commerce (2015). Vision and actions on jointly building Silk Road Economic Belt and 21st-century Maritime Silk Road. Available at: http://www.ndrc.gov.cn/gzdt/201503/t20150330_669392.html.

Qi, X. (2018). Foreign students in Shanghai talk about the Belt and Road Initiative. *Global Times*. 16 May.

Si, Y. (2017). Zhongguo yidaiyilu de fengxian he tiaozhan. [Risks and challenges of China's belt and road initiative]. *Voice of America*, 13 May.

Wu, J. (2015). "One Belt and One Road", Far-Reaching Initiative. *China-US Focus*. Available at: https://www.chinausfocus.com/finance-economy/one-belt-and-one-road-far-reaching-initiative.

Yu, J. (2018). Wunianlai zhongguo tong "yidaiyilu" yanxian guojia maoyie chao 5 wanyi meiyua. [The trading value between China and countries along the BRI exceeded 5000 billion over the past five years]. *Xinhuanet*. 28 August.

Zhang, L. and Lan, Q. (2016). Pushing forward the connectivity construction along with the BRI implementation by means of capital operation. *Nankai Journal* (1), 71–76.

Chapter

2

Economic Historical Development and Leadership Underlying the BRI Strategy

Gary Hawke

1. Introduction

What is new is always challenging. Yet, innovation is needed for economic and social progress. China's Belt and Road Initiative (BRI) is the current feature of the international landscape which most clearly exhibits this familiar dilemma. Its challenge derives from its novelty, and not from its Chinese origins.

2. A Vision, Not a Plan

The basic outline of the BRI is well known. It was introduced by President Xi Jinping personally, initially as a revived Silk Belt and a Maritime Silk Road (MSR), clearly drawing on the historical memories of earlier linkages between China and its Asian neighbours, in Central Asia and Southeast Asia especially but extending to South

Asia, Africa and Europe (Gautrin 2018). It can be described as having several components, such as "Six international economic cooperation corridors — The New Eurasia Land Bridge and routes between China–Mongolia–Russia, China–Central Asia–West Asia, China–Indochina, China–Pakistan and Bangladesh–China–India–Myanmar" (EIU for HSBC 2018). But the anxiety to not miss out produced enquiries more generally and BRI is now best conceived as a Chinese offer of collaboration with any partner who can reach agreement on a specific project. There is a substantial element of continuity with earlier Chinese conceptions and initiatives, but when it is expressed in Chinese terms not always readily translated, it looks far from familiar (Thomas 2018).

The most obvious novelty is that it appeals to a history not dominated by the story of "the expansion of Europe" giving way eventually to the primacy of the USA. Marco Polo is a minor figure in that story while the interaction of the expansion of Europe with China is only too likely to lead directly to study of the "century of humiliation".

Perhaps even more striking is the way the BRI looks westward from China. It does not accept the notion of the "Asia-Pacific Region" which has been fundamental to many conceptions of the international economy and society. The precise nature of "Asia-Pacific" was always contested; was it essentially the Japanese concept of "Pacific Asia", the littoral of Asia from the Russian Far East, coastal China, Korea, Japan, Southeast Asia, to Australia and New Zealand, and through the link of the US–Japan Security Alliance, North America? Or perhaps the Pacific created by Spanish ships which linked Mexico, Peru and California to Philippines and China and reinforced by US Pacific interests following the Japanese war of 1941–1945? Or did it evolve from the British notion of Asia as India and the Far East? Was it the "Pacific Rim" created by geographers and including at least the western edge of Latin America? Or, in Australia and New Zealand especially, did it mean the Pacific Islands as well as the rim of the Pacific Ocean? These variations could coexist and Asia-Pacific institutions varied in their footprints. APEC mostly reflected the Pacific Rim idea, while the Council for Security Cooperation in Asia Pacific included India but not Latin America. Despite these variations, Asia-Pacific was widely regarded as a unit within the international system, a natural component along with Africa, Europe and the Americas (despite its overlap with Asia-Pacific). BRI was not Asia-Pacific in character.

While novelty induced scepticism and doubts if not opposition, BRI also attracted thoughts of possible largesse. Fear of missing out created questions about whether BRI was limited to regions and countries in its westward trajectories (Bisley 2018[1], Young and Lin 2018[2]). Chinese responded that participation was open generally and so the notional map of BRI was extended to include a component which moved through the South Pacific and at least towards Latin America and the Americas generally. That induced other tensions, especially between desire for resources and unwillingness to contemplate disruption of established relationships. But even without these additional considerations, BRI would not have become an Asia-Pacific initiative.

BRI was advanced as a vision. It was not a plan of a kind which was familiar to participants in many international organisations. It was not composed of a specific objective along with components organised in chronological sequence to achieve that objective and with organisational units charged with managing those components. It was much more like the process familiar to ASEAN and APEC, the negotiations of agreed objectives and frequent interaction to compare notes and exchange learnings from the experiences of different courses of action adopted in pursuit of the agreed objective. Such a process is not unknown in the European Union, especially in the area of social policy, but it is much more familiar to those experienced in the "ASEAN way".

All projects and initiatives encounter a "blueprint" dilemma. How far is it worthwhile planning in detail, when learning from experience is likely versus how can there be assurance about any particular choice

---

[1] This is very evident in Australia and New Zealand.

[2] Young and Lin (2018) have a good discussion of thinking about BRI in relation to Pacific Islands. An amusing example is the opportunism of a Maritime Silk Road Universities Consortium (*VUW University News* 2018).

without first elucidating long-term implications? The best choice depends on the nature of the project and especially on the risks and benefits associated with it. That in turn may depend on the particular parties most concerned. BRI was advocated as an opportunity for codirection, for collaboration between China and one or more of its partners. Demands for "transparency" and advanced specification of what and how BRI would consist of were more rhetorical than analytical. The novel did not fit with the familiar.

BRI was never a project. It was an invitation to others to join with China in projects which offered mutual benefit. It was not just for infrastructure development although infrastructure was always prominent in thinking about it. Infrastructure was something which China could do well, and it was always high on the wishlist of any analyst looking for economic growth and progress in Asia. Infrastructure is more than concrete, asphalt and steel even for those who are inclined to forget about airports. The physical infrastructure requires technology which facilitates its use and technology, which ensures that its use is compatible with the intentions of those who provided the infrastructure. And it requires people who are able to manage that technology. The dominant vision is connectivity, facilitating community building among all parties to an interaction.

This is familiar thinking in the discussions of Asian economic integration. It has also spread into wider international discussions. The Asia–Europe meeting has adopted connectivity in the following sense:

> Connectivity is about bringing countries, people and societies closer together. It facilitates access and is a means to foster deeper economic and people-to-people ties. It encompasses the hard and soft aspects, including the physical and institutional social-cultural linkages that are the fundamental supportive means to enhance the economic, political security and socio-cultural ties between Asia and Europe, which also contribute to the narrowing of the varying levels of development and capacities.
>
> ASEM connectivity … should also contribute to the materialisation of the principles, goals and targets of the 2030 Agenda For Sustainable Development. Sustainability is one of the important quality benchmarks for the connectivity initiatives in the ASEM context.

More prosaically, connectivity may be divided into three components: physical infrastructure which permits connections, institutional connectivity or rules and official processes which facilitate use of connecting infrastructure, and person-to-person connectivity which requires popular attitudes permitting collaboration across borders.

Each of the elements of this conception can be related to pieces of thinking more conventional in international economic diplomacy. Infrastructure connectivity has much in common with the projects long familiar in official development assistance (ODA). Institutional connectivity immediately evokes thoughts and debates about "behind the border", "structural reform", especially competition policy and regulation of foreign investment. Person-to-person connectivity overlaps with cultural diplomacy and social interaction. Nevertheless, recognising the context of connectivity facilitates understanding of how different styles of thinking can generate miscommunication.

BRI is not ODA. It neither invades territory well provided for by existing development processes and institutions nor undermines the protections they have developed for borrowing countries. It is not a set of infrastructural developments for which institutions like the World Bank and regional development banks have built up a store of learning by doing (especially on sustainable management) which should not be bypassed. BRI is not a variant on the familiar.

Nor does BRI supplant existing efforts to develop regulatory cooperation across national borders. But it creates a different venue and a changed context for bringing national regulators together and widening their perspective from exclusive concentration on the national interest as traditionally understood. The same is true for the task of reducing suspicions and antagonisms between different peoples. BRI creates novelty.

This is especially disconcerting for those who are accustomed to leadership in international affairs being exercised by "us and our mates".

BRI necessitates reflection on the durability of the current global order with "two pillars: first, a series of essentially liberal international institutions including the UN, the Bretton Woods machinery, the

GATT (later WTO), and the 1948 Universal Declaration of Human Rights; second, the possession and predisposition to use US political, economic, and military power to defend the order it created. Ever since then, the United States has sought to defend this system through its global network of alliances" (Rudd 2018). There is no direct challenge, but the creation of an alternative centre of attention reduces certainty about the future. Certainty is always subject to evolution and change which is likely to proceed on several fronts[3] and have numerous but not always entirely consistent motivations. The Bretton Woods institutions are no longer what they were in 1945, and their original motivations were mixed. American interests genuinely desired a harmonious world, but some American senators were more concerned to ensure that American goods were not shut out of markets by a system of imperial preference. The Marshall Plan which could be added to those specified above was a generous effort to create a more prosperous world, one which would add to US prosperity, but it was also an initiative to generate commitment to US leadership. The big changes in history are seldom simple. That is equally true of BRI. What some see as planning and managing the continuation of economic growth while collaborating with neighbours and international partners, others may see as directed to "trade connectivity, reduce surplus domestic industrial capacity, develop poorer interior provinces, promote energy security, and internationalise Chinese industrial and financial standards", and with escalating intensity of suspicion, "Fundamentally, beyond the 'community of shared destiny for humanity' claimed by Xi, BRI is selling a China-centred *order*, encompassing Eurasia and its maritime periphery." (Graham 2018).

Perceptions will be modified over time, and only for those prepared to recognise experience rather than always claim justification for existing beliefs. It is especially ironic now to see wholehearted commitment to the global order combined with actions by the US administration whose actions must tend to undermine that order.

---

[3]This is most obviously in the use of tariffs contrary to the spirit of the "most favoured nation" character of the World Trade Authority (Feigenbaum 2018).

3. The Economic Dimensions of BRI

The economic growth of China is the outstanding event of the international economy in the last 40 years.

Essentially, the resources of China, natural and human, which had been isolated by political decisions, were brought into the international economy. The experience of the American mid-west and west being added to the international economy centred on the North Atlantic in the 19th century, was repeated 40 years after Deng Xiaoping's opening to the world economy from 1978.

Just as the development of 19th century USA was facilitated by the willingness of Europe to accommodate American imports, the remarkable growth of China was facilitated by the willingness of the international economy to accommodate its rise. Just as Europe benefited from American imports and American markets, so the world economy benefited from Chinese growth. Europe's gains were not equally shared among regions and occupations — European wheat farmers who were unable to adapt were simply displaced by imported American wheat. So, in more recent times, those who were unable to evade direct competition with Chinese imports did not share in the increased prosperity.

The recent experience has been moderated by international institutions and especially the World Trade Organisation. Those countries, like the USA, whose acquiescence was essential for WTO decisions were in a position to frustrate the process. There is a sense therefore in which the willingness of the USA to accommodate Chinese growth was essential, and the same is true of any country large and influential enough to exercise a veto in the consensual decision-making of the WTO. But we might also reflect that the WTO influences trade rather than controlling it. Had China not become a member of the WTO it would still have offered its exports to international markets and its economic growth would have generated attractive markets for international traders. The process of Chinese growth as part of the international economy would have been much less smooth, but it would still have proceeded. Neither the US, nor any other country, made Chinese growth possible.

Just as the rise of the USA in the 19th century, while dependent in the form it took on European acquiescence, was the result of those who managed and provided the workforce for agriculture and the urban infrastructure of the American West, so the rise of China, while facilitated by the accommodation in established institutions and markets, was due primarily to the workforce and management which incorporated Chinese natural and human resources into the international economy. When resources previously unused, whether because they are unknown or because of political restraints, are brought to bear in the world economy, world growth is the natural result.

Chinese growth occurred first in coastal regions with ready access to international trade. The objective of spreading growth among the very large population of China directed attention to central and western China. (In any case, as growth proceeded in eastern China, wage levels there rose relative to those in central and western China creating an incentive to use the resources that existed in those regions.) Consequently, memories of the Silk Road constituted a very natural framework for thinking about how continuation of growth could be assured.

China's economic growth utilised a model of export-led growth such as had proven successful for Japan, the Tigers of Korea, Taiwan, Hong Kong and Singapore, and the "flying geese" of Southeast Asia. China was much too large to be just another goose. Furthermore, the Chinese political system was not inclined to follow all aspects of the "business-led" characterisation of the flying geese model (although that had been compatible with significant government roles, the essential character being that they facilitated change rather than protected existing activities.)

China has observed the rules of the WTO to which it agreed on its accession in 2001, but it has also participated in changes in the distribution and nature of world trade. It is simply too large to do anything else. From using labour which was cheap in international perspective to attract components and assemble them into final products which were exported to make cheaper goods available in world markets, China has itself become a significant final market, and its industries do more of the preparatory production. World production and world trade have become a set of networks in which components cross borders several times before becoming the consumer products found in many markets, including China's. Far from being simply another node in this network of production and trade, China's size and growth made it a hub alongside the existing hubs. Accordingly, neighbouring economies were attracted to engage with China. BRI encouraged this adaptation. Those neighbouring countries were more to the west of China than in the Pacific region. And there was no competing hub in China's neighbourhood to the west.

Inside China, the growth process involved a great deal of building and construction. Steelmaking and construction industries grew especially fast. Consequently, as China looked to spread growth beyond its borders as well as within them, steel and construction industries had the capacity to participate. It is not possible to distinguish industries which respond to a diminishing rate of growth in their "home" market by exploiting opportunities for exports, from using foreign markets to dispose of "excess" capacity — medieval and early modern commentators often thought of exports in terms like "vent for surplus".

The nature of the challenge of Chinese trade to the existing WTO system is contested. There is a very widespread belief in Washington that China cheats against existing rules or at least does not observe their spirit. So even a shrewd and experienced observer like Fareed Zakaria asserts, "on one big, fundamental point, President Trump is right: China is a trade cheat." His argument, however, is unusually confused since it continues by distinguishing China from other economies like Korea and Singapore whose admission to the WTO the US supported, "They were relatively small compared with the size of the global economy, and they also lived under the American security umbrella. Both factors meant that Washington and the West had considerable leverage over these new entrants." (Zakaria 2018). Zakaria almost but not quite acknowledges that the problem is with US expectations rather than Chinese behaviour.

China conforms with WTO rules, but those rules have not kept up with changes in the world trade. The most persuasive judgment is that of former WTO Director-General, Pascale Lamy, "China's trade practices — including opaque, trade-distorting subsidization of high-tech products — need to be disciplined by stronger WTO rules. But technically, Beijing is right to argue that it abides by current WTO restrictions because the rules on industrial subsidies are too vague. And it will probably argue that rules about agricultural subsidies also need strengthening, which U.S. farmers may not like." (Lamy 2018).[4] The trading system involves more than tariffs and subsidies. The really difficult issues are the terms on which foreign direct investment is permitted, the rules for digital trade and especially the management of data and standards generally. In these areas, the problem is not that China is in breach of the rules or even the spirit of the rules, but that it has not been possible to reach agreement on what the rules should be. No new rule can be formulated without China's participation, but then that is true of any other major economy. In response to a query about China's compliance with WTO rules, China-critic, Derek Scissors of AEI concedes "It mostly is. But the WTO no longer works. I'm not arguing that Chinese industrial policy is conventional, I just don't see a clear WTO violation in subsidization of SOE's (if not for export, which they don't) or of market access commitments at accession. WTO IP rules have been violated but they are weak so the violations are minor in comparison to the scope of the harm." (Nelson Report 2018). The US no longer makes international rules, and CPTPP shows that USA is indispensable only for global rules.

BRI is significant because it carries the prospect of creating a network within the international economy which can write rules for its members, and those rules need not be the same as the existing international rules. For a long time, the US, while not having the ability to impose all of its wishes, could prevent the adoption of international rules which it judged incompatible with its interests. BRI is a visible

[4] The headline is misleading — the idea is that Trump's tariffs, while illegal, may stimulate WTO reform. But the process may not be simple: "Keeping the United States within the WTO should obviously be Plan A. But it would be prudent for other members to start thinking about devising a new international trade organization minus the United States in order to avoid the 'my way or the highway' blackmail that has become the American president's signature negotiating style." The evolution of CPTPP as a TPP-USA could well be significant.

symbol of a decline in its power. Its response is causing others to distrust the WTO too, and because the US claims to be acting in response to China, China is blamed for the WTO decline. (Gao 2018). "The China One Belt, One Road is going to be the new W.T.O. — like it or not," said Joe Kaeser, chief executive of Siemens, the German industrial giant, referring to the World Trade Organization." (Bradsher 2018). Like much business comment, this is exaggerated, but decision-making in the WTO is changing and BRI will inject a new powerful voice.

China's rate of growth will slow. This is not so much the result of the limitations of any particular economic system as a matter of arithmetic. China has been growing at 8–9% per annum, and the expectation of its government is for a slowing to something more like 6%. If China, now composing about 15% of world output grows at 6% per year while the rest of the world grows at 2%, then after 10 years China will compose more than 20% of world output and, after 20 years, it will be approaching 30%. Capacity constraints eventually force the fastest growing component to converge to the average.

China's growth will inevitably face challenges. The growth of the US mid-west was not without issues and difficulties. It may well be that Chinese financial institutions will not always cope with servicing debt levels[5] although currently because the debt is mostly internal and because there is still effective centralised monitoring of financial institutions, the risk is far from extreme. The very word, "debt", often raises feelings about moral rectitude instead of being read as a technical term for distributing the ownership of asset accumulation.[6] The challenges which will occur are not the main reason for expecting Chinese growth to converge towards international averages.

BRI will influence the international average as well as provide a safety valve for surplus Chinese capacity. It is, in any case, odd to see

---

[5] Perkins wisely emphasises not debt management but the problems encountered by all developing economies in building effective institutions.

[6] The classic illustration is Stone (1965), which explored the growth of debt among English aristocrats as a reason for social change in England in the 16th and 17th centuries without recognising that the aristocrats were increasing their net worth by using loans to improve the value of their estates.

surplus capacity cited as a reason for curbing China's participation in world trade. The "creative destruction" which drives private enterprise is supposed to eliminate the least efficient competitors in any market, not the "surplus capacity" of the most efficient producer. It is not unreasonable to seek to identify subsidies which distort competition but that is different from alleging "surplus capacity".

4. The Political/Security Dimensions of BRI

The record of China's economic growth and the prospects for its continuation can account for BRI. However, it has political aspects and it has political and security implications for other countries.

Since 1978, China has played a key role in international political and security affairs. Its government has used the image of a "peaceful rise" and after a brief war with Vietnam and except for skirmishes on the disputed Indo-Pacific border, it can justifiably claim that the image is realistic. Even potential pressure on neighbours has generated more alarm in distant quarters than in the countries directly affected, accustomed as they are to a long history of interactions with China. China has been a responsible member of the United Nations becoming a major contributor to peacekeeping operations and observing sanctions imposed by the United Nations. In addition to meeting its commitments from its accession to the WTO in 2001, China has a record of good international citizenship. Most complaints with any coherence are that China has not allowed new international rules to be formulated entirely in the interest of others. China can reasonably claim that while it does not accept the validity of rules, norms or conventions in the evolution of which it has not had a full part, it implements those to which it has agreed.

Why then should the BRI be thought to threaten any political or security interests?

China is large and different. While international institutions have long accommodated many different kinds of political organisation, they have had a common core which is best described as willingness to acquiesce in American leadership. In the years 1945–1990, that leadership meant maintaining an equilibrium in the Cold War. After the collapse of the Soviet Union, it meant maintaining peaceful coexistence, restraining American unilateralism and at least denying it international status in the absence of a genuine consensus. There are always issues of time consistency; any international agreement is likely to be confronted by issues not fully anticipated when the agreement was made. It is not only discrete initiatives which evolve over time. Thus, one of the major Chinese influences in international political events in the last 30 years has been in the development of the Responsibility to Protect doctrine which adjusted general understanding of the boundary between internal affairs and those in which international intervention is justified. Not surprisingly, there was careful attention to the wording of the basic documents (in all the languages of the United Nations). The doctrine is complex, specifying the responsibility of national governments to protect their people, the responsibility on the international community to assist national governments to fulfil their obligations and, where required, the responsibility of the international community to act in a timely and decisive way to prevent and halt genocide, ethnic cleansing, war crimes and crimes against humanity when a state manifestly fails to protect its populations. The last "pillar" of the agreement needs elucidation and it has become apparent that China interprets it to require more consultation with an offending state than most "western" commentators and authorities. China's participation adds to the complexity of ensuring real agreement among governments and commitment to a common understanding of what was agreed.

The issues are exhibited most clearly in economic institutions. China observed the rules of the WTO as they existed in 2001. But the rules of the WTO had been evolving. In the GATT from the 1950s onwards, rules were created first for tariffs — the mfn (most favoured nation) system provided that parties to GATT established tariffs which applied to all other parties to GATT and "bound" them so that they became an upper limit which could not be exceeded. Then as tariffs were recognised as far from the only barriers to goods, disciplines were adopted on subsidies, first for exports and then on the production of goods which were exported or competed with imports. Disciplines were also evolved for sanitary and phytosanitary issues and government procurement. Technical barriers to trade rules were adopted to allow goods to be subjected to required standards for purposes like consumer safety, but to avoid their use to confer advantages on local producers. As each barrier to trade was subjected to international rules, others became more prominent and they in turn were the subject of internationally agreed disciplines. The Uruguay Round of 1986–1994 brought agriculture within the system, strengthened the system for resolving disputes between parties and also generated some disciplines on investment. It also resulted in an agreement on the trade-related aspects of intellectual property, TRIPs.

Even before the accession of China in 2001, the evolution which had characterised GATT and which was expected to continue with the WTO had proven difficult. The Doha Round was launched with the intention of continuing the process and addressing further disciplines on transparency in government procurement, trade facilitation (customs issues), trade and investment, and trade and competition, and with a general notion that the purpose was to promote "development". "Development" was not carefully defined and it became apparent that the belief, dominant in many advanced economies, that economic development was promoted by reducing barriers to international trade and economic integration was not shared in many developing economies which thought that "development" required more special conditions for poorer economies and more transfer of resources from rich to poor. The Doha Round stalled.

China's membership was not why the Doha Round was not successful. Parties like India were much more directly responsible. But while debate about the Doha Round continued, the world did not stand still. The Internet and modern information and communication technologies changed the nature of much trade and interdependence. Services became much more prominent in economic interdependence and were not readily regulated by controls at the borders. While the TRIPs agreement essentially treated intellectual property (IP) as "property" as generally understood in legal systems, the way in which IP should be understood became increasingly contested. IP has components of copyright, patents, trademarks and trade secrets. These are not an amorphous whole. The first two were originally conceived as providing a balance between making knowledge available for economic innovation while providing rewards for those who generated new knowledge. Specific elements of novelty were protected for a limited period. Trademarks were designed as consumer protection against counterfeit, and the law about trade secrets evolved to support private efforts to both maintain exclusive knowledge and use it. The whole area requires fundamental reconsideration in the face of a digital economy. (Revisiting the Machinery Acts by which British industrialists tried to preserve exclusive knowledge of their innovations in the Industrial Revolution would be a useful component, especially for those who think that knowledge can be treated like a physical asset.) Chinese participation is needed and simply asserting that existing practice is sacrosanct is not productive.[7] BRI will promote the needed discussion.

In these issues, China was simply one among many parties to continuing debates, albeit an especially important one because of its size. In other respects, China posed particular issues. The topics of government procurement and subsidies were established issues in GATT and the WTO but they pointed towards the more general topic of the role of government in economic affairs. Nobody outside some political activists and some misguided journalists thinks that the economy can be insulated from government intervention, but to what extent should governments be constrained from frustrating economic interdependence in pursuit of other objectives? No simple answer is available. Nobody doubts that governments can control migration in the interests of social cohesion, but some trade, especially in services, requires movement of natural persons. Nobody doubts that governments can promote the education of their populations, but education is difficult to separate from some aspects of research and development, and there is not a great deal of difference between subsidising some industrial innovation and subsidising the education of professionals and development of knowledge relevant

[7] A valuable brief summary is in Chopra (2018).

to industrial innovation. State-owned enterprises (SOEs) may act like their private sector counterparts or they may pursue non-economic objectives, and subsidies to them are harder to detect and monitor.

China posed challenges in all these respects. In particular, Chinese SOEs were a bigger component of the economy than in most countries, even though they were relatively declining. The Chinese market was attractive to many foreign investors, sufficiently so for them to accept restrictive rules on the governance of Chinese subsidiaries, and also to accept conditions such as the sharing of IP with Chinese interests.

The sequence of events in GATT and the Uruguay Round created an expectation that the international rules would continue to evolve and in particular would accommodate changes in the world economy. Chinese membership was a reason, although far from the only one, which made continued evolution more difficult.

And it was more than a matter of international economic governance. Contests over the content of economic rules became contests between political systems. The appropriate management of SOEs was not only a matter of ensuring that the terms of competition properly reflected resource use but were seen by some as contests between political systems and political philosophies. Pascale Lamy has identified the core issue: "The U.S. system is hyper-capitalist, individualistic and entrepreneurial; China's mixes a strong collectivist state with uneven market competition; Europe's social market system and many others stand somewhere in between. These systems must be able to coexist and exchange goods and services as well as facilitate people's mobility across their divergent economic and social models." (Lamy 2018). That would be obvious to most European observers; it is equally congenial for many others. For example, New Zealand reconstructed its SOEs to clarify the distinction between their social obligations and their business activities only in the 1980s, and even now, it uses a monopolistic organisation, Pharmac, to acquire the pharmaceuticals distributed in its public health system. Pharmac is a natural target for pharmaceutical producers and only a little less natural for the US negotiators of trade agreements. The optimal boundary between economic diplomacy and social policy requires sophisticated analysis, not simple-minded injunctions to "do it our way".

The same is true in considerations of "hard power" if we distinguish that from the predominantly "soft power" nature of economic diplomacy. The Law of the Sea Convention was mostly negotiated before China became a full member of the international community and interpretation of its terms allows room for disagreement. In particular, "freedom of navigation" may refer to commercial vessels or might extend to the movement of naval vessels, with plenty of middle ground such as a distinction between simple movement of a naval vessel and the transit of a military vessel operating armaments or electronic equipment. The US position on these issues would be stronger if it ratified the Convention on the Law of the Sea but, in any case, its interpretation is shared by a minority of those who have ratified. Similar comments could be made about the International Court of Justice.

The "rule of law" is a good guide for domestic jurisdictions where it can be a shorthand for both the superiority of rules to the preferences of any individual and a statement about the enforceability of known rules. Even then it can be difficult to separate the law from political influence, exercised, for example, through the appointment of judges. But its simplistic transfer to the international sphere cannot be sustained. There are few means of enforcing international decisions. "Rule of law" becomes only too easily a disguise for the assertion "I am the Law", substitution of a hegemon for international agreement.

American perspectives are different. Washington seems almost united in the belief that the US permitted China to join the WTO, and accommodated its rise, in return for a promise that China would become like the US, opening its economy to international competition and adopting American practices on IP and investment conditions. Because China is judged not to honour the alleged agreement, the US is obliged to end "strategic engagement" and enter into "strategic competition". The strength of this Washington consensus is remarkable, crossing disciplines and including officials, former officials, think tanks and academics. It is rare to find American dissent but a former Secretary of Treasury injects some realism: "'There's this revisionist myth that some of us who worked to engage China thought it would become a Jeffersonian democracy, or espouse a liberal Western order,' Mr. Paulson said in his interview. 'We never thought that. We always knew the Communist Party would play an important, dominant role.' [NP] The problem now, he says, is that some in the U.S. believe that a clash is inevitable unless China liberalises politically: 'If we make this about their political system, we are really going to be bumping up against a hard place because we are not the ones who are going to change their political system.'"(Nelson Report 2018).

Nobody, who lived closer to China in 2001, could have been as misguided as the current Washington consensus. Listeners to Lee Kuan Yew knew about Chinese attachments to Chinese ways of doing things. Henry Paulson had and has many Chinese contacts and is much closer to the usual regional view than most of Washington.

BRI has become an element in a wider US view of the world. Unilateralism grew during the 1990s and in response to the events of 11th September 2001. During the Obama Administration, the US showed discontent with the operation of the Appellate Body of the WTO, giving succour to those who maintained an old doctrine that American law recognised no outside authority on American citizens. The election of Trump in 2016 brought a clear statement of "America First" and a desire to rely on bilateral relations rather than multilateral institutions. The withdrawal from TPP, and crude negotiating tactics in relation to KORUS, NAFTA and Japan all point towards dissatisfaction with the position of the US as the leader. The US remains the strongest military power in the world and the largest economy but it has lost its position of dominance. The "politics of trade in Washington now raise serious questions about whether the US can ever again undertake a large-scale multilateral deal" (Feigenbaum 2018). The bluster of President Trump about the US producing the best of everything merely underlines its relative decline.

At the end of the 19th century, Europeans watched the rise of the USA but thought that it had essentially divided the world into the Old World dominated by Europe and its empires and the New World, an American preserve. World War I left no doubt that world leadership had shifted, although the refusal of the US to join the League of Nations left the world divided. From 1945, Europe acquiesced in US leadership against the Soviet bloc. Now Europe puzzles as leadership is divided by the USA and Asia. "Europe is no longer most of what matters on the planet. For some 70 years, the centre was the Atlantic, but since the rise of China, within the rise of Asia, the centre of gravity has shifted to the Pacific. Europe was waning, in the periphery of these trans-pacific exchanges, and *de facto* it was dealing with Asia through America. [NP] Europe regained some centrality with the launch of China's new Silk Road, the BRI (Belt and Road Initiative), and all the rival projects coming from India or other competing countries in Asia, but still the individual countries are in no position to play a role in Asia." (Sisci 2018).

It is a peculiarly European perspective to see Europe as the hidden element in a world consisting of the US and China. Others will see the Sino–American tension as an important element not only in the global affairs but also in the regional affairs of Asia, Asia-Pacific or Indo-Pacific. The countries of South and Southeast Asia have no wish to be forced into alignment with either China or USA. Some like Japan and Australia can see a cleavage between their major security ally and their major economic partner; all wish to avoid disruption to any of their economic partners and especially one as important as China while also wanting to avoid any intrusive hegemony.

This is very clear in the response to BRI of Japan and India. Japan had promoted an Asian Monetary Fund which evolved in the Chiang Mai Initiative Multilateralism long before Asian Infrastructure Investment Bank (AIIB) and it used international investment (mostly private) to support the "flying geese" growth of Southeast Asia. While it was sometimes seen as "pushing back" against AIIB and BRI (Johnson 2018), Japanese policy is increasingly dominated by collaboration with BRI, subject to agreement on alignment with international standards for terms and governance (Basu 2017).[8] India's policy has followed a similar trajectory.

[8] Also notice "Fact Sheet: Prime Minister Abe's visit to China, October 26, 2018" issued by the Japanese government which includes "Both Japan and China concurred in seeking Japan–China cooperation at a new stage as equal partners. To this end, Japan will no longer adopt ODA project proposals for China in and after FY2018." The Sino–Japan relationship will remain tender for some time yet, but the movement towards equal collaboration looks promising.

Nor should the Chinese view be discounted. "In China's proposed community, the world would continue in the general direction of economic liberalisation but would also work towards a new global system that is more equitable, inclusive and fair. Beyond the economic implications, the deepening of international economic cooperation and the strengthening of interdependence would hopefully help solve the 'security dilemma'. Xi and others believe that the Belt and Road Initiative (BRI) and the Asian Infrastructure Investment Bank (AIIB) are not only examples of China's increasing leadership in the provision of international public goods, but may also provide a solution for international conflicts by cementing common economic interests among the parties engaged in confrontation." (Wang 2018).[9] It is hard to see anything but the perspective of the speaker in the difference between those claims and responses like "China is in the midst of a significant effort to redraw the geopolitical, economic and security landscape. Its Belt and Road program, initiated in 2013–2014, is not simply a plan for global infrastructure connectivity using Chinese technology, materials and labour. It is also a larger, strategic effort to develop international support for Chinese political values, to expand the reach of the Chinese People's Liberation Army and Navy via control of scores of ports and the establishment of new military bases and to erode the dominance of the US dollar in international trade and investment settlements. In addition, Beijing is working to establish a community of politically like-minded countries to challenge western liberal democracies on issues such as Internet sovereignty and human rights". (Economy 2018). The contest is not about BRI but about anxieties over who will have the advantage in applying the next stage of technology to their economy (Barfield 2018a, Barfield 2018b, Segal 2018, *Stratfor Worldview* 2018).

BRI, with its major infrastructure projects, and its concomitant intensification of relationships, is necessarily a venue where political-security challenges have to be played out.

[9] Like most IR specialists, Jan Yong Wang uses "public goods" in a normal language sense — thing valued by the public — rather than in the technical sense of economics.

5. Implementation Issues

Worries expressed about BRI tend to concentrate on implementation issues. It is hard to find a convincing reason to decline offers of collaboration. The most common complaints are that governance is opaque and that interest rates create issues of debt infringing sovereignty. Both of these are little more than objections to the novelty.

China responded to claims that its decision-making could be arbitrary by treating proposals as invitations to agree on a common objective and understanding of what was to be done. Inevitably, when one party is a petitioner and the other a benefactor there is likely to be some dissatisfaction but having a proposal declined or varied is not a reason for complaint. It is not that there is a model of governing projects which can be copied. The World Bank dates from before the evolution of modern ideas of a separation between governance and management and full-time executive directors who look to national capitals rather than to the interests of the Bank itself; it is not a model which would be constructed now.

Debtors usually think that interest rates are excessive. When effective interest rates have to be discerned from apparently concessional terms, or are embedded in project definitions which limit providers of components, there is a fruitful ground for disagreement. But there is nothing to suggest that BRI projects are in any way exceptional. It is worth remembering that in any earlier time, Japan was much criticised for providing interest-bearing loans rather than grants; there is now more support for its argument that loans rather than grants attracted more commitment by the recipients, although this argument was often sugared with the observation that repayments could frequently be the basis of further development assistance.

Chinese decision-making is more difficult to follow from outside. Characterization of it as "lacking transparency" is justified. To put that in perspective, it is worth remembering the specific expertise in "Kremlinology" which was used to decipher Soviet decision-making, and it pays to think critically about the extent to which the processes of decision-making in Washington are public. The latter conjectural exercise suggests that the major point about Chinese decision-making is not that it is lacking in transparency relative to decision-making elsewhere as that there is less follow-up by journalists and scholars in reconstructing decisions sometime after they were made. We might expect that as Chinese influence in international decision-making grows, other countries will develop more expertise in reconstructing its processes.

Claims about both governance and interest rates can often be characterised as paternalism or even a colonial mentality. An implicit suggestion is that countries collaborating with China on BRI projects are unable to manage their own affairs and, without the intervention of some benevolent outsider, they will be exploited. It is not only the governments of developing economies which can make mistakes. National governments can be beset by special interests so that "One risk is that political elites would, with easy Chinese financing, implement infrastructure projects with high political gains and limited economic benefits that are doomed to become 'white elephants'" (Gautrin 2018), but that is hardly unique to BRI initiatives and it is best addressed directly rather than through outside management of foreign loans. The same point applies to worries such as the use of Chinese labour and also inexperienced Chinese security forces (Legarda 2018, Lim 2018). Partners in the BRI should indeed do due diligence, ensure they know what is offered and accepted, and make careful and deliberate decisions about their national interest — but then that is what they should do with any venture, international or national. The same point applies to Australian and New Zealand worries about Chinese initiatives with Pacific islands, with the additional point that Pacific Islanders, while drawing on benevolent advice from traditional sources, can make their own decisions (Young and Lin 2018).[10]

Discussion of implementation issues is dominated by debates about infrastructure projects. The World Bank, other development

[10]There is a particular conundrum about decisions by Nauru and Cook Islands which are parts of the "realm" of New Zealand, internally self-governing but with New Zealand managing external relations on their behalf. There are often questions over whether control of foreign investment is an internal or external matter and what was a convenient device in the 1960s and 1970s has to evolve with changes in the world and regional environments.

banks and other providers and managers of ODA directed to infrastructure benefited from learning by doing, especially in anticipating environmental impacts. Learning by doing is substantially a public good, available to all prepared to put in an effort to exploit it. There is no reason to think that BRI projects will be distinctive at all in this regard, while the degree of international scrutiny of BRI projects makes it more likely that available learning by doing will be exploited.

BRI is not exclusively about physical infrastructure. We can expect that the technological and personal aspects of managing infrastructure so as to benefit from connectivity will gradually become more prominent. BRI can be expected to promote trade among partners by reducing transit times and trade costs (De Soyres *et al.* 2018). Institutional connectivity will be as influential as infrastructure in that impact. We can also assume that issues already present in the international economic debate will then be debated in the context of BRI. Will the information and communication technology used in BRI projects be subject to claims of cyber conflict and IP theft? If the Sino–US conflict continues, it is only too likely that it will, but there is nothing unique to BRI.

6. Conclusion

BRI is a new element in world affairs, and it takes time for the new feature to become familiar. In a situation where one economy is gaining a leadership position while another's is declining, the novel is especially threatening. The big issue is whether BRI can be absorbed into an international economic architecture which can accommodate various economic systems in a way which permits exploitation of synergies within and among those systems.

References

Barfield, C. (2018a). Targeting China's high-tech protectionism: CFIUS is not enough. *Nelson Report*, 5 July.

Barfield, C. (2018b). The dual goals of the Trump administration's new attack on Chinese intellectual property theft. *AEIdeas* , 8 November.

Basu, T. (2017). Japan's belt and road puzzle, decoded. *The Diplomat*, 28 February.

Bisley, N. (2018). Melbourne joins the Belt-and-Road. *Lowy Institute Interpreter*, 31 October.

Bradsher, K. (2018). At Davos, the real star may have been China, not Trump. *New York Times*, 29 January.

Chopra, S. (2018). End intellectual property. *Aeon*, 12 November.

De Soyres, F.M.M.R., Mulabdic, A., Murray, S., Gaffurri, N.P.R. and Ruta, M. (2018). How much will the Belt and Road Initiative reduce trade costs? World Bank Policy Research Working Paper No. 8614.

Economy, E. (2018). By backing China into a corner, Trump may end up diminishing US power. *Nelson Report*, 4 June.

EIU for HSBC (2018). The role of BRI in developing trade corridors: The improvement of trade corridors for Chinese and foreign companies is a key component of the Belt and Road Initiative (BRI), 10 April. Circulated by *qz.com*.

Feigenbaum, E. A. (2018). Reluctant stakeholder: Why China's highly strategic brand of revisionism is more challenging than Washington thinks. *The Paulson Institute* circulated by *Nelson Report*, 13 May: "It's tough to critique another country's obvious revisionism when you're a revisionist yourself.".

Gao, H. (2018). Broken promises set a bad example for China in the WTO. *East Asia Forum*, 9 March.

Gautrin, J.-F. (2018). One Belt One Road and the risks behind the win-win situation. *ADB Asia Pathways*, 9 March.

Graham, E. (2018). Belt and Road: More than just a brand. *Lowy Institute Interpreter*, 14 September.

Johnson, K. (2018). Japan takes the lead in countering China's Belt and Road. *Foreign Policy*, 9 February.

Lamy, P. (2018). Trump's protectionism might just save the WTO. *Washington Post*, 12 November.

Legarda, H. (2018). Chinese mercenaries are tightening security on the Belt and Road. *East Asia Forum*, 16 October.

Lim, L. (2018). The BRI needs fewer Chinese characteristics. *East Asia Forum*, 9 May.

Nelson Report (4 April 2018).

Nelson Report (8 November 2018).

Rudd, K. (2018). How Xi Jinping views the world: The core interests that shape China's behaviour. *Foreign Affairs*, 10 May.

Segal, A. (2018). When China rules the web: Technology in service of the state. *Foreign Affairs*, September–October.

Sisci, F. (2018). A German elephant in the room with Trump and Xi. *Nelson Report,* 8 November.

Stone, L. (1965). *The Crisis of the Aristocracy 1558–1641*, Oxford, London.

Stratfor Worldview (2018). The coming tech war with China, August.

Thomas, N. (2018). Chinese foreign policy under Xi Jinping. *East Asia Forum,* 21 October.

Varrall, M. (2018). Belt and Road: China's biggest brand. *Lowy Institute Interpreter,* 29 August.

VUW University News (25 October 2018).

Wang, J.W. (2018). China's vision for a new world order. *East Asia Forum,* 25 January.

Young, J. and Lin, J. (2018). *The Belt and Road Initiative A New Zealand Appraisal*, CCRC, Wellington.

Zakaria, F. (2018). *Washington Post* circulated by *Nelson Report,* 6 April.

Chapter 3

Frontier Infrastructure: OBOR and Northern Sea Route (NSR) in Comparative Perspective

Christopher M. Dent

1. Introduction

For most of recorded human history, Asia has been a primary hub of the world economy. The nations of China and India have, for many centuries, hosted the highest concentrations of human population, and thereby economic activity. Trade with Asia played a notable part in prosperity generation, commercial development, and the rise of European and Middle Eastern societies. When the European maritime powers first established direct sea routes with Asia from the 15th century onwards, regionalised trade networks were already well established among Asian merchants (Chanda 2006, Frank 1998, Sakakibara and Yamakawa 2003). While land-based cargo traffic along the Eurasian "Silk Route" continued to be important at this time, inter-regional trade progressively expanded as European maritime nations became more imperially and commercially ambitious. This would not have been possible without the development of infrastructure.

While the importance of infrastructure has always been acknowledged when explaining this rise of new economic powers and facilitating economic development generally, it has most recently become part of a contested norms discourse covering many aspects of economic governance: trade, development and industry. This specifically relates to China's "Belt Road Initiative" (BRI) initiative, which at its core comprises a set of infrastructure projects traversing the Eurasian landmass and cross-regional sea route links. Some perceive the BRI's "hardware" approach to economic diplomacy as a direct challenge to the Western "software" rules and institutional governance approach. Whatever the case, the BRI represents a historic example of "frontier infrastructure", namely an infrastructure-based project that could establish new frontiers of global economic development with game-changing effects on international trade and economic relations.

The same could be said of the Northern Sea Route (NSR), the shortest maritime link between the global economic hubs of East Asia and Europe, where in a climate changing world Asian nations are looking to develop the NSR over the long term into a major shipping lane. The NSR too is ultimately a frontier infrastructure project, and some interesting and useful comparisons can be made between it and the BRI. This chapter introduces the concept of "frontier infrastructure" as an analytical device to explain both the nature and historic significance of the BRI and NSR, and their position in current debates about how to best govern and promote international trade in the 21st century.

2. Frontier Infrastructure

As one of many possible definitional approaches, infrastructure may be fundamentally understood as the creation of systems that help expand, connect, organise and sustain human activity. It possesses both technical and material attributes, as well as different network and modal features, and may also involve singular or multiple systems that are linked or integrated. The development of infrastructure has been a defining feature of many civilisations throughout history (Edwards 2003, Neuman 2006, Turner 2018, Wheeler 1956). Karl Marx was one of the earliest users of the term "infrastructure", referring to it to describe the founding of civilisations. Harrison (2016) theorises that civilisation became possible when societies advanced beyond subsistence economies, where the net income generated by buying and selling surplus products provided the income for public good investments in shared infrastructure, leading to urban settlements. This infrastructure in turn enabled public cost saving and further generated surplus income that, if properly reinvested in further infrastructure development, helped that civilisation flourish.

Infrastructure is embedded in the socio-economic structures and systems they serve and is commonly perceived as synonymous with notions of "modernity" and "modern development", and as a proxy measure for the latter. In recent centuries, infrastructure has been closely associated with scientific- and technology-driven *modernisation*, more specifically to humanity's subjugation and "taming" of nature (Alexander 1990). It can thus be viewed as an anthropological concept, and is often criticised in contemporary times for causing severe ecological damage and other environmental pressures by the very acts of its construction and associated expansion of human activity. Infrastructure creates systems that facilitate greater aggregate consumption rates of natural resources, but it can also improve resource use efficiency (e.g. smart grids) and other economic efficiencies. Much of the infrastructure development involves the upgrading or replacing of incumbent systems, or creating new links between systems.

As Turner (2018) argues, infrastructure has become an increasingly amorphous concept due mainly to the flexible, evolving nature of technologies that comprise it as well as the systems of human activity which infrastructure supports. Neuman (2006) notes that "infrastructures provide life to the structures they infiltrate and perfuse", and that functionally they "serve triple roles as network creators, flux conveyors, and change inducers" (Neuman 2006: 3–4). In using the term "flux", Neuman articulates the original Latin meaning of the word, referring to the simultaneous dual process of "flow" and "change". In a similar vein, Edwards *et al.* (2009) contend that infrastructure facilitates, channels and, at times, processes flows through its network hubs and links across the spaces within its reach. In this sense, they create "human space".

Following on from this, infrastructure may be viewed from different geographic or spatial perspectives. In terms of economic geography, it is a defining functional element in the development of urban, regional and national economies, as well as the formation of trans-border economic zones and development corridors. Infrastructures thus "organise space" and create structures of territoriality through enabling social, political and economic relations between state and civil societies (Brenner 1999a, 1999b). The greater and more dynamic the flows of circulation around infrastructural networks, the more prosperous society is likely to become, and the more secure the "infrastructured space" and state is likely to be (Krüger 1969, Van der Vleuten 2004).

The political and socio-cultural geographies of infrastructure offer a more critical view of its "civilisational" aspects. From the perspective of the civilisational power, building its infrastructures has been instrumental to consolidating and extending its own frontiers, be this in a state control or empire-building territorial sense, or more simply relating to political and socio-cultural influence (Hugill 1995). There are connections here to the exercise of hard and soft power, respectively. The close historic association between empire-building and infrastructure-building explains the levels of suspicion that persist today regarding foreign infrastructure investors and their grand projects. This is relevant to both the BRI and NSR, and the ways in which they have been critically framed by some observers. It is worth noting that the etymological origins of the word "infrastructure" suggest it was first applied in a military sense in the late 19th century.[1] Many of the well-known defining features of the Roman Empire were infrastructural: roads (a network totalling 170,000 kilometres at its peak), aqueducts, viaducts, communications, forts, border walls, and

[1] See http://www.dictionary.com/browse/infrastructure. According to this source, "infrastructure" is French in origin and first used in 1875.

so on that helped maintain the integral cohesion of the empire itself while defending and pushing out its boundaries. Both Collins (2012) and Luttak (1976) mention the term "frontier infrastructure" in the context of consolidating Rome's imperial boundaries. China's Great Wall was built to both defend and define the frontiers of the Chinese civilisation. It also served as an elevated transportation route for people and goods to pass along the nation's outer cities and towns.

In more modern historic times, continental and intercontinental infrastructure projects have created new frontiers of internationalisation. The Suez and Panama Canals are perhaps the most well-known examples of frontier infrastructure from the so-called "proto-globalisation" period of the latter half of the 19th century to the early 20th century. This was when significant technological and commercial advances in an internationalising world economy were achieved, which in turn gave birth to modern multinational enterprises. Both canals created new important trans-oceanic maritime routes by creating "continental shortcuts" in world trade and communications. The Suez Canal became operational in 1869, allowing ships between Europe and Asia and parts of the Middle East a far more direct route and avoiding having to sail around the huge African continental landmass. Today, around 20,000 ships annually pass through the Suez Canal carrying about 10% of the world trade. Constructed some decades later and opened in 1914, the Panama Canal provides a vital shortcut link between the Pacific and Atlantic Oceans, with around 15,000 ship transits a year and carrying on average 7% of global trade, most of this comprising trade between Asia and America's eastern and gulf seaboards.

Around the time of the Suez Canal's final construction phase, Britain led the way in founding the basis of the world's first truly global communication system (Finn and Yang 2009). In 1866, the British firm Cable and Wireless laid a working durable submarine telegraph cable along the Atlantic seabed that connected London to New York. After its success, other trans-oceanic cables followed that connected different parts of the British Empire in Africa, Asia and Oceania into the same intercontinental telecommunication network. Other leading industrial powers such as France and the United States also contributed to this development of a global communication system. Over time, new cable technologies superseded older ones (e.g. telephone replacing telegraph), allowing companies to communicate across vast distances with greater efficiency and more effective coordination and organisation of their activities, helping facilitate the emergence of transnational businesses. These were historic game-changing developments in the global economy.

Meanwhile, the development of railway and telegraph systems in the continental-scale countries of the United States and Russia helped make them rising international powers. The Trans-Siberian Railway linked Europe and Asia by mechanised transport for the first time. Between 1850 and 1900, railroad companies laid around 300,000 kilometres of track in the United States, thereby extending the nation's expansion and coherence progressively westward. Both Russia and the US were able to eventually become players in Pacific geopolitics as a consequence of these frontier infrastructure projects. At the same time, from a national or domestic perspective, they enabled each country's dominant centre to subjugate "peripheral" indigenous peoples. This provides further lessons of the socio-cultural and political sensitivities associated with ambitious infrastructural schemes.

Frontier infrastructure is, then, essentially about creating major new "game-changing" advances in international connectivity that bring about paradigm shifts in world economic development. Many frontier infrastructure projects fail due to investment capital constraints, political obstacles, technical overambition, scientific misconception, or other factors. The "Atlantropa" project, proposed by the German technocrat Herman Sörgel in the 1920s, for example, was based on the idea of constructing a huge hydropower dam across the entire Gibraltar Straits to supply enormous base load electricity to Europe, as well as drain the Mediterranean Sea up to 200 metres below sea level, thus in theory creating vast new plains of cultivatable land. If this hyper-ambitious plan had been realised, current scientific knowledge tells us that most of the newly created landmass would have been desolate salt flats, and the shrinking of the Mediterranean Sea would have caused disastrous ecological damage and significant lasting changes to European weather patterns. A Soviet plan proposed in 1956 to build a dam across the Bering Strait could have had similarly catastrophic ecological effects, in its case on the Arctic.

Key lessons can be learned from the above. The first is that any frontier infrastructure project based on ambitious techno-utopian objectives can pose huge environmental risks. Second, those embarking on frontier infrastructure projects today must remember how in retrospect their past examples have been understood in a colonial or post-colonial context, where dominant world powers are seen to impose their will on the international stage. Both the Suez and Panama Canals were essentially exercises of imperial power, built and subsequently owned by foreign nations and business enterprises in host nations, initially serving the needs of imperial commerce. Atlantropa was also conceived as a Euro-centric plan in which North Africa's resources and land space would be made subservient to Europe's needs. A sensitivity to the historic context of past frontier infrastructure projects is thus advised.

3. The NSR and BRI in Focus

3.1. *The Northern Sea Route*

The NSR may be conceived in frontier infrastructure terms, situated in the very sparsely populated Russian Arctic but which connects Northeast Asia and Europe by the shortest maritime routes (Blunden 2012, Liu and Kronbak 2010, Pruyn 2016). As with the BRI and the Silk Route, the NSR too has a "historic echo". European explorers such as Willem Barentz, Vitus Bering and Henry Hudson from the 15th century onwards attempted to find far-north sea routes to Asia, but it was not until 1879 that the first such successful transit was achieved, by the Swedish sailor, Nils Nordenskjöld (Mason 1940, Østreng 1991). In the 1930s, the Soviet Union began to invest in the development of its northern territorial frontier, establishing the Arctic coastal port cities of Murmansk, Pevek, Dikson, Tiksi, Magadan, Arkhangelsk, as well as connected inland river ports at Yakutsk and Norilsk. However, during the Soviet period, the NSR maritime trade was exclusively domestic. After the collapse of the Soviet Union and subsequent contraction of the Russian economy in the 1990s, NSR trade grounds to a virtual halt.

In more recent times, the combination of a resurgent Russia and strong, internationalising Asian economies looking to extend their global reach has led to a reevaluation of NSR's commercial prospects and trade route potential. There was much initial excitement about the rapid growth of international NSR traffic in the early 2010s. Yet, this still involved less than a hundred transits (compared to tens of thousands through the Suez Canal over the same period) and was largely based on bulk energy cargo shipments. There have, to date, only been a handful of container ship transits made over the route since its revival. Geopolitical tensions over Russia's foreign policy have contributed to a more erratic pattern of NSR trade since the mid-2010s, but the development of huge energy sector projects in the Yamal Peninsula region based on considerable Asian investment has the potential to establish more substantive and predictable levels of trade into the 2020s and beyond.

The NSR can reduce shipping delivery times between East Asia and Europe by up to 40%. If more fully developed over time into a multipurpose international maritime route, it could revolutionise trade between these two major centres of the global economy. The NSR infrastructure mainly requires the development of Russia's far northern port cities and their maritime shipping facilities, other transportation functions such as roads and airports, energy utilities and communication networks. There are obvious similarities here with the BRI. At present, though, NSR's infrastructure hubs have extremely limited or virtually no economic critical mass. Many of the route's port towns have very small and much diminished populations (Dikson around 1,000, Dudinka 22,000, Pevek 5,000 and Tiksi 5,000), dilapidated Soviet-era infrastructure and no economic hinterland in their northern Siberian districts. The largest NSR seaports of Arkhangelsk (350,000 population) and Murmansk (300,000 population) are located in the far west of the route in "European" Russia. More importantly, is the NSR a frontier being pushed too far and too hard? The Arctic is of great global ecological importance. Any infrastructural development in this part of the planet could not only have or lead to significant environmental damages but also be indicative of humankind's disregard of the environment generally, a continuation of modernisation's excesses and short-sightedness.

3.2. *The Belt Road Initiative*

Whereas the NSR involves developing an "outer frontier" in terms of organising space, the BRI is focused on an "inner frontier", this being the vast landlocked core of Eurasia that remains largely peripheral in the global economy. It has been referred to as "China's Marshall Plan",[2] a hugely ambitious multitrillion dollar programme of economic development and aid directed at multiple linked countries, and is arguably the country's most important foreign policy initiative in modern times (Cheng 2016, Du 2017, Huang 2016). The BRI aims to strengthen trans-continental infrastructures, and thereby commercial connections between Asia and Europe, reviving the old Silk Route links between them, and as Yu (2017) observes to some extent also China's tributary system of relations with neighbouring nations and peoples.

The BRI's origins lie in an initiative launched in September 2013 during the Chinese President Xi Jinping's visit to Kazakhstan, where he then specifically presented the idea of a "Silk Road Economic Belt" as a new regional cooperation model. A month later in October 2013 in Indonesia, President Xi followed this up with a proposal for a "21st Century Maritime Silk Road" and creating an Asian Infrastructure Investment Bank (AIIB) to help finance it. These were combined into the "One Belt, One Road" (OBOR), later rebranded as the Belt and Road Initiative, which in November 2013 was endorsed as formal policy by the Party leadership and made a strategic priority. In March 2015, the State Council passed the BRI action plan document in which it was stated that the initiative "aimed at promoting orderly and free flow of economic factors, highly efficient allocation of resources and deep integration of markets; encouraging the countries along the Belt and Road to achieve economic policy coordination and carry out broader and more in-depth regional cooperation of higher standards; and jointly creating an open, inclusive and balanced regional economic cooperation architecture that benefits all", while

[2] OMFIF News, "China 'Belt' plans criticised — Belt and Road met with resistance in Eurasia", John West, 10 May 2017. Available at: https://www.omfif.org/analysis/commentary/2017/may/china-belt-plans-criticised.

its official objectives were to "maintain closer economic ties, and deepen political trust; enhance cultural exchanges; encourage different civilizations to learn from each other and flourish together; and promote mutual understanding, peace and friendship among people of all countries" (National Development and Reform Commission 2015).

One could argue that the BRI is an extension of the three preceding Chinese government policy platforms. The first of these is the Western Development Strategy (WDS) introduced in 2001 that sought to develop the country's own interior "frontier zones" and close income gaps in the Chinese society. Promoting the economic development of border countries to those zones also serves WDS goals (Ferdinand 2016). The second is the Going Out strategy launched in 2005 as a bid to internationalise Chinese enterprises mainly through promoting their overseas investments. Fostering economic growth and industrial capacity in BRI-linked countries primarily through infrastructural development provides new market and supply chain opportunities for Chinese firms generally (Cheng 2016, Yu 2017). This has been referred to as the "geoindustrial strategy" where China is engaged in "docking" with economies along BRI routes by infrastructure connectivity and investment in economic corridors, export processing zones and industrial parks (Kenderdine 2017). Third, the BRI provides opportunities to more firmly establish China's development assistance model in the international community, a prime aspect of this being investment in infrastructures. This may be understood in a wider East Asian developmental context where the state strategises investment towards building development capacity, in contrast to Western models of market liberal policy reform and the legal-contractual fixes embodied by free trade agreements (FTAs) and other international treaties — a subject of discussion to which we later return. Furthermore, the BRI was formulated during a time of burgeoning discourses on Asian infrastructure connectivity. A few years earlier, the Asian Development Bank (ADB) produced a landmark work on the subject (ADB 2012), focusing on the growing importance of international supply chains, production networks and transnational business logistics.

There are many low-income, underdeveloped states and zones of Central and South Asia that are some distance from containerised seaports, these being key hubs in the global trading system. The costs and constraints on firms of trading internationally in these locations are considerable. For example, according to World Bank (2015) figures, the average cost of export per 20-foot standard container in Bangladesh was US$1,515, in Kazakhstan US$5,265, Afghanistan US$5,680, Uzbekistan US$6,452 and Tajikistan US$10,650. This compares to Singapore US$440, South Korea US$695, Japan US$1,021 and for China itself US$800. Many parts of Central and South Asia thus represent difficult patches within the conceived BRI space but by the same token new substantive infrastructure investment would bring significant logistical-based improvements to these countries' commercial competitiveness.

3.3. *The NSR and BRI: Links and Comparisons*

Like the NSR, the BRI is also focused on strengthening links between East Asia and Europe, the two major economic poles of the Eurasian landmass. Moreover, there is a link between both frontier infrastructure initiatives. In January 2018, the Chinese government published its new Arctic Policy white paper where the concept of a "Polar Silk Road" was afforded particular attention with regard to promoting of Arctic shipping lanes, especially related to the NSR, and working more closely together with Russia and other Arctic powers. The NSR and BRI are both founded on historic trans-continental passage routes and associated infrastructure development to help them function as such. In this sense, they are centuries-old dreams of linking up great landmasses and human settlements.

There is also an interesting relationship between maritime and land-based connectivity in both cases. The NSR is essentially maritime frontier infrastructure, but its future is almost entirely dependent on two key developments in Russia's northern land territories, namely Asian investment-driven energy projects and the expansion of its cities and towns in the area. The first of these developments can advance the second, and it is therefore energy trade that is currently the prime determinant of NSR's frontier prospects. The BRI itself has both maritime and land-based frontier infrastructural dimensions, and there may be some degree of competition between its "Silk Road Economic Belt" (land) and "Maritime Silk Road" (sea) in terms of which proves the most effective at strengthening Eurasian connections and development capacity building, although of course the two elements are supposed to work in a complementary manner.

Both the BRI and NSR also entail high degrees of various risks: political/geopolitical, environmental, commercial and human safety (especially in NSR's case). China's more confident recent territorial claims in the South and East China Seas have in some way raised foreign suspicions and geopolitical anxieties generally concerning Chinese forays into international spaces, and this has affected how many outsiders have viewed the risks associated with supporting the BRI. This, in some way, could impact on how the Chinese leadership balances its future economic and political ambitions, and own foreign policy risk assessments. Thus, in order to bolster the necessary international support required to advance the BRI over the long term, Beijing may be compelled to dial down its maritime claims in its critically important regional neighbourhood. Finally, both the BRI and NSR may take decades to achieve their ultimate goals and fully realise their potential, and their paths ahead face a number of significant challenges. Yet, this is the historic norm for frontier infrastructure projects.

4. Liberalisation or Logistics? Rules or Railroads?

4.1. *Managing and Governing Trade*

Frontier infrastructure's main functional purpose is to advance international trade and economic development, two factors that are themselves codeterminant in that one spurs the other. Trade enables nations and people to connect to the wider world around them. While this can pose risks, history shows that it creates, on balance, greater opportunities for economic and social betterment. How to promote and manage or govern trade has been a key issue in international relations for many centuries, and subject to many competing discourses, norms and theories on this matter. This is highly relevant to the BRI and NSR as arguably the most important fundamental objective of both frontier infrastructure initiatives is to facilitate greater trade between Asia and Europe. Each has been introduced at a particular historic time with its extant circumstances regarding global economic development and dominant ideas on trade governance. It is a time or era of globalisation where a global liberal order was consolidated after the end of the Cold War in the early 1990s, giving momentum to a new historic phase of international trade liberalisation. In addition to the Uruguay Round global trade deal signed in 1993, the number of FTAs worldwide began to proliferate, centred mainly in Europe as the European Union (EU) signed pre-accession FTAs with East European nations, while over in the American hemisphere various new bilateral and regional agreements were brokered among its constituent states.

4.2. *The Rise (and Fall?) of FTAs*

By the early 2000s, a more global pattern of FTA activity became established as most notably Asian countries joined the trend, and more substantive trade deals were also agreed in Africa (Dent 2006). Another decade on, the number of FTAs globally had risen to around 400 by the early 2010s (up from just 16 in 1990), and the Asia-Pacific was by this time where this new pattern was densest. While securing a new World Trade Organization (WTO) global trade deal has proved elusive, the world's trade diplomats have been extraordinarily busy negotiating FTAs. However, have these agreements actually satisfied the main client or customer base at which they are targeted, namely business? In a globalising world economy, are FTAs what companies want most from governments in assisting them manage and expand their transnational operations? Is trade liberalisation the priority service they require from policy-makers in this regard, or are they more interested in receiving support on logistics? These are key questions in the state–business relationship.

One frustration the business community has repeatedly expressed in the Asia-Pacific zone is the complex regulatory compliance arising from the so-called "spaghetti bowl" or "noodle bowl" tangle of numerous bilateral FTAs that defines the trade liberalisation landscape in the region (Kawai and Wignaraja 2011). Take the original Trans-Pacific Partnership (TPP) set of 12 nations for example, where before the talks began there were already 38 bilateral FTA links among them from a possible permutation total of 66. Furthermore, each bilateral FTA is determined by the unique political–economic interaction of the two parties concerned, producing a bespoke agreement of rules, schedules and exemptions that is invariably very different to others. Evidence from the "utilisation" rates of FTAs among companies (i.e. the percentage of trading firms actually applying for the preferential tariff, customs procedures and other beneficial treatments offered by the agreements) seems to indicate that business was often indifferent towards these trade deals brokered by governments on their behalf (Dagooc 2013, Kawai and Wignaraja 2009, Takahashi and Urata 2008, Tambunan and Chandra 2014, Zhang 2010). A joint Thomson Reuters and KPMG International (2016) report found from a global survey of firms that only 23% of trading companies actually used the FTA options available to them. In Asia, this rate was just 20%. Compliance with rules of origin regulations and complex customs documentation were cited by surveyed business as the main obstacles.

4.3. *The Western "Software" Approach to Economic Diplomacy*

Modern sophisticated FTAs are not just about tariffs and trade liberalisation *per se*, but arguably more focused on commercial regulation and governance. For the US, for example, these agreements have been more about meeting the needs of foreign investor firms with embedded interests in FTA partners' markets rather than that of its exporters. The United States economy is now predominately services-based, and American firms generally sell most of their products to other countries within those countries themselves rather than through exporting to them. Thus, the US-led TPP was essentially an endeavour to shape the Asia-Pacific business regulatory environment as closely as possible to United States' commercial laws and rules. The intellectual property rights (IPR) chapter of the TPP perhaps most clearly revealed this, which is also very similar to most other IPR chapters negotiated by the US in other FTAs it has signed in the last decade or so (Allee and Lugg 2016). The EU has signed even more FTAs than the US, and has similar market access objectives and proclivity for complex "behind-the-border" commercial regulatory provisions but generally does not push as hard to impose its business rules on trade partners (Dent 2010).

Two conclusions can be drawn from the above. First, while many governments have been busy negotiating a myriad of largely bilateral FTAs, their actual usefulness to business is questionable. Second, for the US and EU in particular, these agreements have been arguably more about exporting their own commercial regulations and regulatory norms than exporting their products to their trade partners. As the long-serving US Trade Representative Robert Zoellick said at the outset of the United States' new FTA policy in the early 2000s: "each [FTA] agreement made without us may set new rules for intellectual property, emerging high-tech sectors, agriculture standards, customs procedures or countless other areas of the modern, integrated global economy — rules that will be made without taking account of American interests."[3] This remained the strategic principle driving US economic diplomacy generally up until the end of the Obama administration (2009–2017), where the United States proactively pushed a liberalisation agenda but where possible on American regulatory terms.

Fast forward to today, since the inauguration of the Trump administration the United States has largely withdrawn from this engagement, reverting back to what might be understood as a "19th century" position and worldview of zero-sum national competition where tariffs have become again — in the somewhat bizarre archaic

---

[3] USTR Robert Zoellick addressing the US Senate to advocate approval of Trade Promotion Authority (a.k.a. "fast track") legislation in April 2002. Cited in *New York Times*, 14th April 2002.

thinking of the country's leaders — the preoccupation of US trade policy. However, notwithstanding the introduction of new protectionist tariffs to achieve "fairer trade" as singularly determined by the US Presidential Office, the goal of opening up foreign markets to American products has not changed. The same applies more importantly to the "software" approach on economic diplomacy in which ultimately rules, regulations and treaties such as FTAs remain vital to maintaining the Western liberal order.

4.4. *China's "Hardware" Economic Diplomacy: Logistics over Liberalisation?*

China has, of course, also signed FTAs, but the BRI and its overseas development assistance strategy has offered an alternative "hardware" approach to economic diplomacy, with infrastructure development at its core. China's leaders fully appreciate the importance of commercial rules and regulations. They also understand that rules and regulations aimed at promoting free trade and the increased flows of goods across borders will prove ineffective if the interconnecting roads and other transportation links between countries are dilapidated or underdeveloped. Furthermore, this "hardware" economic diplomacy approach of improving the infrastructure of trade partner economies has a palpable direct benefit on their development capacity, as well as boosting the capacity of the domestic business community to trade. In addition, it is more direct in taking into account the economic geography of business development, with infrastructure targeted at industry cluster and economic corridor development. Transnational infrastructure leads to the creation of new economic "gateways" between nations. Multimodal transportation infrastructure is particularly important here to facilitate the rapid, high-volume and cross-border movement of people and goods over large distances whether within regions, inter-regionally or across continents. This is in acknowledgement of the ever wider dispersed supply chains and production networks that form the integrated logistical operations of today's firms in the global economy (ADBI 2009, Rimmer and Dick 2012).

This approach could be said to be more broadly Asian in character than uniquely Chinese. The ADB has, for example, long financed a generally successful infrastructure-based programme in the Greater Mekong Subregion (GMS) in Southeast Asia aimed at cross-border economic and transport corridor development. In 2012, the ADB produced its landmark "Infrastructure for Asian Connectivity" study (ADB 2012) that was principally aimed at promoting physical infrastructures in transport, communications, energy and utility services (e.g. water) to improve connectivity in the region. It cited the development of the Silk Road from the 13th century onwards as a historic early example of Asian transport connectivity, and the existence of pan-Asian maritime trading routes that were established many centuries before Europe's seafaring nations arrived on the scene in the 15th century. The ADB study notes that in the early 1990s, the United Nations Economic and Social Commission for Asia and the Pacific (UNESCAP) revived the idea of Asian transport connectivity by promoting projects such as the Asian Highway, and Trans-Asian Railway. The study also notes the complementary importance of "soft" infrastructure: "policies, regulations, systems and procedures, knowledge and capacity, strategies and institutions to support the development and efficient operation of physical structures" (ADB 2012: 4).

Both the BRI and the NSR incorporate such complementary measures into their remit. Just as importantly, frontier infrastructure depends on substantial funding and robust financial instruments to facilitate its development, and a long-term financial commitment. This was true of the Suez and Panama Canals, and trans-oceanic communication cable projects as it is for their counterpart initiatives today. In EU's case, the European Investment Bank (est. 1958) and European Regional Development Fund (est. 1975) have enabled the financing of regional infrastructures underpinning the functioning of the Single Market and deeper regional economic integration more generally. There are many challenges involved in financing ambitious infrastructure projects. For example, difficulties can arise in the design, cost estimation and technical preparation of bankable projects, including understanding the full scope, type and level of potential risks involved, and pricing those risks accordingly into the technical preparation process to strengthen investor confidence. There may also be deficiencies in appropriate legal, regulatory and governance frameworks to encourage investment and mitigate political, legal and regulatory risks (Bhattacharyay 2012). Of the two frontier infrastructure projects under study in this chapter, the BRI has well-developed financial support mechanisms whereas the NSR has nothing coherent, coordinated or substantial.

In concluding this section, there are some interesting and important issues arising from China's "hardware" approach to economic diplomacy as best exemplified by the BRI frontier infrastructure initiative. First of all, does it better serve what businesses in today's ever-globalising world economy need from government support and economic diplomacy? Do trading firms on the whole want more help from policy-makers on matters of liberalisation or logistics? Would they prefer governments to spend more time on making international rules or constructing cross-border railroads? Of course, this is a simplification and not such a binary choice, rather an issue of what businesses think governments should be prioritising in terms of their efforts to support trading and foreign investing firms.

4.5. *A Challenge to the Western Liberal Hegemony?*

Relatedly, a debate has arisen concerning how China's BRI initiative and its broader "hardware" approach to economic diplomacy, backed up by substantive development-oriented financing, represents a challenge to the West or more specifically to the US-led global liberal order. This perceived "challenge" takes many forms. At the very least, the BRI is seen as an exercise of "internationalised Keynesianism" or state-directed capitalism involving the funding of public works programmes, and therefore a departure from US championed market-liberal capitalism. In this context, it is seen as creating new norms for promoting the development of global trade through this state interventionism or activism, thus seen to rival the Western intellectual hegemonic discourse of liberalisation. Similarly, China's BRI is being framed as an alternative way of affecting change in international development and commerce, not through rules and legal institutional mechanisms — the long preferred method of Western powers — but rather an emphasis on physicalised actions, exemplified by infrastructure construction. From a geopolitical perspective, the sheer ambition and scale of the BRI for many embodies both China's new assertiveness and broader challenge to Western hegemony that has largely defined the world order over recent centuries.

Realist observers often cite the "Thucydides trap" in this context, where a rising power always poses a serious security threat to the incumbent lead power, where gradually ramped up tension and conflict inevitably leads to war between great powers (Kynge 2017). However, this may take the form of a "trade war" between China and the United States, or possibly create new rival economic and strategic regions, such as the BRI in the long term forming a Eurasian bloc that over time undermines the significance of a Euro-Atlantic one (Rachman 2017). Complex economic interdependencies that form the underlying basis of the contemporary global system means the economic costs of any future "great power" war would be so vast for all parties concerned to the extent to make such a war inconceivable. Moreover, there is a qualitative difference between the functionally integrated nature of today's transnational business interdependencies compared to the simple export–import trade links that existed between the major economies prior to World War I. Politically powerful multinational enterprises from all sides with a strong vested interest in stable prospering markets could also be relied on to seriously pressure governments to maintaining the peaceful status quo.

Furthermore, coexistence is possible. The BRI is not trying to replace the rules-based system of international economic order, nor rewrite those rules. It is simply offering an alternative path forward to strengthen that order. Regarding trade, it is not seeking to bypass or challenge the WTO, rather improving the development capacity of weak, lesser developed economies so that they can better engage in international trade and more fully benefit from WTO rules-based trade governance. In the infrastructure sector, some may view the BRI as providing China with the opportunity to shape global standards in critical emerging industries such as high-speed rail and data networks (White 2017). However, this is just consistent with past history of how standards are competitively established among nations. It is possible for any perceived dichotomy or competition between Western and Chinese "models" of economic governance and diplomacy to coexist in parallel without a significant conflict arising, although some believe in the longer term this may come to a head as the layers of global governance progressively thicken and the need to establish firmer global rules, norms and institutions become far more imperative (Kynge 2017). By then, though, whole new political and economic conditions may exist both domestically and internationally, and the geopolitical landscape may look very different.

Some Western observers are worried about China's inexorable economic rise, and how the BRI helps it consolidate its position at the centre of global production and supply chains. Yet, this is not a direct challenge as such to how the world economy is currently governed, instead simply being consistent with how it has been organised of late with "public good" benefits for other nations, such as competitive Chinese production leading to historically low inflation and interest rates over the last two or so decades. Finally, the perceived challenge or threat posed by China's proactive economic diplomacy to promote international development and trade through the BRI initiative would be far more muted if the United States under President Donald Trump was not at the same time disengaging itself from both the international stage and addressing global challenges such as climate change. As one major nation steps forward on this stage, another is stepping back, or even off it, creating an even greater mind-space for a perceived "China challenge", whether this actually exists or not.

5. Conclusion

In this chapter, we have examined two quite different but linked frontier infrastructure initiatives — the BRI and NSR — where China and other Asian nations are playing key roles. It has defined frontier infrastructure as essentially about creating major new "game-changing" advances in international connectivity that bring about paradigm shifts in world economic development. Both the BRI and NSR are focused on forging stronger and more efficient trade connections and other economic linkages between Asia and Europe.

Like all past historic examples of frontier infrastructure, they are not without their controversies and major challenges. Development of the NSR, made possible by the progressively receding Arctic polar ice cap, poses a number of significant environmental and other risks, including the geopolitical risks of Asian nations working in partnership with Russia's Putin government. The BRI, on the other hand, is perceived by some Western observers as China's bid to challenge the Western global liberal order and hegemony by presenting an alternative "hardware" approach to economic diplomacy, where its emphasis on cross-border infrastructure and development capacity building is seen to supplant the Western "software" approach of international rules, regulations and institutions. It has been argued, though, that both approaches can and should coexist.

Furthermore, like the NSR, the BRI is just another way of strengthening connections between distant nations and people, this being consistent with past historic examples of frontier infrastructure. Yet, it was also noted that sometimes frontier infrastructure projects are overambitious, misconceived, trying to push boundaries and frontiers too hard, or viewed as imperially motivated. These are lessons from history to remember when designing, developing and implementing frontier infrastructure, and thus relevant to both the BRI and NSR.

Of the two, the NSR's future as a frontier infrastructure project looks much less assured. Russia has proven itself to be an unpredictable and often volatile international partner for governments and businesses alike. The network nodes and hubs on which future NSR development ultimately depend are small, weak and dispersed with very limited linkages between them. There are also laudable environmental reasons for limiting the scope of NSR's future as pushing the human civilisation "frontier" yet harder into the Arctic could cause serious long-term ecological damage to an already increasingly fragile zone of the planet. For now NSR's prospects will remain dependent on energy sector developments, where Asian enterprise investments in a project such as the Yamal Peninsula LNG are key. This will most likely lead to an erratic pattern of NSR development for decades to come, unless the Arctic warms considerably and becomes ice-free over a much longer seasonal window, making Asia–Europe container shipping traffic far less risky and more far commercially viable: yet this is a scenario that international society will hopefully wish to avoid.

BRI's future looks considerably more promising but ultimately depends on China's own continued burgeoning economic development that will generate both the financial resources and geoeconomic weight the nation's leaders require to implement its plans, forge commercial relationships and realise its goals. China also will need to prove itself a trustworthy international partner interested in multilateral cooperation and solutions, and willing to make concessions in other areas of its foreign policy as hinted earlier. Like the NSR, there are also important questions of sustainable development regarding the BRI as a frontier infrastructure project that China's leaders must take heed of. This too provides China with an opportunity to prove itself an enlightened member of an emerging global community that is seeking to address the great challenges facing all humanity in the 21st century.

References

Alexander, J.C. (1990). Between progress and apocalypse: Social theory and the dream of reason in the twentieth century. In Alexander, J. and Sztompka, P. (eds), *Rethinking Progress: Movements, Forces, and Ideas at the End of the 20th Century*, Unwin Hyman, Boston.

Allee, T. and Lugg, A. (2016). Who wrote the rules for the Trans-Pacific Partnership? *Research & Politics* 3(3), 1–9.

Asian Development Bank/ADB. (2012). *Infrastructure for Asian Connectivity*, Edward Elgar, Cheltenham.

Asian Development Bank Institute/ADBI. (2009). *Infrastructure for a Seamless Asia*, ADBI, Tokyo.

Bhattacharyay, B.N. (2012). Modes of Asian Financial Integration: Financing infrastructure. In Asian Development Bank, *Infrastructure for Asian Connectivity*, Edward Elgar, Cheltenham.

Blunden, M. (2012). Geopolitics and the Northern Sea Route. *International Affairs* 88(1), 115–129.

Brenner, N. (1999a). Globalisation as reterritorialisation: The re-scaling of urban governance in the European Union. *Urban Studies* 36(3), 431–451.

Brenner, N. (1999b). Beyond state-centrism? Space, territoriality, and geographical scale in globalization studies. *Theory and Society* 28(1), 39–78.

Chanda, N. (2006). When Asia was one. *Global Asia* 1(1), 58–68.

Cheng, L.K. (2016). Three questions on China's Belt and Road Initiative. *China Economic Review* 40, 309–313.

Collins, R. (2012). *Hadrian's Wall and the End of Empire: The Roman Frontier in the Fourth and Fifth Centuries*, Routledge, London.

Dagooc, E.M. (2013). Philippine exporters still not keen on free trade deals, *The Philippine Star*, 9 November.

Dent, C.M. (2006). *New Free Trade Agreements in the Asia-Pacific*, Palgrave Macmillan, Basingstoke.

Dent, C.M. (2010). Freer trade, more regulation? Commercial regulatory provisions in Asia-Pacific Free Trade Agreements. *Competition and Change* 14(1), 48–79.

Du, M.M. (2016). China's "One Belt, One Road" Initiative: Context, focus, institutions, and implications. *The Chinese Journal of Global Governance* 2(1), 30–43.

Edwards, P. (2003). Infrastructure and modernity: Force, time, and social organization in the history of sociotechnical systems. In Misa, T., Brey, P. and Feenberg, A. (eds), *Modernity and technology*, MIT Press, Cambridge, MA.

Edwards, P., Bowker, G., Jackson, S. and Williams, R. (2009). Introduction: An agenda for infrastructure studies. *Journal of the Association for Information Systems* 10, 365–374.

Ferdinand, P. (2016). Westward Ho: The China Dream and 'One Belt, One Road': Chinese foreign policy under Xi Jinping. *International Affairs* 92(4), 941–957.

Finn, B. and Yang, D. (2009). *Communications Under the Seas: The Evolving Cable Network and Its Implications*, MIT Press, Boston, MA.

Frank, A.G. (1998). *ReOrient: Global Economy in the Asian Age*, University of California Press, Berkeley.

Harrison, F. (2016). *The Infrastructure of Civilisation: Public Goods, Private Rents, and the Existential Dilemma*, DOC Research Institute, Berlin.

Huang, Y. (2016). Understanding China's Belt and Road Initiative: Motivation, framework and assessment. *China Economic Review* 40, 314–321.

Hugill, P. (1995). *World Trade since 1431: Geography, Technology, and Capitalism*, John Hopkins University Press, Baltimore.

Kawai, M. and Wignaraja, G. (eds) (2011). *Asia's Free Trade Agreements: How Is Business Responding?*, Asian Development Bank, Manila.

Kawai, M. and Wignaraja, G. (2009). The Asian 'noodle bowl': Is it serious for business? *Economic Working Paper Series*, No. 136, Asian Development Bank, Manila.

Kenderdine, T. (2017). 13th Five-year Plan on International Capacity Cooperation — China Exports the Project System, *Global Policy*, 17th October 2017, available at: http://www.globalpolicyjournal.com/blog/17/10/2017/13th-five-year-plan-international-capacity-cooperation%E2%80%94china-exports-project-system.

Krüger, H. (1969). *Marktwirtschaftliche Ordnung und öffentliche Vorhaltung der Verkehrswege*, Metzner, Hamburg.

Kynge, J. (2017). China's Ancient Strategies Create a New Challenge to the West, *Financial Times*, 26 December 2017.

Liu, M. and Kronbak, J. (2010). The potential economic viability of using the Northern Sea Route (NSR) as an alternative route between Asia and Europe. *Journal of Transport Geography* 18, 434–444.

Luttak, E. (1976). *The Grand Strategy of the Roman Empire from the First Century AD to the Third*, John Hopkins University Press, Baltimore.

Mason, K. (1940). Notes on the Northern Sea Route. *The Geographical Journal* 96(1), 27–41.

National Development and Reform Commission (2015). Vision and actions on jointly building Silk Road Economic Belt and 21st-century Maritime Silk Road. Beijing: NDRC.

Neuman, M. (2006). Infiltrating infrastructures: On the nature of networked infrastructure. *Journal of Urban Technology* 13(1), 3–31.

Østreng, W. (1991). The Northern Sea Route: A new era in Soviet policy? *Ocean Development and International Law* 22(3), 259–287.

Pruyn, J.F.J. (2016). Will the Northern Sea Route ever be a viable alternative? *Maritime Policy and Management* 43(6), 661–675.

Rachman, G. (2017). An Assertive China Challenges the West, *Financial Times*, 23 October 2017.

Rimmer, P.J. and Dick, H. (2012). Economic space for transnational infrastructure: Gateways, multimodal corridors and special economic zones. In Asian Development Bank, *Infrastructure for Asian Connectivity*, Edward Elgar, Cheltenham.

Sakakibara, E. and Yamakawa, S. (2003). Regional Integration in East Asia, Challenges and Opportunities: Part I — History and Institutions, *Policy Research Working Paper 3078*, World Bank, Washington DC.

Takahashi, K. and S. Urata. (2008). On the use of FTAs by Japanese firms, *RIETI Discussion Paper Series*, No. 08-E-002, Research Institute of Economy, Trade, and Industry, Tokyo.

Tambunan, T. and Chandra, A.C. (2014). Utilisation rate of Free Trade Agreements (FTAs) by local micro-, small- and medium-sized enterprises: A Story of ASEAN. *Journal of International Business and Economics* 2(2), 133–163.

Thomson Reuters and KPMG International (2016). *Global Trade Management Survey*, Thomson Reuters and KPMG International, London.

Turner, C. (2018). *Regional Infrastructure Systems: The Political Economy of Regional Infrastructure*, Edward Elgar, Cheltenham.

Van der Vleuten, E. (2004). Infrastructures and societal change: A view from the large technical systems field. *Technology Analysis & Strategic Management* 16(3), 395–414.

Wheeler, S.M. (1956). The first towns? *Antiquity* 30(119), 132–136.

White, H. (2017). China's Belt and Road Initiative to Challenge US-led Order, *East Asia Forum*, 8 May.

World Bank (2015). *Statistics Database*, World Bank, Washington DC. Available at: www.data.worldbank.org.

Yu, H. (2017). Motivation behind China's 'One Belt, One Road' initiatives and establishment of the Asian Infrastructure Investment Bank. *Journal of Contemporary China* 26(105), 353–368.

Zhang, Y. (2010). The Impacts of Free Trade Agreements on Business Activity: A Survey of Firms in the People's Republic of China, *ADBI Working Paper Series*, No. 251, Asian Development Bank Institute (ADBI), Tokyo.

Chapter

4

The Belt and Road Initiative: Case of Kazakhstan

Batzhan Akmoldina, Sara Alpysbayeva and Zhanna Kapsalyamova

1. Introduction

China's initiative, proposed in 2013 by the Chairman of the People's Republic of China (PRC), Xi Jinping, "One Belt, One Road" (OBOR) is aimed at improving the existing and creating new trade routes, transport corridors linking more than 60 countries of Central Asia, Europe and Africa, which will promote the development of trade and economic relations between the countries. This initiative consists of two components: first, the "Economic belt of the Silk Road" (EBSR) that aims to strengthen cooperation between the countries in the Eurasian space and, second, the "Silk Road" to strengthen cooperation between China and the Association of Southeast Asian Nations (ASEAN) countries.

Xi proposed five necessary measures to implement the OBOR initiative, such as political coordination, the interconnection of country infrastructure, trade liberalization, free movement of capital and the strengthening of mutual understanding among people.

Participation of Kazakhstan in this initiative is related to the development of trade routes from China through Central Asia, Russia to Europe (to the Baltic Sea).

The concept of the EBSR, in which Kazakhstan is involved, is designed for several decades to come; currently its implementation is at an early stage, covering mainly the construction and reconstruction of highways in the direction of "Western Europe–Western China" and is one of the vectors in promoting China to a new global role.

In addition, negotiations have been held between countries and their regional unions to support the OBOR initiative. So, in May 2015, the Agreement of the Eurasian Economic Union (EEMA) and the Chinese initiative of the EBSR was signed. The work has been expanded both at national and supranational levels, on the identification of and in some places already on the implementation of projects representing the joint interests with China. These are the infrastructure projects, but there are projects in other economic activities. At the supranational level, the EAEC agreements on free trade with partner countries are concluded, which resulted in a reduction in customs duties that enabled simplified market access for partners.

For Kazakhstan, economic cooperation with China entails both benefits and risks; therefore, it is vital to compare the benefits from the implementation of the OBOR initiative with probable costs. Infrastructure investment is crucial for Kazakhstan due to the low population density and the long distance between regions. Moreover, in recent years, the rate of economic growth in Kazakhstan has slowed, which led to a reduction in the investment of the private and public sectors. One of the important areas of cooperation between Kazakhstan and China within the framework of the OBOR initiative is the construction of the highway "Western Europe–Western China". On the one hand, this infrastructure project creates an impetus for the development of the regions in inland China and the Sinzan–Uygur District; on the other hand, it provides an opportunity for the development of settlements in Kazakhstan along the main road. In Kazakhstan, the road is laid through Aktyubinsk, Kyzylorda, South Kazakhstan, Almaty and Zhambyl regions. The main road sections are constructed from the funds of international organizations, such as the European Bank for Reconstruction and Development (EBRD), International Bank for Reconstruction and Development (IBRD), Asian Development Bank (ADB), Islamic Development Bank (IDB) and Japan International Cooperation Agency (JICA), partially covered by the republican budget of Kazakhstan and through concession mechanisms. Kazakhstani section of the Western Europe–Western China transport corridor with the length of 2,787 kilometres connects China through Russia with the countries of Western Europe.

The direct economic benefits of this project include reduction in travel time for road haulers and a reduction in the cost of operating vehicles (improving road quality reduces repair costs and reduces breakdowns). Also, the likelihood of road accidents is reduced. Indirect benefits are associated with the development of related industries: there is a positive effect for road construction companies, manufacturers of building materials (crushed stone, bitumen, sand) for entrepreneurs developing roadside service (cafes, campgrounds, tire repair shops) and for the development of domestic tourism. In turn, these benefits are multiplied by increasing tax revenues to the budget from these industries, through creation of temporary and permanent jobs (increase in employment of local people and labour migrants from China).

Also, the transit potential of Kazakhstan can be strengthened within the framework of the OBOR initiative and through the development of rail transportation from China to the countries of Europe by expanding the infrastructure, enabling the development of container transportation and multimodal transportation.

Kazakhstan directly participates in three directions of the Eurasian transcontinental corridor EBSR: China–Kazakhstan–Russia–Europe, with access to the Baltic Sea; China–Kazakhstan–Azerbaijan–Georgia–Turkey–Europe, within the framework of the international Transport Corridor Europe–Caucasus–Asia (TRACECA) program, with access to the Black and Mediterranean Seas; China–Kazakhstan–Turkmenistan–Iran–Pakistan, with access to the Persian Gulf and the Indian Ocean.[1]

---

[1] https://forbes.kz/finances/markets/popast_vkoleyu_1/?utm_source=forbes&utm_medium=mlt_articles&utm_campaign=119909.

This paper has six sections. Section 2 proposes an assessment of investment cooperation between Kazakhstan and China. Section 3 presents an analysis of foreign trade in goods and services. Section 4 covers the migration processes between the two countries. Section 5 presents analysis and key recommendations.

2. Investment of China to Kazakhstan

To assess the prospects for Kazakhstan's cooperation with China within the framework of the OBOR initiative, we will consider their cooperation in investment, trade and migration.

China's investment to Kazakhstan: From 2005 to 2012, Chinese direct investments in Kazakhstan increased by more than 10 times reaching US$2.4 billion (Figure 1). Since 2013, the volume of direct investment from China began to decline, for two years the economy experienced relatively low rates and then in 2015, there was a sharp decrease to US$0.5 billion. In 2016, there is again a rise in the volume of direct investment from China, but it has not yet reached the previous volume of 2012. The share of Chinese investment in the structure of foreign direct investment (FDI) in Kazakhstan in 2005–2016 ranged from a minimum level of 2.3% in 2007 (from total FDI) to 9.3% in 2013. In 2016, China's contribution in the

Figure 1. Inflow of direct investment from China to Kazakhstan in 2005–2017

Source: National Bank of the Republic of Kazakhstan.

structure of FDI was 4.6%. China is one of the 10 largest foreign investor countries investing in the economy of Kazakhstan.

As can be seen from the analysis of the dynamics of direct investment from China to Kazakhstan, the OBOR initiative did not bring a substantial rise in investment activity between countries. China's international investment position in Kazakhstan as of 1st October 2017 was US$10.7 billion, while assets amounted to US$4.4 billion; Kazakhstan's obligations to the PRC equalled to US$15.1 billion, of which direct investments were US$9.5 billion and other investments were US$5.6 billion.

China's investments in Kazakhstan are mainly directed to the oil-extracting industry, oil refining and construction of pipelines. Also, Chinese investments in a less significant amount are invested in the financial sector in Kazakhstan and in the development of networks of gas stations.

In May 2016, China and Kazakhstan announced plans to implement 51 projects that amounted to more than US$26 billion, including the transfer of excess production capacity from China. Priority is given to six industries: manufacturing, the productive services sector (including engineering and personal services, transport and logistics services, geological exploration, health and education services), agro-industrial complex and infrastructure development, public–private partnerships, attraction of investment in the advanced sectors of the economy, such as information technologies.[2]

The governments of Kazakhstan and China reached an agreement on the establishment of enterprises in the following sectors: chemical industry — 14 projects, mining and metallurgical complex — 10 projects, machine building — six projects, infrastructure — six projects, electric power and RES — six projects, agro-industrial complex — five projects, light industry — one project, oil refining and oil and gas industry — two projects, production of building materials — one project.

For example, China National Machinery Import and Export Corporation signed an agreement on intending to acquire 51% of common shares of the Kazakhstan carmaker AllurGroup in the Kustanai region.

[2] Source: https://ia-centr.ru/publications/kitay-kazakhstan-perspektivy-vzaimodeystviya/.

The construction of a new briquette iron plant for US$1.2 billion will be carried out by the Chinese metallurgical company MCC Baosteel in partnership with the Kazakhstani mining company Eurasian Resources Group, in which the state owns 40% of the shares.

Also, within the framework of the development of cooperation between Kazakhstan and China, KazTransGas jointly with Trans-Asia Gas Pipeline Company Limited launched the gas compressor unit at the Bozoya compressor station of the Beyneu–Bozoy–Shymkent gas trunk line. Commissioning of the station "Bozoy" will expand the transportation of up to 6 billion cubic meters of gas per year, and with the commissioning of the station "Karaozek" — up to 10 billion, increasing the efficiency of the main gas pipeline "Beineu–Bozoy–Shymkent" and ensuring uninterrupted supply of gas to the southern regions of the country.

Also, among the projects of the Kazakh–Chinese cooperation, there is a plant for the production of powder polypropylene, cement and rapeseed oil. Among the infrastructure projects within the framework of the OBOR initiative, it is also important to highlight the construction of the light rail train (LRT) in the city of Astana. This is one of the key projects, implemented with the participation of Chinese contractors and investment. The contractor for the construction of LRT in Astana is a consortium consisting of three Chinese companies: China Railway No. 2 Engineering Group Co. Ltd, Beijing State-Owned Assets Management Co. Ltd and China Railway Asia–Europe Construction Investment Co. Ltd.

As of 1st April 2018, 3,072 enterprises with Chinese foreign capital were registered in Kazakhstan, more than half of them have businesses in Almaty (1,913 enterprises). For comparison, on the same date more than 14,000 enterprises with participation of capital from Russia were registered in Kazakhstan.

3. Foreign Trade of Kazakhstan with China

In 2015, the volume of exports of goods from Kazakhstan to China fell by almost half compared to the previous year (a 44% decrease), in 2016, the decline in exports continued (compared to the previous

Table 1. Foreign trade between Kazakhstan and China

	2014	2015		2016	
	Mln USD	Mln USD	Growth rate relative to the previous year	Mln USD	Growth rate relative to the previous year
Export	9,799.4	5,483.8	−44.03%	4,228.4	−23.1%
Import	7,357.8	5,082.8	−30.92%	3,668.0	−28%
Trade balance	2,441.6	401		560.4	
Trade volume	17,157.2	10,566.6	−38.41%	7,896.4	−25%

Source: Committee on Statistics of Kazakhstan.

year, a decrease of 23%) (see Table 1). The volume of imports of goods also fell: in 2015 by 31% compared to the previous year, in 2016 by another 28%. Accordingly, over the past three years, there has been a significant decrease in the foreign trade turnover for goods between countries. The share of exports to China in the total exports of goods from Kazakhstan is 11.5–12%; the share of imports from China in the import structure of Kazakhstan was 17.8% in 2014, 16.8% in 2015 and 14% in 2016.

The main articles of Kazakhstan's export to China are mineral products and raw materials: 65% — oil, oil products and natural gas, 20% — metals. In the commodity structure of imports from China, machines, electrical equipment and electronic devices, and textiles dominate.

In general, according to the expert opinion, there is a discrepancy in statistics in the foreign trade of goods between Kazakh and Chinese sides, the so-called distortion of "mirror statistics". For instance, the volume of exports of goods from China to Kazakhstan in China's statistics is much higher than the volume of imports from China to Kazakhstan, as indicated by Kazakhstan's statistical authorities.

In foreign trade of services, Kazakhstan in 2014–2016 maintained a positive balance. The export of Kazakhstan's services to China has seen a steady growth (Table 2), in 2015, exports of services amounted to US$1,747.5 million which is 10.8% higher than in 2014 and

Table 2. Foreign trade in services between Kazakhstan and China

	2014	2015		2016	
	Mln USD	Mln USD	Growth rate relative to the previous year	Mln USD	Growth rate relative to the previous year
Exports	1,577.3	1,747.5	10.8%	19,440	11.2%
Imports	654.4	389.6	-40.5%	502.1	28.9%

Source: National Bank of the Republic of Kazakhstan.

similarly, growth was observed in 2016 (an increase of 11.2%). Mostly, the export of Kazakhstani services to China is represented by the transport of goods, which indicates the use of the advantages of the transit potential of bilateral cooperation, by Kazakhstan. The import of services from China to Kazakhstan in 2015 has seen a sharp decrease in volume by 40% compared to 2014, but in 2016, the import of services increased by 29% compared to the previous year.

4. Migration between Kazakhstan and China

4.1. *Labour Migration*

Kazakhstan is mainly a host of migrant workers, although there is an outflow of emigrants in the country, mainly to the Russian Federation. According to the migration service in the Russian Federation, 110,000–180,000 citizens of Kazakhstan were engaged in the Russian labour market at the end of 2014 and 2015.

Labour immigration to Kazakhstan from other countries can be divided as regulated and unregulated. The regulated labour migration is represented by the following: (1) foreign labour force (FLF); (2) labour migrants working for individuals under the permissions of the migration police; (3) foreign workers who independently obtain work permits in the Republic of Kazakhstan on the basis of certificates on the list of demanded professions in the Republic of Kazakhstan; and (4) citizens of the EEA countries who freely move through the participating countries and have the right to seek employment without obtaining permits.

Unregulated migration is represented by the following: (1) foreigners who enter legally the territory of Kazakhstan, but who carry out informal labour and entrepreneurial activities in the Republic of Kazakhstan; and (2) foreign citizens illegally staying in Kazakhstan, who also work illegally or engage in entrepreneurial activities without official registration and due legal protection.

The account of labour migrants is conducted in Kazakhstan mainly only on a stream of the FLF involved by the enterprises under the permissions of local executive bodies. According to the database of the Ministry of Labor and Social Protection, the peak of labour migration approvals fell in 2007 and 2008, when 58.8 and 54.2 thousand foreign citizens performed their work under these permits (Figure 2). In 2012, there is a decrease in the number of foreign workers, attracted by the permits of local executing agencies, to 24,000 people. Then until 2015–2016, there was an increase in their numbers to 36,000–38,000 people.

The majority of foreign workers attracted though the permits of local executing agencies is represented in 2014–2016 by Chinese citizens (38% of all permits in 2014, 46% in 2015 and 41% in 2016). This is followed by Turkey (11–13% of all permits), India, UK, Italy and Ukraine (see Figure 3).

From Central Asia, Kazakhstan attracted workers from Uzbekistan: during the last years, the number permits increased from 1,778 to 4,202 (Figure 4). From Kyrgyzstan, prior to its inclusion to Eurasian Economic Partnership (EAEP), 456 workers were attracted in 2014 (see Table 3).

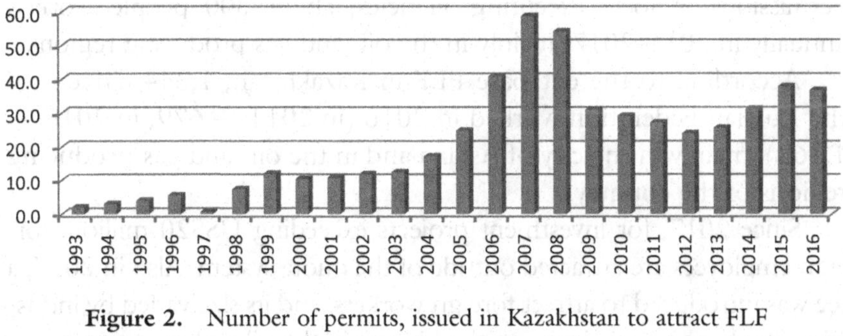

Figure 2. Number of permits, issued in Kazakhstan to attract FLF

Source: Ministry of Labor and Social Protection of Population of the Republic of Kazakhstan.

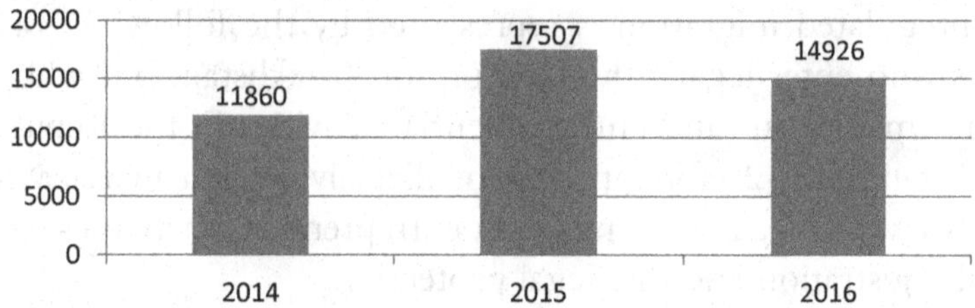

Figure 3. Number of permits issued by local executing agencies to attract FLF from China

Source: Ministry of Labor and Social Protection of Population of the Republic of Kazakhstan.

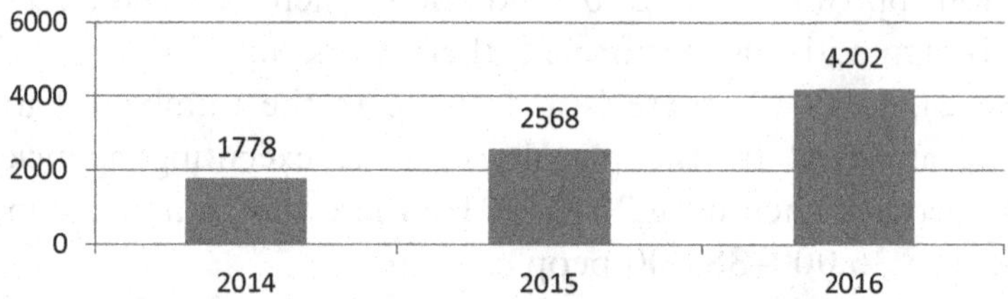

Figure 4. Number of permits issued by local executing agencies to attract FLF from Uzbekistan

Source: Ministry of Labor and Social Protection of Population of the Republic of Kazakhstan.

Starting from 2015, citizens of Kyrgyzstan can work in Kazakhstan as per agreement of EAEP. In 2014–2016, the number of workers attracted from Tajkistan was growing — from 59 in 2014 to 349 in 2016. From Turkmenistan, a small number of foreign workers (20–40 permits per year) are attracted by permits. From Azerbaijan, under the permissions of local executing agencies, about 300 people worked annually in 2014–2017, mainly in the oil- and gas-producing regions.

According to the database FLF in Kazakhstan, 1,344 citizens of the Russian Federation worked in 2016 (in 2014 — 679, in 2015 — 1,162), mainly in the city of Astana and in the oil- and gas-producing regions of the country.

Since 2017, for investment projects exceeding US$20 million, foreign employees are attracted outside of the quota system. Also in 2017, a fee was introduced to attract foreign workers, and its size varied by industries (the lowest in agriculture, the highest in the oil and gas sector).

Table 3. Labour immigration in Kazakhstan in 2014–2016 by permits of local executing agencies

	2014	2015	2016	2014	2015	2016
Total number attracted (FLF)	31,198	37,909	36,792	100.0%	100.0%	100.0%
1st category	1,533	1,705	2,076	4.9%	4.5%	5.6%
2nd category	5,895	5,986	7,043	18.9%	15.8%	19.1%
3rd category	12,811	16,724	16,811	41.1%	44.1%	45.7%
4th category	9,586	11,440	8,542	30.7%	30.2%	23.2%
Seasonal foreign workers	1,373	2,054	2,320	4.4%	5.4%	6.3%
Intracorporate transition	329	603	458	1.1%	1.6%	1.2%
From CIS	3,507	5,121	6,256	11.2%	13.5%	17.0%
Uzbekistan	1,778	2,568	4,202	5.7%	6.8%	11.4%
Kyrgyzstan	456			1.5%		
Kyrgyzstan with no permissions	1	25	76			
Tajikistan	59	223	349	0.2%	0.6%	0.9%
Turkmenistan	32	26	21	0.1%	0.1%	0.1%
Azerbaijan	303	376	300	1.0%	1.0%	0.8%
China	11,860	17,507	14,926	38.0%	46.2%	40.6%
Turkey	4,243	4,536	4,164	13.6%	12.0%	11.3%
India	1,376	1,425	1,709	4.4%	3.8%	4.6%
UK	1,313	1,414	1,654	4.2%	3.7%	4.5%
Italy	1,029	1,186	1,166	3.3%	3.1%	3.2%
Ukraine	810	1,552	1,337	2.6%	4.1%	3.6%
Attracted labour force without permits	1,424	1,498	3,005			
From Eurasian Economic Community (Customs Union)	544	1,209	1,522			

Source: Ministry of Labor and Social Protection of Population of the Republic of Kazakhstan.

In addition to permit system by local executing agencies to attract FLF by enterprises, since 2014, there is a system of permits issued by the migration police to individuals to attract a labour migrant (no more than five migrants per one person). A migrant worker pays a preliminary payment of income tax in the amount of two minimum calculation index (MCI). There is no comprehensive statistics on the number of labour migrants in Kazakhstan, working on the basis of permits for migration police. There is a fragmentary information from statements by representatives of the Ministry of Internal Affairs of the Republic of Kazakhstan on the issue of about 76,000 permits in 2014 (the issuance began in April of that year) and more than 100,000 permits in 2015.

According to the Ministry of Internal Affairs of the Republic of Kazakhstan, over 2 million foreigners arrived in Kazakhstan in 2011–2012, of which about 1 million are citizens from the main donor countries of labour migration from Uzbekistan, Kyrgyzstan and Tajikistan. At the same time, less than 1% of them indicated employment for the purpose of their arrival, 96% named private purposes of stay; therefore, it is difficult to judge the real number of labour migrants from these countries in Kazakhstan. In 2015, out of 1,381,681 registered foreigners, 797,982 were from Uzbekistan (about 58%), 114,385 were from Kyrgyzstan (about 8%) and 33,036 from Tajikistan (slightly more than 2%). And of the registered foreigners only 125,625 people indicated the purpose of their arrival to find a job. The main flow of labour migrants falls on the South Kazakhstan, Mangistau regions and the cities of Almaty and Astana. Most labour migrants do not officially register their work activities and are mainly represented by low-skilled workers. They work at construction sites (mostly citizens of Uzbekistan), in agriculture in the south of Kazakhstan from March to November (mostly citizens of Uzbekistan and Kyrgyzstan), in markets (mostly Kyrgyz and Tajik citizens, to a lesser extent citizens of Uzbekistan), in the service sector services (shops, cafes, restaurants) and individuals as domestic workers.[3] Most

[3]Трудовые мигранты в Казахстане: без статуса и прав. — Международная федерация по правам человека. FIDH, 26 сентября2016 года, № 681 (HDIM.NGO/0207/16/RU).

of the labour migrants from Central Asian countries strive to obtain a higher-paid job than at home.

In the balance of payments of Kazakhstan, the article *Remuneration of Labor to Non-residents* reflects the legal employment of labour outside immigrants. “Peak” wages for non-residents in the dynamics accounted for in 2007 (about US$3 billion), when the country experienced an investment and construction boom. Then until 2010, there was a decline in the flow of labour to non-residents almost two times. From 2010 to 2013, there was a slight increase in activity for non-residents. In 2014–2016, the flow of remuneration of non-residents decreased from US$1.8 billion to US$1.3 billion.

Also, the activity of labour immigrants in Kazakhstan is also partially characterised by the balance of payments item of the host country — “personal transfers”, some of which are transferred by immigrants working in Kazakhstan to their families abroad.

Personal transfers go mainly to the following countries — labour force donors in Kazakhstan:

- The Russian Federation (in the period 2009–2016, 25–50% of all transfers)
- China (8–20% of all transfers)
- Turkey (10–16% of all transfers)
- Uzbekistan (6–13% of all transfers)
- Kyrgyzstan (2–5% of all transfers)
- Tajikistan (0.6–1.2% of all transfers)

The total amount of transfers to these countries from Kazakhstan amounted to 75–90% of all money transfers (personal transfers) in 2009–2016.

Although transfers can characterise not only the effects of labour migration but also include transfers of relatives for students studying abroad, for example, the growth of transfers to Russia may be associated with a large flow of educational migration from Kazakhstan to Russia (see Figures 5 and 6).

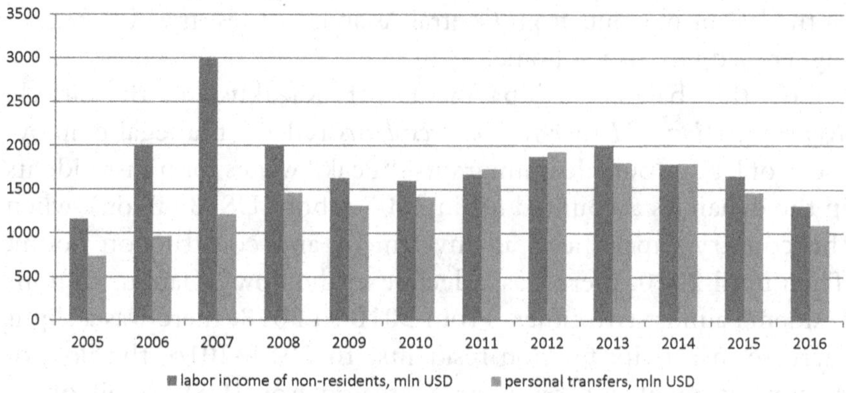

Figure 5. Flows of income and remittances of foreign citizens in the BoP
Source: National Bank of the Republic of Kazakhstan.

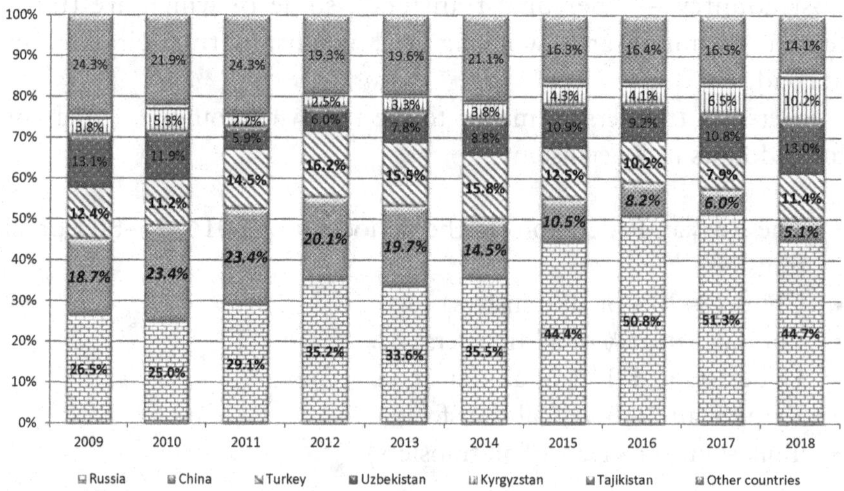

Figure 6. Country structure of transfers (private transfers) from Kazakhstan
Source: Committee of Statistics of Kazakhstan.

4.2. *Student Migration*

According to UNESCO, most of the students from Kazakhstan go to study to Russia (about 35,000 in 2015) (see Figure 7). There are small flows of students from Kazakhstan to Kyrgyzstan (more than 4,000 people), the Czech Republic, the United States, Great Britain

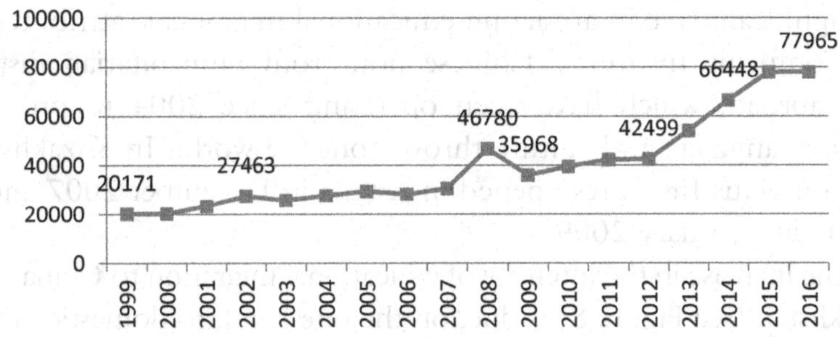

Figure 7. Student migration from Kazakhstan

Source: UNESCO Institute for Statistics.

(1,000–2,000 people), followed by Germany, Malaysia, Poland, the United Arab Emirates and France (300–600 people).[4] There is no data in UNESCO statistics on students studying in China (the PRC does not provide information).

Sadovskaya[5] finds that in the 2003–2004 academic year, within the framework of the development of contacts, the two countries began the exchange of students (20 students from higher education institutions of Kazakhstan); in 2006, about 1,200 Kazakhstani students were educated in China, in 2010, 7,874 students were studying in China, and in 2011, it was around 8,287 students (according to the PRC Embassy in Kazakhstan). The students were trained both within the framework of state agreements on the exchange of students, and within the framework of the SCO University (University of Shanghai Cooperation Organization), the Bolashak program (in 2004–2011, 344 students studied in China). In addition, a large influx of students was also due to private financing of education — at the expense of enterprises and self-financing. In general, the first year of study in China is devoted to learning the Chinese language. After the language courses, students pass the *Hanyu Shuiping Kaoshi* (HSK) exam to certify the level of Chinese language proficiency and access education in the system of higher education in China.

[4] http://uis.unesco.org/indicator/edu-mobility-in-country.

[5] https://cyberleninka.ru/article/n/kitayskaya-migratsiya-v-kazahstane-prichiny-osnovnye-tendentsii-i-perspektivy.

Significant role in attracting educational migrants is attributed to the Confucius Institutes, Chinese non-profit humanitarian institutions abroad, which have been operating since 2004 to promote Chinese language and culture throughout the world. In Kazakhstan, the Confucius Institutes opened in Astana in December 2007 and in Almaty in February 2009.

The increase in the intensity of educational migration to China from Kazakhstan (see Figure 8) is due, on the one hand, to domestic factors in Kazakhstan — the relatively expensive cost of training in leading Kazakhstani universities, relatively low level of quality of vocational education in Kazakhstan and to some extent studying abroad is an attempt to escape from a unified national testing (UNT), which requires the accumulation of the threshold score for admission to a university. On the other hand, there is also an external attracting factor — a policy of "soft power" in China in education and culture, within the framework of which grants for education in China are offered.

In January 2017, the Research Institute "Public Opinion" and the Confucius Institute at the Eurasian National University named after Gumilyov (Astana) presented a joint report on the study of educational migration from Kazakhstan to China. The research is titled *Educational Migration from the Republic of Kazakhstan to the People's Republic of China as One of the Aspects of Strategic Cooperation between Countries.* This study examines the quantitative and qualitative characteristics of the process of obtaining higher education in the PRC by

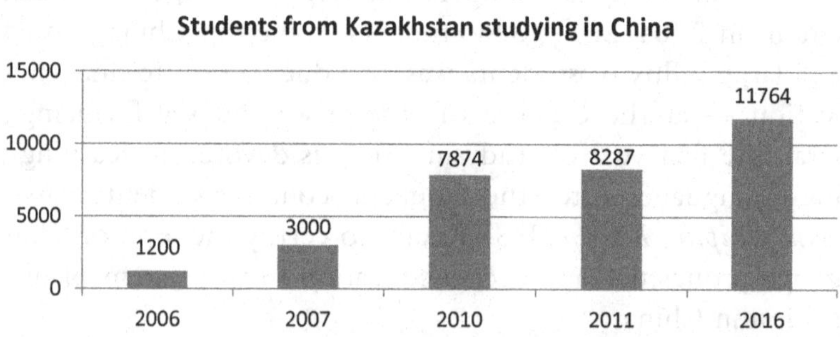

Figure 8. Student migration from Kazakhstan to China

Source: Koshanova and Rakisheva (2016).

Kazakh students. The authors of the survey interviewed more than 400 Kazakhstani students from 14 cities of China. The share of self-studied students is 64.6%. The share of Kazakhstani students studying for a grant from China is 32.7%, for a grant of 2.7% from Kazakhstan.

The study finds that the popularity of teaching in China is a worldwide trend. China ranks third in the world after the United States and Great Britain in terms of the number of foreign students studying in the country. In 2014, more than 370,000 foreign students from 203 countries of the world were studying in China. And there are plans by the government of China to bring this number to half a million by 2020. Most of the foreign students studying in China are citizens of South Korea. The list is followed by the United States, Thailand, Russia, Japan and Indonesia. Kazakhstan ranks 9th in this list.

Further, from the report, it follows that as of today, Kazakhstan holds the second place after Russia in the list of countries most popular for educational migration. And, moreover, studying in China is becoming more popular. While in 2007, about 3,000 Kazakh students were studying in China, as of February 2016, their number had grown almost fourfold, amounting to 11,764 people.

Applicants acquire information about education in China from their relatives, friends, etc. Students who studied in China based on information from friends were 76.8%. Only 12.5% of the respondents received information from the Internet and slightly more than 5% from the Kazakh media (Koshanova and Rakisheva 2016).[6]

Though the flow of educational migration from Kazakhstan is growing in China, the Russian Federation still attracts a high number of Kazakh students (from 2011 to 2015, migration doubled) (see Figure 9). This is the so-called "brain drain" from the country, since largely educational migration can grow into a non-return form. Other Central Asian countries and Azerbaijan are also donors of educational migration to Russia.

To the countries of Central Asia, educational migration is significant in Kyrgyzstan (about 5,000 students in 2016), and there is a small number of Kazakhstanis travelling to study in Uzbekistan and

[6] http://www.opinions.kz/wp-content/uploads/2017/06/um-rus-kaz.pdf.

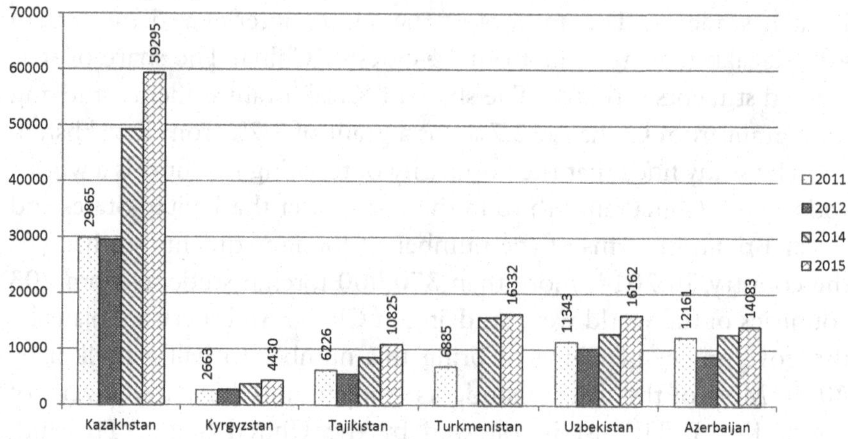

Figure 9. Student migration from Central Asia and Azerbaijan to Russia
Source: UNESCO Institute for Statistics.

Table 4. Student migration from Kazakhstan to other Central Asian countries

Destination region	2011	2012	2014	2015
Azerbaijan	25	17	45	51
Kyrgyzstan	2,700	2,941	4,535	4,828
Mongolia	4	11	19	16
Tajikistan	188	193	123	131
Uzbekistan	47	75	111	119

Source: UNESCO Institute for Statistics.

Tajikistan (100–200 students per year). A small number of migrants from Kazakhstan study in Azerbaijan and Mongolia (see Table 4).

Student migration from China to Kazakhstan until 2004 was not significant and was not regulated by state agreements. After agreements were signed between the countries on the exchange of students, 20 Chinese students were sent to Kazakhstan in response to that 20 Kazakhstani students were sent to study in China.

Students from China were mainly ethnic Kazakhs sent through the framework of the state program to support compatriots living abroad. If in 2000, only 127 students from China studied, 61 of them were oralmans, then by 2006, the number of students from China had grown to 1,995, and 1,735 of them were oralmans (ethnic Kazakhs). In the subsequent years, the number of students from China declined and amounted to 1,037 in 2012. In 2013, the state order for training representatives of the Kazakh diaspora from China was 1,400 people, out of them only 1,101 people were enrolled, and 299 seats were not occupied.

For students from China, studies in Kazakhstan are associated with difficulties due to the lack of knowledge of Cyrillic alphabet of Kazakh and Russian languages. Due to that, students have difficulties in perceiving materials, and there is also a lack of materials and teaching aids in Kazakh language.

In other countries of Central Asia, only few students travel to learn from China, and their number is declining (see Table 5). In Kyrgyzstan, 600 students from China studied in 2010, but by 2015, their number dropped to 267 people. In 2010, 189 students from China studied in Azerbaijan, by 2015, their number dropped to 130 people.

From China, a significant number of students study in the Russian Federation (about 9.8 thousand people in 2015). Large flows of student migration from China are directed to the USA (291,000 people in 2015), to countries of Western Europe, to South Korea (34.5 thousand people in 2015), to Australia (97,000 in 2015) and New Zealand (15,000 in 2015).

In general, student migration is still mainly oriented towards the Russian Federation as the country of destination, mostly due to the low language barrier (Russian remains the language of interethnic communication in many countries), and second due to the established reputation of the Russian systems of vocational education (e.g. physics, maths, engineering and other technical professions).

Table 5. Student migration of China to other Central Asian countries

	2010	2011	2012	2013	2014	2015
Azerbaijan	189	152	155	110	161	131
Kyrgyzstan	601	539	433	385	255	267
Tajikistan	8	8	12	12	12	17

Source: UNESCO Institute for Statistics.

4.3. *Ethnic Migration*

Since 1991, there has been a large outflow of population in terms of external migration in general. From 1990 to 2004, the balance of external migration was negative (the peak of the negative balance was 406,000 people in 1994), which sometimes blocked the natural growth of the population and contributed to a decrease in the population of the country. Mostly, the people who left were as follows: the Russian population to Russia, Germans to Germany, Ukrainians to Ukraine and Jews to Israel. In many respects, this outflow was promoted by various programs of assistance to ethnic repatriation in the countries of reception of emigrants from Kazakhstan.

From 2004 to 2011, Kazakhstan experienced a positive external migration balance (the peak was in 2006 and amounted to 33,000). From 2012 to 2016, the external migration balance was negative (see Figure 10).

The main influx of immigrants to Kazakhstan was ethnic repatriates — Kazakhs from abroad, or as they are called in Kazakhstan "oralmans". In 2014–2016, Kazakhs among all immigrants to Kazakhstan accounted for 55–60%, followed by Russians (20–25%), the rest share less than 2.5%.

From 1991 to early 2016, 261,104 families or 957,772 ethnic Kazakhs returned to their historical homeland and received the status

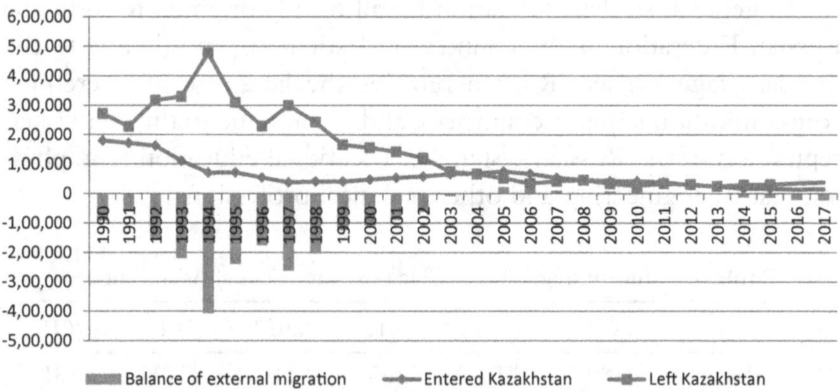

Figure 10. External migration flows to Kazakhstan

Source: Committee of Statistics of the Republic of Kazakhstan.

of oralman. Of these, 61.6% came from Uzbekistan, 14.2% came from China, 9.2% from Mongolia, 6.8% from Turkmenistan, 4.6% from Russia and 3.6% from other countries.

In 2016, 16,417 families or 33,754 ethnic Kazakhs returned to their historical homeland and received the status of oralman. Of these, 65.5% came from Uzbekistan, 25% from China, 3.2% from Turkmenistan, 2.75% from Mongolia and 3.7% from other countries.

For the CIS (Commonwealth of Independent States) countries, the largest flows of immigrants came from Uzbekistan, Russia, Kyrgyzstan and Turkmenistan (see Table 6).

From non-CIS countries (see Table 7), the migrants to Kazakhstan arrive mostly from the following countries:

- 9–11% of all immigrants arrived from China annually until 2013, but in 2014, there was a sharp decline in the inflow from 2,092 people to 630 people, then again there was a revival to 2,102 people. Due to the historically diverse ethnic composition of the Xinjiang Uighur Autonomous Region (XUAR) in the PRC (47 nationalities), in which Uighurs, Kazakhs, Uzbeks, Tajiks, Tatars and Dauri are present, there are long-standing cultural, social and economic ties between Kazakhstan and China.

Table 6. Migration to Kazakhstan from CIS countries

	2009	2010	2011	2012	2013	2014	2015	2016
Uzbekistan	18,793	21,160	20,143	15,321	12,725	8,725	7,592	4,972
Russia	8,942	8,239	6,629	4,935	4,278	3,711	3,905	3,717
Turkmenistan	2,089	1,371	1,039	1,352	932	565	765	385
Kyrgyzstan	1,333	1,501	1,779	1,139	1,455	932	695	584
Azerbaijan	215	699	494	376	296	234	194	185
Tajikistan	163	297	331	323	264	197	210	183
Ukraine	270	258	233	145	138	143	217	276
Armenia	110	219	205	164	130	96	200	101
Belarus	137	131	116	110	99	201	175	155
Moldova	30	41	27	24	14	29	13	13

Source: Committee of Statistics of the Republic of Kazakhstan.

Table 7. Migration to Kazakhstan from non-CIS countries

	2009	2010	2011	2012	2013	2014	2015	2016
China	4,663	4,020	3,296	2,656	2,092	630	1,249	2,102
Mongolia	3,502	2,607	1,939	329	337	271	223	273
Turkey	217	286	376	334	368	200	233	98
Germany	386	366	307	212	169	176	222	214
Georgia	97	333	337	294	185	77	117	65
Israel	45	43	52	53	47	19	21	14
Iran	18	49	59	53	52	104	88	30
USA	48	43	73	65	50	31	64	40

Source: Committee of Statistics of the Republic of Kazakhstan.

- Mongolia (in 2009 — 8% of all immigrants, but by 2014, the inflow has greatly decreased and amounted to only 1.6% of all immigrants).
- There are also small inflows from Turkey, Germany and Iran, minor inflows from the USA, Georgia and Israel.

Across CIS countries (see Table 8), the most active migration is directed towards Russia (85–91% of all emigrants annually), Belarus (2–4% of all emigrants annually), Ukraine (about 1%) and Uzbekistan (about 1%). Russians are the leading number to migrate — 70–80%, followed by Ukrainians, Belarusians and Uzbeks.

Outside of the CIS region (Table 9), destination countries for migrants include Germany (about 3–4% of all migrants per year), less significant outflows to the USA, Canada and Israel. A small number of migrants from Kazakhstan leave to China (in 2009, 65 immigrants).

In general, the migration processes between Kazakhstan and China have a diverse dynamics: the most intensive and rapidly increasing process is the educational migration of students to China, the labour migration from China to Kazakhstan is also increasing, while the ethnic migration from China is decreasing and migration to China for permanent residence and labour migration from Kazakhstan have low intensity.

Table 8. Migration from Kazakhstan to CIS countries

	2009	2010	2011	2012	2013	2014	2015	2016
Russia	30,088	23,499	29,850	26,998	20,839	23,859	25,682	30,274
Belarus	710	705	791	663	1,052	1,605	605	399
Ukraine	323	258	297	270	232	184		276
Uzbekistan	350	318	192	154	219	244	364	208
Kyrgyzstan	131	83	89	97	128	139	164	144
Azerbaijan	68	47	44	62	63	36	20	37
Tajikistan	17	5	3	9	4	10	9	45
Turkmenistan	1	18	22	9	6	5	3	3

Source: Committee of Statistics of the Republic of Kazakhstan.

Table 9. Migration from Kazakhstan to countries outside of CIS

	2009	2010	2011	2012	2013	2014	2015	2016
Germany	1,339	974	971	818	1,206	2,179	2,196	2,679
USA	247	173	196	137	158	198	265	232
Canada	232	145	130	168	92	112	121	179
Israel	117	90	104	106	80	91	84	125
China	62	32	32	48	43	34	32	45
Mongolia	31	4	13	17	30	9	44	16

Source: Committee of Statistics of the Republic of Kazakhstan.

5. Opportunities and Costs Analysis of Belt and Road Initiative (BRI) for Kazakhstan

On summarising the analysis of the relations between China and Kazakhstan in investment, trade cooperation and migration, we obtain the following results:

1. *Investment*: China until 2012 steadily increased the volume of direct investment in Kazakhstan, mainly in the oil and gas production, transportation of oil and gas, then the annual amount of

direct investment fell more than two times by 2016. The implementation of the "Belt-way" initiative opens up opportunities for revitalising Chinese–Kazakh relations in the sphere of production, and as the 51 projects of Chinese enterprises in Kazakhstan are implemented and developed, there may be an increase in investments from China to Kazakhstan. It is vital to evaluate, in addition to the possibility of creating about 15,000 jobs at these enterprises, investment injections of US$26 billion, as well as the potential environmental risks from the implementation of these projects, the risks associated with attracting Chinese expatriates to these projects.

2. *Foreign trade in goods* between Kazakhstan and China in recent years reduced both in terms of the volume of exports of Kazakh goods to China, and imports of Chinese goods to Kazakhstan. In the export strategy of Kazakhstan, much attention is paid to the development of trade with China, as a priority direction for the development of Kazakhstan non-primary exports.
3. *Foreign trade in services* has seen a positive trend in the development of exports of Kazakhstan's services for the transport of goods to China, which indicates the growing benefits from the implementation of the transit potential of Chinese–Kazakh transport. Regarding the import of services from China, the dynamics varied by year, in general there was a positive balance in trade in services (especially for transport services), which is beneficial for Kazakhstan, taking into account the overall negative balance of its foreign trade in services with other countries.
4. There is an intensive *student migration* to China from Kazakhstan, which will likely strengthen further business cooperation between Kazakhstan and China, developing the human resources of Kazakh who studied Chinese and received education, which is recognised by Chinese companies.
5. With the development of Kazakh–Chinese projects in oil and gas extraction, and other projects in transport infrastructure, manufacturing, the number of *labour migrants* from China is growing in the sectors of the agro-industrial complex in Kazakhstan. Labour migration in the future will depend on the policy of the

government of Kazakhstan tailored to regulate the attraction of foreign labour.

6. *Ethnic migration from China* in recent years has been weakening. Decrease in the intensity of ethnic repatriation from China is likely due to the reduction in incentives and support payments for repatriates in Kazakhstan and tightening of the authorities' internal policy in the XUAR of China regarding migration to Kazakhstan.
7. *Migration to China from Kazakhstan*, except for student migration, has a very low intensity. Basically, this is due to language barriers and difficulties in finding employment in China because of the overabundance of labour in the Chinese labour market.

References

FIDH (2016) Трудовые мигранты в Казахстане: без статуса и прав (in Russian). *International Federation for Human Rights*, 26 September, No 681.

Koshanova, S. and Rakisheva, B. (2016). Student migration from Kazakhstan to PRC as one of the aspects of strategic partnership between countries/ the results of the sociological survey — Astana.

Sadovskaya, E. (2008). Китайская миграция в Казахстане: причины, основные тенденции и перспективы (in Russian). *Central Asia and Caucasus* 1(155), 186–196.

Chapter 5

Financing the OBOR Initiative

Joseph Lim and Deborah Lim

1. Introduction

In March 2013, Xi Jinping assumed the post of President of the People's Republic of China. During a visit to Kazakhstan later in the year in September 2013, Xi introduced the Silk Road Economic Belt concept. A month later, the Maritime Silk Road (MSR) was proposed together with the establishment of the Asian Infrastructure Investment Bank (AIIB) to finance the infrastructure projects that would arise from the new Belt and Road initiatives (BRI) (Miller 2017).

With the removal of the two five-year term limits for the Chinese presidency under the 2018 Constitutional Reform, the continuity and political will behind the BRI is assured. It is highly likely that the BRI will be one of the significant legacies of Xi's presidency.

While the will behind the BRI may be strong, the wherewithal has to be considered. Despite the impressive coffers of the Chinese government, other demands for funds as well as the scale of the BRI suggest that sources other than the Chinese government and its institutions may need to be tapped. In particular, a relatively untapped source from private capital should be considered.

This chapter uses the lens of private investors to view the funding requirements of the BRI. It considers the risks and rewards for private investors to participate in this initiative. The advantage of a private investor perspective is that it presents a more objective point of view, namely the economic benefits of the infrastructure projects under the BRI compared to the costs, countering the concern that "some Beijing-funded infrastructure projects do not appear likely to justify their price tag" (Kynge 2018). Hence, the merits and viability of projects can be considered apart from the political, social and other imperatives common to infrastructural development.

In assessing investments, private investors typically adopt a top-down approach, starting from the macroeconomy and moving down to the micro level of the entity and the particulars of the project. We adopt this approach and consider the BRI financing in a wider context.

At the macro level, large infrastructure projects typically use US dollar loans. This adds another dimension to the loan recipients' management of the project as exchange rate risks have to be considered. In recent years, China has moved towards using the Chinese yuan to denominate loans for infrastructure projects. We will look into the ramifications of this move away from the standard practice of US dollar denominated loans.

When infrastructure projects are linked or related, for example, railways that cut across different countries, any disruption in one part could translate to disruption along the whole network. Such systemic and contagion risks cannot be managed at the local level. Coordination at the macro level is required. Presumably China, as the promoter of the BRI, will have to take the lead in developing mechanisms for consultation and coordination to mitigate systemic risk.

In this chapter, we also consider the micro aspects of infrastructure financing. In addition to the macro-risks that pervade cross-border and large-scale projects, the specifics of the project have to be considered. As the nature of cash flows derived from the project and the risks that impact on the cash flows are different from what private investors encounter in their other investments, we will discuss financial arrangements that allow investors with different risk appetites to participate in the project.

Finally, we combine the insights from the macro and micro perspectives to look at how the financing of the BRI projects can be structured to assuage the concerns of private investors. The issues of transparency, liquidity and legal arrangements that encompass the financial instruments will also be discussed.

Much discussion of the BRI has focused on its geopolitical ramifications such as China using it to further its foreign policy goals. At the extreme, some quarters have even accused China of being a neocolonist. Further discussion of whether the BRI initiative is geostrategy or geoeconomics, and other geopolitical considerations may be found in Cai (2017) and Yu (2017a, 2017b). We recognise the intertwining of politics and economics in the BRI and broach any discussion involving politics from the perspective of how it impinges on risk assessments by private investors.

2. The Need for Private Investors' Involvement in the BRI

The scope and scale of the BRI are very impressive and ambitious. It is "a network of projects that span the transportation, finance, telecom and power industries, the economic corridors and maritime roads that span Eurasia [that] could fundamentally change the dynamics of global business" (Tweed and Engle 2018). Encompassing 65 countries, the completion of the BRI would establish a network that links and integrates many of the less-developed countries more effectively into the global economy. This initiative would also uplift the many less-developed economies and accelerate the achievement of the United Nations Sustainable Development Goals (Rosellini and Brahm 2018).

While the aims of the BRI are laudable, implementing the strategy is formidable. In particular, the "Cost of funding 'Belt and Road Initiative' is [a] daunting task" proclaims a South China Morning Post (2017) article headline. The article goes on to quote estimates of US$4 trillion to US$8 trillion to fund the projects. While China has foreign reserves estimated to be about US$3 trillion (Barbones 2018), much of it may not be available to fund the BRI projects. The reserves, as the name suggests, are needed to stabilise the Chinese currency, to serve as a backstop to failing financial institutions and to bolster the economy in times of financial crisis. With a debt-to-GDP ratio of 299% in the first quarter of 2018 (Wolf 2018), the option of increasing leverage to fund BRI projects is more limited now than in the past when that ratio was much lower. Indeed, if we accept McMahon's (2018) dire picture of "China's Great Wall of Debt" where "the economy has added about US$12 trillion worth of debt, roughly the size of the entire US banking system" since 2008, the BRI may take longer to come to fruition.

Funding for infrastructure projects is often done through transnational organisations like the World Bank and the Asian Development Bank (ADB). However, the remit of these organisations go beyond the BRI countries and encompasses the whole world in the case of the World Bank and the whole of Asia where the ADB is concerned. Further, the range of financing extends beyond infrastructure projects to include investments in non-tangible assets like education, health and social development.

For the world as a whole, spending for infrastructure is considerable, amounting to US$9.5 trillion in 2015 and accounting for 14% of global GDP, according to the McKinsey Global Institute's 2017 executive briefing (Woetzel *et al.* 2017). The Institute estimates that US$3.7 trillion of investment would be needed every year till 2035 for economic infrastructure. For Asia and the Pacific infrastructure, the ADB projects the need for funds of US$1.7 trillion a year through 2030 (Asian Development Bank 2017). As the promoter of the BRI, China is well aware of the vast funding requirements. For a start, it helped launch the Asian Infrastructure Investment Bank (AIIB) in October 2014 with, presumably, a BRI thrust. However, the US$100 billion in pledged capital from its members seems modest in comparison to the requirements enumerated above. (See Shi (2017) for a comprehensive survey of financing the BRI through transnational and governmental institutions). Hence, alternative sources of financing have to be explored, making the case for harnessing the relatively untapped private capital compelling. However, enticing private capital can be a challenge.

The use of private capital to finance infrastructural projects is not new. However, its participation has been somewhat limited to projects in the developed countries. Besides the very long-term nature of such projects and the ensuing uncertainty and risk of cash flows that emanate from these investments, the BRI projects present quite formidable challenges when soliciting private capital. Many of the projects are located in developing countries where quite a few struggle with their national finances. An example is Pakistan which is host to many of the BRI projects along the China–Pakistan Economic Corridor (CPEC). It was reported by the *Financial Times* in October 2018 that Pakistan was seeking a bailout from the IMF as its foreign reserves have fallen to very low levels (Stacey *et al.* 2018).

3. Macro Considerations

3.1. *Currency Risks*

Large-scale infrastructure funds in Asia are typically denominated in US dollars, since they tend to be syndicated by investors from various markets (ASIFMA-ICMA 2016). Further, 67% of the World Bank's infrastructure loans are issued in US dollars (IFC Annual Report 2017). Despite the prominence of the dollar in such financing schemes, China has shifted towards the use of the Chinese renminbi (RMB) for infrastructure projects. Since 2016, the AIIB and New Development Bank have issued RMB-denominated bonds earmarked for infrastructure projects both locally and abroad, while the China Development Bank and China Exim Bank continue to provide extensive RMB-denominated infrastructure loans (Liu *et al.* 2017).

This shift away from the dollar-denominated financing is particularly prominent in the BRI, which is expected to "expedite the use of the RMB for … financing and investment" (China Construction Bank 2018). On a national level, President Xi's exhortation to Chinese financial institutions to establish outbound, RMB-denominated investment funds at the 2017 Belt and Road International Cooperation Forum (Plubell and Liu 2017) has piqued private sector interest in RMB financing. Sovereign use of the RMB for reserve and investment purposes has also been bolstered by China's RMB-denominated bilateral swap agreements with several overland route nations for the BRI, such as Belarus, Kazakhstan, Mongolia, Russia, Tajikistan and Uzbekistan (International Monetary Institute 2017). Additionally, China has tapped into the offshore financial centres to raise capital in RMB for the BRI — besides its sale of one-year RMB debt in cities such as London. The Chinese administration has also withdrawn approval requirements for Chinese corporate bond issuances overseas (Kynge 2015), thereby assuaging investor concerns on the lack of RMB liquidity to purchase issued debt. With the expanded range of mechanisms in place to facilitate broader RMB use, both domestic and foreign firms have followed suit, utilizing the currency for cash management, trade and consequently financing.

From a private investor's standpoint, greater exposure to the RMB presents opportunities to participate in its upside as an increasingly internationalised currency. In October 2016, the IMF announced the inclusion of the RMB in the basket of Special Drawing Rights (SDR), alongside the US dollar, Euro, Yen and Sterling pound. The currency presently constitutes the third-largest weight within the SDR (International Monetary Fund 2018b). These milestones point to the mounting international use of and trade in the RMB, and have also strengthened the currency's credibility among international investors seeking to hold RMB-denominated assets as reserves (Liu *et al.* 2017). Moreover, offshore RMB clearing centres have emerged in prominent economies such as the United Kingdom, Korea, Germany and the United States (SWIFT 2018), catapulting the RMB to the sixth most-used currency for domestic and international payments (SWIFT 2017). The coalescence of China's burgeoning economic heft, growing cross-border investments and flourishing trade volumes bears great promise for the RMB finding favour among private investors across the board.

Despite these inroads, several currency risks remain regarding the adoption of RMB-denominated investment and financing. Unlike the US dollar which is managed by the US Federal Reserve, which is commonly viewed as an independent and politically bipartisan body, the RMB is perceived by the investing public as strongly subject to the hands of the Chinese government. Despite the reassurance from the People's Bank of China (PBOC) that it would relax its active management of the RMB, its foreign exchange policies continue to pervade the monetary system. While other major currencies such as the dollar and the Euro trade freely, the RMB is regularly monitored by the central bank to ensure that it trades within a 2% daily range, in either direction of the US dollar (Shane 2018). Additionally, the PBOC in August 2018 resumed its slew of countercyclical measures (Bloomberg 2018) — it reinstated "a reserve requirement ratio for financial institutions settling foreign exchange forward dollar sales to clients" (Reuters 2018b), and barred banks "using some interbank accounts to deposit or lend yuan offshore through free trade zone schemes" (Reuters 2018b). According to the State Administration of Foreign Exchange, the tightening of such "micro-level supervision" and "macro-prudential management" measures (Reuters 2018a), are set to remain as China attempts to curb foreign exchange volatility. Such auguries suggest a need for private investors to be cognizant of the relevant exchange rate risks when investing in RMB-denominated financial products.

3.2. *Sovereign Risk*

As many of the BRI projects are owned by national governments, private investors place much weight on the issue of sovereign risk. Private investors do not enjoy the clout of supranational institutions like the World Bank and the IMF whose threats of withholding funds give them leverage in negotiations with national governments. Unlike private entities, governments cannot be easily sued. Even if lawsuits can be brought against a government, the success of legal redress is low if the independence of the judiciary is suspect. Unfortunately, governance and transparency are not strong suits for many of the countries which the BRI encompasses.

Sovereign risk runs the gamut of governments postponing projects, reneging on or contesting the terms of earlier agreements, to expropriation of private assets and interests. An example of the first occurred after a new government was voted into power in Malaysia in

May 2018. In July 2018, the *Financial Times* reported that Malaysia had suspended three of the largest China-backed projects worth $22 billion (Palma 2018). These projects included the massive East Coast Rail Link, a BRI project. Similarly, in March 2015, the newly elected Sri Lankan government suspended construction on the Port City, a key port along the "Road" in the BRI, and announced investigations into whether the loan rates were unfavourable and deals overpriced (Fairclough 2015).

Sovereign expropriation of private assets and interests can take various forms. In 2011, the Greek government in trying to resolve its debt crisis imposed a massive 50% haircut on the sovereign bonds that it issued. All bonds issued under Greek law were exchanged for bonds worth half the face value of the old ones. However, creditors possessing US$6 billion out of US$28 billion of bonds issued under foreign law held out and managed to get repaid in full (Manuelides 2017). For Cyprus, the expropriation took the form of a haircut on bank deposits. As part of its agreement to receive a €10 billion loan from the IMF and some European countries, Cyprus agreed that depositors in its largest bank would suffer a haircut of 47.5% on deposits exceeding €100,000 (Hadjicostis 2013).

3.3. *Systemic Risk*

This year (2018) marks the 10th anniversary of the Great Financial Crisis (GFC) of 2008. The GFC began when prices in the US housing market reached sky-high levels and turned downwards quickly creating problems in the mortgage market and affecting the rest of the financial markets. The contagion soon spread to the global financial markets and "[e]ach in its own way, economies abroad marched to the American drummer. By the end of the year, Germany, Japan and China were locked in recession, as were many smaller countries" (Havemann 2009).

The GFC illustrates the risks that can result if a lynchpin — the US in this case — in the global financial system fails. Similarly, the importance and potential systemic risk China poses, as the lynchpin of the BRI, cannot be underestimated. Most BRI projects have China in the driver's seat, initiating, guiding and fuelling (financing) the investment vehicle. Infrastructure projects have long gestation periods and are sequentially financed as the project progresses. Until the project is completed and starts to deliver cash flows, any interruption of the financing risks postponing the completion of the project and delaying any payments to the financiers. In fact, Kynge (2018) reports that "critics fear it [the BRI] could become the conduit through which some of China's debt problems are transmitted overseas."

On a smaller scale, projects that are linked, for example, through a railroad that runs through different countries, are also faced with systemic risk. Any adverse development in one or more of the nodes through which the network is connected could render the network inoperable. An example could be the railroad that runs through the BRI's CPEC which was launched in 2015, and stretches from the Pakistani port at Gwadar to the Kashgar province in China's Xinjiang region. Parts of the Corridor pass through the less-developed Pakistani provinces of Balochistan and Sindh. These provinces are greatly concerned that the BRI projects mainly benefit the rich and powerful province of Punjab. The ensuing tensions resulted in "several attacks on Pakistanis employed in the CPEC projects" (World Economic Forum 2018).

3.4. *Transparency*

One of the major concerns of investors in emerging economies is transparency. While many countries have laws and regulations governing business and investments, the implementation of those laws and regulations may not be consistent and are often subjective. Those who do business in such countries often resort to paying officials to facilitate approval of permits, grant of licences and award of contracts.

Transparency International publishes its annual Corruption Perceptions Index. The index "ranks 180 countries and territories by their perceived levels of public sector corruption according to experts and businesspeople, us[ing] a scale of 0 to 100, where 0 is highly corrupt and 100 is very clean". From Table 1, we note that all the BRI

Table 1. Country debt ratings, risk classifications, debt-to-GDP ratio and risk premiums

Country	GDP (billions)	Moody's rating	OECD risk class.	Public debt/GDP	Corruption Perceptions Index 2017 Score xx/100	Corruption Perceptions Index 2017 Rank xx/180	Adjusted default spread
Azerbaijan	37.85	Ba2	5	48.8%	31	122	3.08%
Bangladesh	221.42	Ba3	5	33.4%	28	143	3.69%
Cambodia	20.02	B2	6	31.7%	21	161	5.64%
Indonesia	932.26	Baa3	3	29.8%	37	96	2.26%
Kazakhstan	137.28	Baa3	6	17.8%	31	122	2.26%
Kyrgyzstan	6.55	B2	7	55.0%	29	135	5.64%
Laos	15.9	NA	7	66.7%	29	135	1.06%
Malaysia	296.54	A3	2	55.1%	47	62	1.23%
Mongolia	11.18	Caa1	6	no data	36	103	7.69%
Myanmar	63.23	NA	6	33.2%	30	130	6.67%
Pakistan	278.91	B3	7	72.5%	32	117	6.67%
Papua New Guinea	20.21	B2	6	35.7%	29	135	5.64%
Philippines	304.91	Baa2	3	39.8%	34	111	1.95%
Sri Lanka	81.32	B1	6	78.0%	38	91	4.62%
Tajikistan	6.95	B3	7	52.7%	21	161	2.56%
Thailand	407.03	Baa1	3	41.9%	37	96	1.64%
Vietnam	205.28	B1	5	62.3%	35	107	4.62%
China	11,199.15	A1	2	50.1%	41	77	0.72%

Sources: Damodaran (2018), International Monetary Fund (2018a) for Public Debt/GDP Ratio, OECD (2018) for Country Risk Classification and Transparency International (2018) for Corruption Perceptions Index.

countries listed, with the exception of China and Malaysia, have scores below 40 and are ranked in the bottom half of the 180 countries, for 2017. By way of comparison, New Zealand was ranked first and had a score of 89. Corruption increases the costs of projects and dilutes the operational cash flows. This results in investors either staying away or demanding large risk premiums when they invest in countries ranked poorly on the Corruption Perceptions Index.

4. Micro Considerations

Schroders (2017) suggests a typical financing structure for infrastructure projects (Figure 1). This is based on European projects ranging in size from €500 million to €2 billion and are mainly bank financed. From the figure, it can be seen that debt forms the major portion of financing. Since BRI projects are likely to be much more risky than European projects, private investors will come in as lenders, with national governments serving as equity holders. As such, we will restrict all discussions of private capital financing to debt financing.

4.1. *The Credit Model*

Lenders typically assess a borrower's creditworthiness according to the "four C's", namely Capacity, Collateral, Covenants and Character.

Capacity is the borrower's ability to service the debt. An indicator, where countries are concerned, is the government debt-to-GDP ratio. The higher the ratio, the lower the likely ability of the borrower to service the debt. From Table 1, we see that among some of the BRI countries, the two with the highest ratios are Sri Lanka and Pakistan, with debt-to-GDP ratios of 78% and 72.5%, respectively. Sri Lanka financed the building of the port at Hambantota with debt from the Chinese but had difficulties servicing it. Unable to service the debt, Sri Lanka "handed over the port and 15,000 acres of land around it for 99 years [to the Chinese government]" (Abi-Habib 2018). For Pakistan, the debt overhang was highlighted in the Nikkei Asian

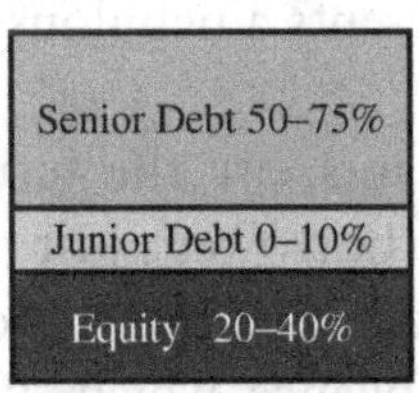

Figure 1. Typical infrastructure financing structure (Schroders 2017)

Review headlines: "Pakistan goes to polls as debt reckoning looms. Islamabad likely to need bailout from IMF and Beijing" (Bokhari 2018). A more technical approach to capacity may be found in Blanc-Brude *et al.* (2018).

The second "C", collateral, refers to the value and quality of the assets backing the loan. The machines in an infrastructure project tend to have more specialised uses and are mainly fixed in place. These attributes result in liquidation values being very substantially lower than their corresponding costs. For example, if an electricity generation plant is shut down, some of the machinery can be dismantled and sold in the used market. As these equipments are highly specialised, the used market is rather small and consequently, they can only be sold at a steep discount to the replacement cost, after incurring hefty dismantling costs.

Further, there are few alternative uses for the buildings and space that house those machinery, and rehabilitation to other uses may be costly. Infrastructure financing is certainly not the place where lenders can seek comfort in the collateral attached. As such, apart from property and assets that are pledged as collateral in the case of default, project lenders often include a "step in rights" clause in the financing agreement (Turley and Sample 2013). These terms allow the lender to seize control of the assets in question and operate them until debt obligations from the borrower have been fulfilled, thereby ensuring another layer of internal financial controls. However, it is important to note that a host of factors might limit or even nullify such lender protection strategy. In particular, projects involving public authorities not only require technical expertise for immediate step-in, but are also contingent on whether a jurisdiction considers step-ins a "violation of public procurement rules" (Madykov 2015). It is thus evident that the notion of collateral presents a nebulous area within infrastructure financing.

The third "C", covenants, are the terms and conditions in the loan agreements which the borrower must observe. If the borrower is in breach of those terms and conditions, the lender is entitled to take legal action to force compliance which, if not forthcoming, could result in the lender taking control over the entity that was granted the loan. Terms and conditions are only effective if they can be enforced. Herein, lies the problem with many of the BRI projects where the borrower is a government-owned entity. Often, it is practically impossible to seek legal redress against a sovereign government. This is borne out by the experience of investors involved in buyouts of state-owned entities. Typically, the seller of the company makes certain representations and warranties relating to the state of the business that is being acquired and any breach of those representations and warranties can be a cause for legal action. However, investors who recognise the futility of suing government entities often take out representations and warranties insurance when buying state-owned firms. Thus, should the representations and warranties about the acquired business not pan out, the investor would then be compensated by the insurance policy.

Argentina's bond default in 2001 aptly illustrates the challenge private investors face in seeking litigation against sovereign debt default. Despite more than 180 separate law suits filed for the repayment of the bonds within the subsequent 12-year period in New York courts, none of the cases were successful (Schumacher 2015). In fact, the courts ruled that assets could not be seized for enforcements, and 93% of bondholders consequently accepted a 65% haircut on the face value of the bonds (Schumacher 2015). Such limitations to debt covenants may perpetuate recalcitrant behaviour, evidenced from Argentina's issue of 100-year bonds amounting to US$16 billion in June of 2017 (Mander and Wigglesworth 2017).

Finally, the last "C" is character, which in this case refers to a borrower's track record of repaying loans. Many of the governments with BRI projects have mainly borrowed from development banks like the World Bank and the ADB. The information regarding a country's record of repayment of loans is often confidential. This information would include situations where the loan terms and conditions are modified and the maturity of the loan extended. Even if some of the information is available, the user is not privy to the political considerations affecting the terms and conditions. This makes it difficult to compare deals with politics intruding when transnational organisations and governments are involved, unlike debt workouts in the private sector which are solely based on commercial considerations.

From our discussion of the 4 "C's" earlier, private investors would be loathed to participate in the financing of projects like those of the BRI as the only viable threat against a government not complying with the terms and conditions of a loan is the denial of access to future financing. As private investors may not speak with one voice nor act in concert, such a threat may carry little weight. Further, as a survey by the IMF of emerging market sovereign debt restructurings (International Monetary Fund 2012) showed, "market access could be restored relatively quickly after restructuring. However, post-restructuring access could come at a cost .... Greater haircuts were associated with larger post-restructuring bond spreads". It appears, then, that the threat of access to future financing would not deter a sovereign bond default if the government is prepared to pay higher interest costs. If private investors are to be attracted to the table to discuss the financing of government-related infrastructure projects, their reservations about the terms and conditions need to be addressed. Mechanisms which can ameliorate the risks private investors face will be discussed later.

4.2. *Bond Ratings*

Bond investors typically rely on bond rating agencies, like Moody's Investors Service, Standard and Poor's Global Ratings and Fitch Ratings, to provide assessments of the riskiness of bonds. The ratings that the agencies produce help investors determine the returns commensurate with the risks, with higher-rated bonds paying lower rates of return than lower-rated bonds. Rating agencies also monitor, over time, the likelihood that the bond issuer would default on their payments to bondholders, and adjust their ratings with either an upgrade or downgrade as the case requires.

Moody's (2018) reports that credit loss rates were low and credit quality stable for US$2.7 trillion of infrastructure sector debt, comprising US$2 trillion of corporate infrastructure debt and preferred stock and US$0.7 trillion of US municipal obligors. Moody's study was based on its own rated bonds over the period from 1983 to 2017.

The low loss rates are not unsurprising as over 75% of the corporate bonds were rated single-A and Baa.

The results of Moody's study augur well for potential investors of infrastructural bonds in general. However, the fact that the public sector bonds in the study consist of US municipal bonds, suggests that few non-US public entities have tapped the bond market to finance their infrastructure projects. If BRI countries were to include bonds in their financing mix and seek a rating, they may find that the bond rating agencies may err on the side of caution with slightly lower ratings than those countries desire, given fewer relevant comparables and a lack of history. Further, if private investors are constrained to invest in investment grade bonds (Baa and above), then not many of the countries involved in the BRI may qualify due to ratings much lower than the threshold (see Table 1).

5. Possible Solutions

5.1. *Risk Reduction*

For potential private investors, many BRI infrastructure projects bear the following characteristics: long gestation period, long payback period, situated in relatively less-developed and possibly less politically stable countries with weak public finances. As such, measures to reduce the risks associated with investing in the projects are key to attracting private investors. However, risk reduction at the project level is not what we are concerned about and is outside the scope of our analysis, although this would help. What we are talking about are the ways to redistribute the investment risks among the fund providers. This concept is not new. In fact, when an enterprise is funded by debt and equity, equity holders undertake to bear more of the risks the enterprise faces for a higher expected return for their investment. We discuss some of the mechanisms for redistributing the risks that debt holders face, as well as other risk amelioration measures, in the following:

- *Portfolio Diversification*:

At the level of the individual investor, portfolio diversification is a useful tool to reduce and manage risk. By spreading the portfolio funds across different investments, risk can be reduced. Hence, if investment in infrastructure comprises a small proportion of the portfolio, the contribution to overall portfolio risk may not be that significant even though infrastructure investments are much more risky than the other investments in the portfolio.

Key to risk reduction through portfolio diversification is the correlation of returns among the different investments in the portfolio. The lower the correlation, the greater the reduction of risk through diversification. In this regard, the relatively low correlation of returns of infrastructure investments with the returns of the other investments in the portfolio makes investing in infrastructure an attractive addition to the portfolio.

• *Tranching*:

One way to redistribute the risk that debt holders face is by dividing the total amount of debt into tranches, starting with the safest tranche and followed consecutively by more risky tranches. The first tranche is the safest as it has the highest priority to the cash flows received by the debt holders, and after this tranche has been fully paid does the remainder go to the next tranche, in a cascading fashion like a waterfall, as illustrated in Figure 2. This arrangement has been used successfully in the Collateralised Mortgage Obligations (CMO) and Collateralised Debt Obligations (CDO) markets, and is known as credit tranching. In the mortgage market, for example, mortgage

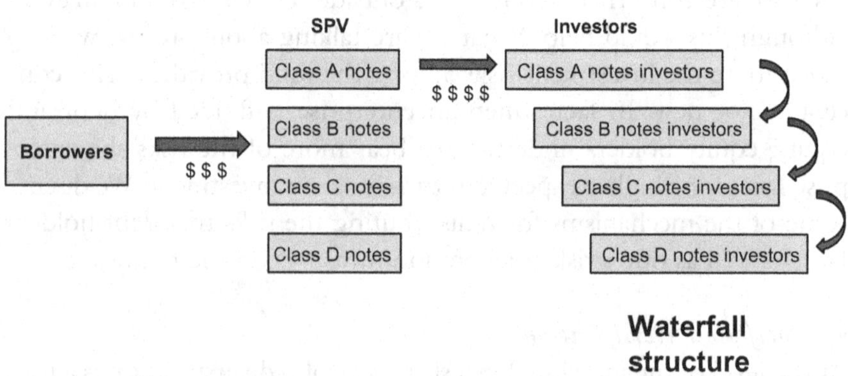

Figure 2. An illustration of tranching

loans that were taken out by homeowners were aggregated and the aggregate periodic payments received from the homeowners were distributed according to the priority of the tranches. Consequently, the safest tranche yields the lowest expected return while the last tranche will have the highest expected return. Investors choose the tranche that matches their risk appetites.

One may ask about the necessity of the waterfall structure given that the issuer can issue bonds with different seniorities. The problem is that if the issuer fails to make payment on any of the bonds, default occurs. However, with the waterfall structure, the failure of lower tranches to receive any payments does not result in a default. Afterall, it is an internal arrangement, so to speak, among the bondholders.

Another advantage the waterfall arrangement brings to the BRI is that the bonds issued to fund the projects may not command an investment grade rating of BBB, or Baa and above. This is significant as it shuts out private investors who are constrained to invest in investment grade bonds. However, through tranching, it is possible that the highest tranches achieve a rating of at least BBB, making it possible to tap a wider spectrum of investors with differing risk appetites.

Private investors may also see the merit of investing through a special purpose vehicle (SPV) which is an entity incorporated for the purpose of investing in the bonds of the BRI project. In any negotiation with the issuer, the SPV speaks with one voice and commands more clout than a disparate group of bondholders with their different objectives and motivations.

- *First Loss*:

Separate from the discussion previously, risk can be further reduced for the private bond investors if any impairment to the aggregate bond value of the entity is first borne by the government involved. In other words, the first loss does not fall on the private bond investors. With regards to the various tranches in the financing structure discussed earlier, the government would assume the riskiest tranche.

Why is there a need to insert the government into the equation? After all, the equity in an entity serves as a buffer to absorb losses in the asset value before bondholders are affected. If bondholders need more comfort, just increase the proportion of equity in the entity. The reason for having the government bear the first loss in bond values is that it has an incentive to monitor the entity. Further, as the government has a final say in approval and regulations, having the government involved in this manner reduces the systemic risk on the part of government actions that may negatively affect the project.

- *Cornerstone Investors*:

Cornerstone investors are "that class of investors who commit in advance to invest a fixed amount of money or for a fixed number of shares, in an IPO" (Tan and Ong 2013). The benefits of having such investors lie in the signalling and halo effects they provide, namely to "significantly raise the profile of the transaction ... by lending credibility and stimulating demand, thereby increase the chances of favourable pricing and of the transaction closing successfully" (Tan and Ong 2013). The cornerstone investors in Asian IPOs have generally been sovereign wealth funds and state investment holding companies.

The concept of using cornerstone investors can be similarly applied to BRI project bonds. Private investors can look towards these cornerstone investors performing the role of lead investors in doing the due diligence and attesting to the "soundness" of the offering with regards to the terms and governance issues. Private investors can take comfort that, if the need so arises, these cornerstone investors, given their size and clout, can advocate on their behalf in negotiations with the issuer.

A potential cornerstone investor for BRI projects is the Hong Kong Exchange Fund which has reserves of about US$500 billion. The *South China Morning Post* reported on 1st November 2018 that "the city's de factor central bank mulls the idea of ... using part of the fund to back infrastructure projects under Beijing's 'Belt and Road Initiative'" (Yiu 2018). Other potential cornerstone investors would be the large infrastructure funds which have the capacity and the expertise to determine the merits of the bond offering.

- *Contingent Convertible (CoCo) Bonds*:

A CoCo bond is a hybrid security which is a cross between a stock and a bond. CoCos have high yields because of the high risk that they face. Unlike conventional convertible bonds which can be converted into stock when the stock price rises to a level at which the bondholder finds favourable to exercise the conversion feature, CoCo bonds are converted into stock when the stock price has fallen, and the CoCo bondholder has no say regarding whether and when the bond is converted. A comprehensive explanation may be found in Jeffery (2018).

Banks turned to CoCos to bolster their capital adequacy ratios (capital divided by assets) which were raised following the 2008 GFC (Paisner 2010). Should a bank fail to meet those requirements, it either has to raise equity or sell assets. Instead, if the bank had issued CoCos, those convertible bonds would convert into shares should the bank's capital adequacy ratio fall to a predetermined level, helping the bank meet its capital adequacy ratio requirements.

Incorporating CoCos into the financing mix of BRI projects imposes a cap on the debt-to-equity ratio of the project. A write-off of some of the project's assets increases the debt-to-equity ratio prompting an increase in the required rate of returns of bonds since leverage has increased. With CoCos in place, bondholders are protected from impairments of asset values.

- *Legalities — Governing Law and Arbitration*:

An earlier section on sovereign risk discussed the difficulty of bringing legal proceedings against a governmental entity. Private investors have concerns whether they could get a fair hearing since the governmental entity and the court are from the same country. Lawyers may also be reluctant to represent parties going to court against the governmental entity for fear of antagonising the government. One way to overcome this issue is for the parties to the bond issue to agree that the law governing the bond issue be designated as those of either New York or London. These jurisdictions accounted for 69% and 22%, respectively, of the law governing emerging market bonds in 2009, according to Das *et al.* (2012).

Another avenue of legal redress is the use of arbitrators from a neutral third party. The merits of arbitration are that the process is usually less costly and the case can be decided much faster as there are fewer formalities, unlike a court hearing. For the BRI projects, efforts are underway to facilitate this avenue for dispute resolution. An inaugural conference on "Effective Resolution of Belt & Road Disputes" was held in Beijing in October 2018. It was jointly organised by the

Singapore International Arbitration Centre (SIAC) and the China International Economic and Trade Arbitration Commission (CIFTAC) who signed a memorandum of understanding "[a]imed at promoting international arbitration for business... and also 'to extend our outreach efforts to existing and potential users of international arbitration in China and Belt and Road economies'" (Vijayan 2018).

- *Credit Default Swap*:

As highlighted in an earlier section on bond financing, typical ratings for private public partnership infrastructure projects range from BB+ to BBB–, which might deter private institutional investors with the mandate to invest in bonds with an investment grade rating (Li *et al.* 2017). Thus, credit enhancement in the form of a credit default swap (CDS) would alleviate poor bond ratings and ensure sustainable financing costs (Li *et al.* 2017). In simple terms, a CDS is like an insurance policy — the buyer of the CDS, like a buyer of an insurance policy, makes periodic payments to the seller of the swap to insure against some event. For the bond investor, the event would be a default of the bond issue.

The use of CDSs for sovereign debt is not new. In 2003, JP Morgan and Morgan Stanley launched *Trac EM*, a tradable portfolio of five-year CDS for emerging sovereign credits. However, there are very few CDSs for the BRI countries. In fact, of the countries in Table 1, only China and Indonesia are in the sovereign CDS list on the "World Government Bond" website (World Government Bond 2018).

- *Infrastructure Funds*:

Infrastructure funds, like other mutual funds, are investment vehicles which raise funds from investors and invest them in "essential public assets such as toll roads, airports and rail facilities ....[which] are typically characterised by low levels of competition and high barriers to entry" and "are often attractive to investors looking for predictable returns" (ASX 2018).

According to The Infrastructure Investor, US$388 billion was raised in 2017 by the top 50 infrastructure funds that it tracked. The amount raised represented a 23% increase over the previous years. If BRI projects were to seek investment from private investors, the infrastructure fund industry would certainly be a prime candidate.

Besides the availability of investable funds, infrastructure funds bring with them a familiarity about the nature, process and risk of infrastructure investments. Their expertise about such investments ensures that proper due diligence and subsequent monitoring of the project would be conducted. This would also help increase the liquidity of investments in the BRI projects.

6. Conclusion

The BRI initiative is a major undertaking which will have significant impact on the countries involved. The connectivity to the vast supply chain network will bring development to many areas which were left out of the growth brought on by globalisation in the past few decades because of the lack of communication and transport access. However, infrastructure projects are capital-intensive. Many of the countries involved in the BRI face challenges generating enough revenue to meet their own need for funds from the many competing sectors in their economy. Hence, the success of the BRI lies in a sponsor who can coordinate the development along the routes envisaged in the BRI, as well as lead in the financing of those infrastructure projects.

China has played the role of the sponsor of the BRI and has initiated many projects including those in Pakistan, Sri Lanka and Laos. It has also been the key financier of those projects. However, as the BRI gathers momentum, China will find it increasingly difficult to shoulder the financing burden alone. Apart from deflecting criticisms of neocolonialism if it brought in other partners to the BRI, the reality is that, for the BRI to succeed, the available funds from China may not be enough. Given that partnership with other governments or transnational agencies have political ramifications, private capital seems an attractive alternative.

From the perspective of the private investors, the BRI offers an opportunity to participate in the potential untapped growth in Asia and beyond. This comes on the heels of projections by pundits such as *The Economist* which suggests "[w]hy low returns are inevitable" (The Economist 2018) in traditional investments in the future. While the promise of higher returns is tempting, the private investor is well aware of the risks. Sovereign risk, particularly those of countries which do not have a good record of transparency, is a big concern. In addition, the interconnectedness of the projects as well as having the same key sponsor, China, for most of the projects, heighten the systemic risk for any investment. Finally, the liquidity of the investments and the exchange rate risks add another layer of risk premiums that the private investor may require.

We have discussed many of the challenges as well as proposed some solutions. Many of our suggestions are based on examples in the well-developed capital markets. How viable is the BRI financing from the private sector depends to a large extent on how far those models and practices that worked elsewhere can be adapted to the particular needs and circumstances of the BRI projects.

While the focus of the BRI has been on infrastructure and the logistics supply chain, the opening up and development of the nodes along the "belt and road" will see a parallel development of the financial infrastructure. Much as many of the financial centres like New York, London, Shanghai and Singapore had their roots in commerce, the opening of new trade routes through the BRI will usher in the development of the financial sector in these countries.

References

Abi-Habib, M. (2018). Paying China with territory. *The New York Times*, 28 June.

Asian Development Bank (2017). Meeting Asia's infrastructure needs. ADB, Philippines. Available at: http://www.oecd.org/trade/xcred/cre-crc-current-english.pdf (Last accessed: 4 November 2018).

ASIFMA-ICMA (2016). Guide to infrastructure financing in Asia. Available at: https://www.cbd.int/financial/infrastructure/icma-guideasia2016.pdf (Last accessed: 17 October 2018).

ASX (2018). Infrastructure funds. Available at: https://www.asx.com.au/products/managed-funds/infrastructure-funds.htm (Last accessed: 4 November 2018).

Barbones, S. (2018). China is sitting on $3 trillion in currency reserves, but is that enough?" *Forbes*, 24 May. Available at: https://www.forbes.com/sites/salvatorebabones/2018/05/24/china-is-sitting-on-3-trillion-in-currency-reserves-but-is-that-enough/#6b1d0ded5fce (Last accessed: 19 October 2018).

Blanc-Brude, F., Hasan, M. and Whittaker, T. (2018). Calibrating credit risk dynamics in private infrastructure debt. *Journal of Fixed Income* 27(4), 54–71.

Bloomberg (2018). China Central Bank signals renewed action to support the Yuan. *Bloomberg*, 24 August. Available at: https://www.bloomberg.com/news/articles/2018-08-24/china-resumes-counter-cyclical-factor-in-yuan-fixing (Last accessed: 18 October 2018).

Bokhari, F. (2018). Pakistan goes to polls as debt reckoning looms. *Nikkei Asian Review*, 24 July. Available at: https://asia.nikkei.com/Politics/Pakistan-goes-to-polls-as-debt-reckoning-looms (Last accessed: 20 October 2018).

Cai, P. (2017). *Understanding China's Belt and Road Initiative*, Lowy Institute for International Policy, Sydney, Australia.

China Construction Bank (2018). Optimism towards "Belt and Road" raises cross-border use of RMB. Renminbi Internationalisation Report 2018. Available at: http://www.ccb.com/cn/ccbtoday/news/upload/20180525_1527240298/20180525172450401450.pdf (Last accessed: 17 October 2018).

Damodaran, A. (2018). Country default spreads and risk premiums. Available at: http://pages.stern.nyu.edu/~adamodar/New_Home_Page/datafile/ctryprem.html (Last accessed: 20 October 2018).

Das, U.S., Papaioannou, M.G. and Trebesch, C. (2012). Restructuring sovereign debt: Lessons from recent history. In Classens, S., Kose, M.A., Laeven, L. and Valencia, F. (eds.). *Financial Crises: Causes, Consequences and Policy Responses, IMF 2012*. Available at: https://www.elibrary.imf.org/page/financialcrises?redirect=true#view3.

Fairclough, G. (2015). Sri Lanka halts Chinese-backed construction project. *Wall Street Journal*, 5 March. Available at: https://www.wsj.com/articles/sri-lanka-halts-chinese-backed-construction-project-1425564657 (Last accessed: 17 October 2018).

Havemann, J. (2009). The financial crisis of 2008. *Encyclopaedia Britannica*. Available at: https://www.britannica.com/topic/Financial-Crisis-of-2008-The-1484264 (Last accessed: 18 October 2018).

Hadjicostis, M. (2013). Bank of Cyprus depositors lose 47.5% of savings. *USA Today*, 29 July. Available at: https://www.usatoday.com/story/money/business/2013/07/29/bank-of-cyprus-depositors-lose-savings/2595837/ (Last accessed: 17 October 2018).

IFC Annual Report (2017). Available at: http://documents.worldbank.org/curated/en/686891507514704349/pdf/IFC-AR17-Vol-1-Complete-for-BOD-09292017.pdf (Last accessed: 17 October 2018).

International Monetary Fund (2012). A survey of experiences with emerging market sovereign debt restructurings. Available at: https://www.imf.org/external/np/pp/eng/2012/060512.pdf (Last accessed: 20 October 2018).

International Monetary Fund (2018a). IMF DataMapper. Available at: https://www.imf.org/external/datamapper/GGXWDG_NGDP@WEO/OEMDC/ADVEC/WEOWORLD/BGD/BMU/KHM (Last accessed: 20 October 2018).

International Monetary Fund (2018b). Factsheet: Special drawing right, 19 April. Available at: https://www.imf.org/en/About/Factsheets/Sheets/2016/08/01/14/51/Special-Drawing-Right-SDR (Last accessed: 18 October 2018).

International Monetary Institute (2017). Strengthen the financial function of RMB. RMB Internationalization Report 2017. Available at: http://www.imi.org.cn/en/wp-content/uploads/2017/07/%E3%80%90IMI-Research-Report-No.-1702-EN%E3%80%91RMB-Internationalization-Report-2017-Press-Release.pdf.

Jeffery, E. (2018). AT1 capital/CoCo bonds: What you should know. *Euromoney*, 31 May. Available at: https://www.euromoney.com/article/b12kqjlwvsz26k/at1-capitalcoco-bonds-what-you-should-know.

Kynge, J. (2015). "One Belt, One Road" set to turbocharge renminbi usage. *Financial Times*, 30 November. Available at: https://www.ft.com/content/6f105c2a-7f02-11e5-98fb-5a6d4728f74e (Last accessed: 18 October 2018).

Kynge, J. (2018). China's Belt and Road projects drive overseas debt fear. *Financial Times*, 8 August. Available at: https://www.ft.com/content/e7a08b54-9554-11e8-b747-fb1e803ee64e (Last accessed: 4 November 2018).

Li, S., Abraham, D.M. and Cai, H. (2017). Infrastructure financing with project bond and credit default swap under public-private partnerships. *International Journal of Project Management* 35(3), January.

Liu, D., Gao, H., Xu, Q., Li, Y. and Shuang, S. (2017). The "Belt and Road Initiative" and the London market — The next steps in Renminbi internationalization. *Chatham House*. Available at: https://www.chathamhouse.org/sites/default/files/publications/research/2017-01-17-belt-road-renminbi-internationalization-liu-gao-xu-li-song.pdf (Last accessed: 17 October 2018).

Mander, B. and Wigglesworth, R. (2017). How did Argentian pull off a 100-year bond sale? *Financial Times*, 20 June. Available at: https://www.ft.com/content/5ac33abc-551b-11e7-9fed-c19e2700005f (Last accessed: 13 November 2018).

Madykov, M. (2015). Step-in right as a lender protection mechanism in project financed transactions. *De Paul Business and Commercial Law Journal* 13(2). Available at: https://via.library.depaul.edu/cgi/view content.cgi?referer=https://www.google.com/&httpsredir=1&article=1308&context=bclj (Last accessed: 14 November 2018).

Manuelides, Y. (2017). Overview: Restructuring of Greek sovereign debt. *Global Restructuring Review*. Available at: https://globalrestructuring review.com/benchmarking/the-european-middle-eastern-and-african-restructuring-review-2017/1137879/overview-restructuring-of-greek-sovereign-debt (Last accessed: 17 October 2018).

McMahon, D. (2018). *China's Great Wall of Debt*. Little Brown, London.

Miller, T. (2017). *China's Asian Dream: Empire Building Along the New Silk Road*. Zed Books Ltd, London.

Moody's (2018). Moody's: Infrastructure sector demonstrates low credit loss rates, stable credit quality for $2.7 trillion of rated debt. Moody's Investor Service Research Announcement, 28 September 2018. Available at: https://www.moodys.com/research/Moody's-Infrastructure-sector-demonstrates-low-credit-loss-rates-stable-credit-PBC_1143896.

OECD (2018). Country risk classification of the participants to the arrangement on officially supported export credits. Available at: http://www.oecd.org/trade/xcred/cre-crc-current-english.pdf (Last accessed: 4 November 2018).

Paisner, N. (2010). Swiss CoCo. *Reuters, Breakingviews*, 4 October. Available at: https://www.breakingviews.com/considered-view/swiss-regulators-place-faith-in-coco-bonds/ (Last accessed: 14 November 2018).

Palma, S. (2018). Malaysia suspends $22bn China-backed projects. *Financial Times*, 5 July. Available at: https://www.ft.com/content/409942a4-7f80-11e8-bc55-50daf11b720d (Last accessed: 17 October 2018).

Plubell, A.M. and Liu, S. (2017). A snapshot of Renminbi internationalization trends under One Belt One Road Initiative. *EMPEA Legal & Regulatory Bulletin*. Available at: https://www.empea.org/app/uploads/2017/10/Snapshot-of-Renminbi-Internationalization-Trends-Under-One-Belt-One-Road-Initiative.pdf (Last accessed: 17 October 2018).

Reuters (2018a). China to use "counter-cyclical" measures to curb FX volatility. Available at: https://www.reuters.com/article/us-china-economy-forex/china-to-use-counter-cyclical-measures-to-curb-fx-volatility-idUSKBN1K9089 (Last accessed: 18 October 2018).

Reuters (2018b). China central bank adjusts yuan fix factors to keep FX market stable, 24 August. Available at: https://www.reuters.com/article/us-china-yuan-factor/china-central-bank-adjusts-yuan-fix-factors-to-keep-fx-market-stable-idUSKCN1L91EH (Last accessed: 18 October 2018).

Rosellini, N. and Brahm, L. (2018). Peace and development with the Belt Road Initiative. *China Daily*, 9 February. Available at: http://www.chinadaily.com.cn/a/201802/09/WS5a7cee14a3106e7dcc13bb13.html (Last accessed: 17 October 2018).

Schroders (2017). Infrastructure financing — An overview. Available at: https://schroders.com/en/sysglobalassets/digital/hong-kong/institutional/201704_infrastructure_financing_an_overview.pdf (Last accessed: 12 October 2018).

Schumacher, J. (2015). Sovereign debt litigation in Argentina: Implications of the *Pari Passu* default. *Journal of Financial Regulations* 1, 143–148.

Shane, D. (2018). This is how China controls its currency. *CNN*, 16 August. Available at: https://www.cnn.com/2018/10/01/economy/china-currency-yuan-rmb/index.html (Last accessed: 18 October 2018).

Shi, J. (2017). Financing China's "Belt and Road" initiative. In Larcon, J.-P. (ed), *The New Silk Road: China Meets Europe in the Baltic Sea Region*, World Scientific.

South China Morning Post (2017). Cost of funding 'Belt and Road Initiative' is daunting task, 27 September. Available at: https://www.scmp.com/special-reports/business/topics/special-report-belt-and-road/article/2112978/cost-funding-belt-and (Last accessed: 17 October 2018).

Stacey, K., Bokhari, F. and Giles, C. (2018). Pakistan to seek IMF bailout as foreign currency dwindle. *Financial Times*, 9 October. Available at: https://www.ft.com/content/a6cbe2d4-cb1b-11e8-9fe5-24ad351828ab (Last accessed: 10 October 2018).

SWIFT (2017). Will the belt and road revitalise RMB internationalisation? *SWIFT RMB Tracker*. Available at: https://www.swift.com/resource/rmb-tracker-july-2017-special-report (Last accessed: 18 October 2018).

SWIFT (2018). RMB Internationalisation: Where we are and what we can expect in 2018. *SWIFT RMB Tracker*, January. Available at: https://

www.swift.com/resource/rmb-tracker-january-2018-special-report (Last accessed: 18 October 2018).

Tan, T.-G. and Ong, J. (2013). Cornerstone investors in IPOs — An Asian perspective. *Capital Markets Law Journal* 8(4), 427–449.

The Economist (2018). Why low returns are inevitable. Buttonwood's notebook, 21 February. Available at: https://www.economist.com/buttonwoods-notebook/2018/02/21/why-low-returns-are-inevitable (Last accessed: 14 November 2018).

Transparency International (2018). Corruptions Perceptions Index 2017. Available at: https://www.transparency.org/news/feature/corruption_perceptions_index_2017.

Turley, L. and Sample, A. (2013). Financing sustainable public-private partnerships. *International Institute for Sustainable Development*, February. Available at: https://www.iisd.org/pdf/2013/ppp_financing.pdf.

Tweed, D. and Engle, S. (2018). China is undertaking the 'Project of the Century'. *Bloomberg*, 11 September. Available at: https://www.bloomberg.com/news/articles/2018-09-11/china-is-undertaking-the-project-of-the-century?srnd=belt-and-road-initiative (Last accessed: 17 October 2018).

Vijayan, K.C. (2018). Two MOUs inked in China to boost S'pore arbitration profile. *Straits Times*, 16 October. Available at: https://www.straitstimes.com/singapore/two-mous-inked-in-china-to-boost-spore-arbitration-profile (Last accessed: 8 November 2018).

Woetzel, J., Garemo, N., Mischke, J., Kamra, P. and Palter, R. (2017). Bridging infrastructure gaps: Has the world made progress? *McKinsey Global Institute Executive Briefing*, October.

Wolf, M. (2018). China's debt threat: Time to rein in the lending boom. *Financial Times*, 25 July. Available at: https://www.ft.com/content/0c7ecae2-8cfb-11e8-bb8f-a6a2f7bca546cv (Last accessed: 3 October 2018).

World Economic Forum (2018). Opportunities and risks — The China-Pakistan trade corridor. China-Pakistan Economic Corridor: Opportunities and Risks. *International Crisis Group*, 3 July. Available at: https://www.weforum.org/agenda/2018/07/opportunities-and-risks-the-china-pakistan-economic-corridor/(Last accessed: 19 October 2018).

World Government Bond (2018). Sovereign CDS table. Available at: http://www.worldgovernmentbonds.com/sovereign-cds/.

Yiu, E. (2018). Hong Kong's search for higher returns leads Exchange Fund down risky Belt and Road Plan. *South China Morning Post*, 1 November. Available at: https://www.scmp.com/business/companies/article/2171025/hong-kongs-search-higher-returns-leads-exchange-fund-down-risky (Last accessed: 7 November 2018).

Yu, H. (2017a). Motivation behind China's "One Belt, One Road" initiative and establishment of the Asian Infrastructure Investment Bank. *Journal of Contemporary China* 26(105), 353–368.

Yu, H. (2017b). Infrastructure connectivity and regional economic integration in East Asia: Progress and challenges. *Journal of Infrastructure, Policy and Development* 1(1), 44–63.

Chapter

6

Explaining Irreconcilable Sino–Japan Rivalry

Shintaro Hamanaka

1. Introduction

Suppose that there are two countries that have totally different policy preferences. The two countries may sit down and have constructive negotiations and agree to assume co-leadership complementing each other's strength. There is, however, a possibility that they end up with insisting upon negotiation modalities convenient to themselves, without initiating substantial negotiations. This is what I call as the elevation of rivalry to the "meta-level". Negotiations often become irreconcilable not because of fierce disagreement on substance but because of the elevation of disagreement to the meta-level. The purpose of this chapter is to depict the meta-level rivalry between countries that aspire for international leadership.[1] The following analysis

[1] Having a fundamental difference in policy preference (disagreement at the non-meta level) is a necessary, but not sufficient condition for meta-level rivalry. To identify the

will show how difficult it is to set negotiation modalities acceptable to concerned parties in competition.

It is during the negotiation preparation stage that such an elevation of rivalry may happen. Once the negotiations on substance is launched, the game is nearly over; the negotiations for the negotiation modalities *before* the launch of negotiation on substance is the main battlefield for countries that aspire leadership. The negotiation preparation stage starts with the formation of a group of countries that share the idea of establishing institutions and ends with the launch of substantial negotiations for institution building, to be followed by the actual negotiation stage. The "negotiation" during negotiation preparation stage is intense and complex because negotiation modalities set during this period affect the entire course of negotiations. During the negotiation preparation stage, the modalities of forthcoming negotiations on substance should be agreed upon or at least shared among concerned parties. There are three meta-level factors that are important in shaping negotiations: *membership* (which countries can and cannot participate in negotiations), *agenda* (what can and cannot be discussed in the negotiations) and *sponsorship* (which country can claim the credit as a "founder" and can hold the chairmanship at negotiation meetings).

We will use the case study of Sino–Japan relations in regional cooperation building in examining irreconcilable meta-level rivalry. The two countries certainly compete at the non-meta-level, having totally different ideas regarding regional cooperation, including free trade agreements (FTAs) and international financial institutions (IFIs). China emphasises trade facilitation and, at most, trade liberalisation. It does not like "deep" integration that requires regulatory reform in services and investment sectors. Hence, China prefers goods-centric FTAs and supports IFIs to finance infrastructure development beneficial to trade facilitation such as transport infrastructure. China is not of the view that IFIs should assist the development of regulatory framework of the recipient country; IFIs

---

determinants that enhance the rivalry to the meta-level is beyond the scope of this chapter.

making "profit", given the regulatory standards in place, is acceptable just like private sectors (note that regulatory standards such as environmental standards are sometimes absent). In contrast, Japan emphasises the significance of regulatory reform in services trade and investment, rather than tariff reduction. It prefers comprehensive approaches to development (not just infrastructure development), including the establishment of regulatory standards (e.g. environmental standards) of partner countries. Hence, Japan supports service/investment-centric FTAs. It holds the idea that IFIs should help develop environmental standards of recipient countries, not just lending money — it prefers a development bank. However, interestingly, the two countries seldom have substantial discussion on those substantial issues of regional cooperation in a quiet room; the real problem is that disagreement on substance is elevated to the meta-level, which results in the situation wherein no constructive negotiation takes place.

Note, however, that I do not argue that the meta-level rivalry of institutionalising negotiation modalities is unique to China and Japan. It is certainly a worldwide phenomenon. In fact, as we will see later, such a meta-level rivalry also exists between China/Japan and the US. However, the manoeuvre of negotiation process to achieve convenient negotiation modalities seems be to be more important to China and Japan, and perhaps other Asian countries than the West because Asians value the process of negotiations or institutionalisation in addition to substance (Acharya 1997). In particular, the sponsorship of negotiations, such as which country originally proposed the new institution is very critical for Asian countries in making a decision whether or not to support the proposal. This is because many countries accept the norm that the founder's voice should be respected.

This chapter is structured as follows. Section 2 provides the overview of the analytical framework of empirical examinations, namely, meta-level institutionalisation of negotiation modalities. More specifically, I will explain the way in which the meta-level rivalry takes place with regard to membership, agenda and sponsorship of negotiations. Then, irreconcilable rivalry between China and Japan in regional cooperation in the field of finance and trade will be discussed in turn. We will review the irreconcilable rivalry between China and Japan, using specific cases of regional cooperation, such as the Regional Comprehensive Economic Partnership (RCEP) and the Trans-Pacific Partnership (TPP) from trade, and Asian Infrastructure Investment Bank (AIIB) and Asian Development Bank (ADB) from finance. Section 5 concludes with some observations regarding the future prospects of rivalry between the two countries on regional cooperation.

2. Irreconcilable Rivalry: Meta-level Institutionalisation

The negotiations for institution building have two stages. The first one is the negotiation preparation stage, which starts with the formation of a group of countries that share the value of establishing an institution and ends with the launch of negotiations on substance of institutions to be established. During the negotiation preparation stage, a loosely formed group of states starts to institutionalise its modality of decision-making rules and norms. The second is the actual negotiation stage, which starts with the launch of negotiations and ends with the conclusion of negotiations to be followed by the establishment of institution. This is the stage when negotiations are actually conducted to agree upon details of the institution to be established.

Existing studies do not make a clear distinction between the negotiation preparation stage and the actual negotiation stage. At best, they regard the negotiation preparation stage as a tiny or insubstantial part of the whole negotiation process. As a result, they tend to oversimplify negotiations and overlook critical negotiation dynamics that can be observed at the outset of the entire negotiation processes. First, it is often assumed that negotiation is conducted in an anarchical setting, and the fact that even negotiations for new institution building have some institutional context is overlooked. In particular, liberal leadership literature argues that leadership is necessary to overcome the so-called prisoners' dilemma situation or collective action problems in an anarchical world which impedes the supply of international public goods, namely, institutions.[2] Second, it is assumed that negotiation suddenly takes place and everything is negotiated at once through issue linkages. However, an attempt to establish regional institutions involves a more nuanced politics.

The real negotiation, especially that during the negotiation preparation stage, is a very dynamic process mainly caused by the two factors associated with the problems discussed earlier. First, negotiations usually start at the meta-level, not on substance. The main task to be accomplished during the negotiation preparation stage is to conduct "negotiations to launch negotiations". The modality of negotiations should be negotiated and agreed upon or at least shared among concerned parties before the launch of actual negotiations on substance. Second, negotiations usually have some institutional context, even when it looks that negotiations for a newly proposed institution started from scratch.[3] Countries spend huge amount of resources so that the favourable rules of the game during the actual negotiation stage can be institutionalised during negotiation preparation stage. Because countries attempt to institutionalise convenient negotiation modalities, no negotiation can take place in a vacuum.

The rivalry among countries that aspire for leadership culminates during the negotiation preparation stage, not the actual negotiation stage because the rules of the game are institutionalised during the negotiation preparation stage. It is often the case that the launch of actual negotiations is delayed because countries are unable to agree upon negotiation modalities to be institutionalised. Once negotiations are launched, the game is nearly over. Hence, the meta-level rivalry in institutionalising negotiation modalities during the negotiation preparation stage tends to be irreconcilable.

There are at least three meta-level modalities of negotiations to be institutionalised during the negotiation preparation stage. The first factor is membership. The question regarding which country

---

[2] Along this line, Young (1991) argues that there are three types of sources for leadership: material resources (structural leadership), intellectual capacity (intellectual leadership) and entrepreneurship (entrepreneur leadership).

[3] Lukes (1974) argues, leadership often requires institutional context, not *ad hoc*.

can and cannot participate in negotiations is critical. In other words, who is inside and outside the group of "like-minded" countries is the question. There is a strong incentive of exclusion, rather than inclusion because exclusion of rivals is necessary to assume leadership during negotiation in the group. Second, agenda-setting is important. In particular, suppression of collective decisions (the so-called non-decision) is important. Concerned parties should share some ideas regarding both what can and cannot be negotiated. Agenda to be prioritised are often called as built-in agenda, while items to be dropped from negotiations is treated as *fait accompli*. A framework agreement and memorandum of understanding (MOU) are often used to confirm what became no longer negotiable. Third, the sponsorship of a group or negotiations significantly affect the decision-making of the group at an early stage of negotiation. Sponsorships such as which country proposed, which country chairs the meeting and which country (location) hosts the organisation or secretariat, among others, affect the decision-making norms of the group.

3. Regional Free Trade Agreements (FTAs)

3.1. *Chinese Approach to Regional FTAs: EAFTA*

China seems to already have a capacity to conduct proactive regional trade diplomacy by the late 1990s, but the situation was complicated because of the interaction between its regional trade diplomacy and its World Trade Organization (WTO) membership application. China applied for the WTO membership in July 1986, but the process was a very long and difficult journey. China's regional trade diplomacy was nearly absent, until it secured the WTO membership. This is because, the pursuant of FTAs at a critical juncture of WTO accession process would only make the prospect of its WTO membership slim. China and the US bilaterally agreed upon the terms of WTO accession in November 1999, but it was only in September 2000 when the US Congress agreed to render Permanent Normal Trade Relations (PNTR), namely, the most-favoured-nation (MFN) status to China. The then President Bill Clinton signed the bill for the Chinese PNTR in the following month.

This means that the Chinese membership in WTO was secured by then as long as the US–China relations are concerned.

The idea of ASEAN–China FTA was informally floated by China around 1998 partly to cope with "China threat" sentiment in ASEAN (Aslam 2012). China became very serious to realise this ambitious project soon after it secured the WTO membership in 2000, despite the fact that East Asia Vision Group (EAVG) formed in December 1998 was discussing East Asia-wide cooperation, including East Asia Free Trade Area (EAFTA).[4] China aggressively lobbied for ASEAN counterparts during the ASEAN-related meetings held late November 2000. The ASEAN side, however, considered that it was necessary to keep the same distance from China and Japan. In fact, at the ASEAN+3 Summit on 24th November, Thai Prime Minister Chuan Leekpai expressed the view that FTA which involved not only China but also Japan and Korea was desirable. Partly because Goh Chok Tong, the Singaporean Prime Minister, successfully guided the discussions among ASEAN+3, the leaders agreed to establish East Asia Study Group (EASG), consisting of government officials, and to include the EAFTA as a group's study item (Hamanaka 2008). China, however, strongly demanded the initiation of feasibility study on ASEAN–China FTA, at the ASEAN–China Summit held on the next day. As a result, the Statement of ASEAN Informal Summit released on 25th November 2000 emphasised the significance of East Asian cooperation, while it also spelled out the initiation of study on ASEAN–China FTA.[5] At the ASEAN–China Summit in November 2001 in Brunei Darussalam, China and ASEAN agreed to establish FTA in 10 years time. In November 2002, ASEAN–China Summit delivered Framework Agreement on ASEAN–China FTA while ASEAN+3 Summit, held back-to-back to this, simply requested their Economic Ministers to study options for EAFTA.[6] In November

[4] EAVG produced a report in which it recommended the establishment of EAFTA. The report was submitted to ASEAN+3 Summit in Brunei in 2001.

[5] http://asean.org/?static_post=the-fourth-asean-informal-summit-22-25-november-2000-singapore.

[6] http://asean.org/?static_post=press-statement-by-the-chairman-of-the-8th-asean-summit-the-6th-asean-3-summit-and-the-asean-china-summit-phnom-penh-cambodia-

2004, China and ASEAN already signed Agreement on Trade in Goods of the ASEAN–China FTA. To summarise, ASEAN was unable to refuse the strong request from China, and the project of ASEAN–China FTA moved very quickly, while the progress of EAFTA discussion was slow.[7]

At the ASEAN+3 Summit in November 2004, leaders exchanged views on the establishment of EAFTA, and they welcomed the decision by the ASEAN+3 Economic Ministers to set up an expert group to conduct the feasibility study of EAFTA. The first meeting of Joint Expert Group for Feasibility Study on EAFTA (JEG) was held in April 2005 in Beijing, which means that China was leading the project. The idea of China was to establish goods-centric FTA among ASEAN+3 members alone (Teh 2011). The Chinese emphasis on trade in goods was natural given the fact that the service and investment components of ASEAN–China FTA were still under negotiations as of 2005.[8]

One may wonder why China's position with regard to EAFTA that included Japan, suddenly changed. As we saw, in 2000, China made every effort to facilitate the establishment of ASEAN–China FTA, excluding Japan. In 2005, China already insisted upon the creation of EAFTA that includes Japan. One of critical reasons is that the trade of China quickly expanded during this period and overtook that of Japan. In fact, as Figure 1 shows, the Chinese trade grew much faster than Japan's and the total trade of China and Japan became almost the same in 2003. While the Chinese trade was 55% of that of Japan in 2000, it became 30% more than that of Japan in 2005. By the mid-2000s, China became confident to assume leadership in negotiations for FTA that covers the entire Asia, provided that it is a goods-centric agreement.

4-november-2002-3.

[7] In 2003, the statement for ASEAN+3 Summit was merged with that of ASEAN Summit. The statement for ASEAN and ASEAN+3 Summit does not specifically mention EAFTA.

[8] Trade in Services Agreement and Agreement on Investment for ASEAN–China FTA were signed in 2007 and 2009, respectively.

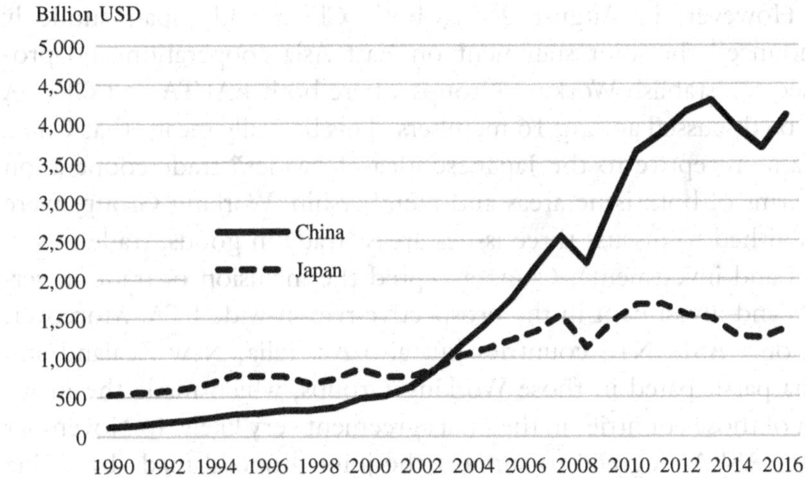

Figure 1. Total trade of China and Japan

Source: Author's compilation based on UNCTAD STAT.

China was not really keen to support the idea of Comprehensive Economic Partnership for East Asia (CEPEA) proposed by Japan in 2006 (see Section 3.2 for the Japanese motivations for proposing CEPEA). Unlike EAFTA, CEPEA emphasises the significance of trade in services and investment. Those are the areas where Japan has competitiveness via-a-vis China and has large commercial interests. Moreover, China had a very clear policy about the membership of regional FTA — CEPEA is problematic because it includes members beyond ASEAN+3 (Teh 2011). The Chinese proposal on EAFTA and the Japanese proposal on CEPEA competed; feasibility studies for the two proposals were conducted separately, one led by China and the other led by Japan. While ASEAN made a desperate effort to bridge the two proposals in 2010, such an attempt was unsuccessful because the two countries stuck to their own initiatives (Hamanaka 2014).[9]

[9] In 2010, ASEAN established Working Groups on rules of origin, tariffs, customs procedures and economic cooperation. The participants of those Working Groups

However, in August 2011, both China and Japan suddenly announced the joint statement on East Asia cooperation and proposed to establish Working Groups where both EAFTA and CEPEA can be discussed among 16 members. This basically means that China became receptive to the Japanese idea of "wider" trade cooperation in terms of both issue areas and membership. Working Groups were established to discuss three issues areas (trade in goods, trade in services and investment); China accepted the inclusion of trade in services and investment in the prospective region-wide FTA. Moreover, not only ASEAN+3 countries but also Australia, New Zealand and India participated in those Working Groups, which made the inclusion of those countries in the final agreement very likely. In November 2011, ASEAN agreed to support the joint proposal made by China and Japan and establish Working Groups to conduct preparatory work for the negotiations for the prospective region-wide agreement, which was given a new name, Regional Comprehensive Economic Partnership (RCEP). Hence, we can say that by 2010 China agreed to negotiate a region-wide FTA covering not only goods but also services and investment, which is very similar to CEPEA originally proposed by Japan.[10]

How to explain such as a rapid shift in Chinese regional economic diplomacy, especially its positive attitude towards the investment negotiations? There are mainly two reasons. First, there is a possibility that regional trade diplomacy in Asia would be dominated by the US-led TPP. In fact, Japanese Prime Minister Naoto Kan for the first time expressed the interest in Japanese membership in TPP at the Diet Session in October 2010. China did not like to see regional trade diplomacy dominated by TPP that is jointly led by the US and Japan. It was necessary for China to attract Japan so that its regionwide FTA project became successful. Second, it is again the rise of China. As Figure 2 shows, the rise of China in the investment field was very significant after 2005. In particular, having a large amount of outward

---

were ASEAN+6. From the Japanese perspective, the ASEAN proposal was too goods-centric. For China its membership was too wide.

[10] The RCEP negotiation was formally launched in November 2012.

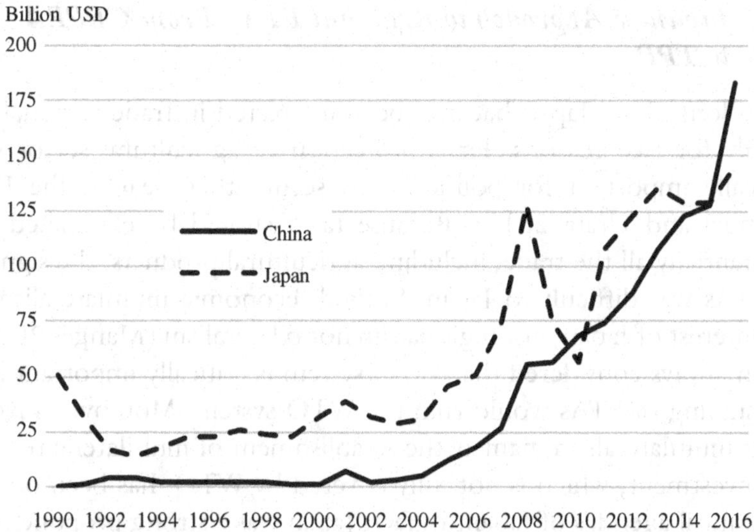

Figure 2. Outward investment of China and Japan

Source: Author's compilation based on UNCTAD STAT.

investment is critical to have a large voice in investment agreement negotiations because many countries are in an attempt to attract investment. While investment flows fluctuate across years, the Chinese outward investment grew very quickly and this is especially true for the period after 2005. It is very symbolic that the Chinese outward investment for the first time surpassed that of Japan in 2010. In short, while China was unconfident to negotiate investment with Japan in 2005, such a situation totally changed by 2010.

Since the time around 2010, from the Chinese perspective, the only condition that any regionwide agreement should satisfy is that the US should be excluded from there. As far as US was absent, China can dominate regional trade negotiations even if it included Japan. In November 2012, ASEAN and its FTA partners formally agreed to launch RCEP negotiations, and the Guiding Principle and Objectives for Negotiating RCEP was announced. Principle 6 of the Guiding principle states that only ASEAN FTA partners can join the RCEP negotiations. Note that the US does not have an FTA with ASEAN as a group, hence it cannot be a part of RCEP negotiations.

3.2. *Japanese Approach to Regional FTAs: From CEPEA to TPP*

For a long time, Japan had not been interested in trade regionalism mainly for two reasons. First, protection of agricultural sector was critically important for politicians to secure their seat at the Diet (Pempel and Urata 2013). Because tariff should be eliminated for substantially all the trade, including agricultural products, the signing of FTAs was difficult to Japan. Second, economic multilateralism is the interest of Japan, not regionalism nor bilateralism (Manger 2005). Japan always considered that WTO system is critically important and the signing of FTAs would ruin the WTO system. Moreover, investment multilateralism, namely the establishment of multilateral regime for investment, which is not fully covered by WTO, has been one of the critical agendas of Japan. In fact, Japan was a strong proponent of Multilateral Agreement on Investment (MAI), which was negotiated at the Organisation for Economic Co-operation and Development (OECD) in the 1990s.

Japan's pursuit of regionalism and bilateralism started in the field of investment, rather than trade. As Japan started having huge amounts of investment assets abroad, both investment protection and liberalisation became an immediate problem by the late 1990s, especially after the MAI became unlikely. Japan launched negotiations of bilateral investment treaty (BIT) with Korea[11] in November 1998, immediately after the collapse of MAI negotiations. Japan also agreed to start BIT negotiation with Vietnam in March 1999. Those are predated to the launch of Japan's first FTA negotiation with Singapore; the two countries agreed to start negotiations only in January 2001. Hence, we can say that Japan's investment bilateralism started even before its trade bilateralism (Hamanaka 2017).

[11] Until 2001, Japan signed only nine BITs. The first one was with Egypt signed in 1977. For almost all Japanese BITs signed in early days, the partner side approached Japan expecting BITs are helpful in attracting Japanese investment. Those BITs are classified as the first generation of Japanese BITs — they cover only investment protection, not liberalisation. In contrast, Japan–Korea BIT covers both investment protection and liberalisation. See Hamanaka (2017).

Japan's regional trade diplomacy, however, quickly reacted to the Chinese proposal on FTA with ASEAN made in November 2000. In January 2001, Japan and Singapore agreed to launch bilateral negotiations for Economic Partnership Agreement (EPA). After the agreement was made to launch ASEAN–China FTA negotiation in November 2001, Japan's regional trade diplomacy became even more proactive (Hamanaka 2008). In January 2002, Japanese Prime Minister Junichiro Koizumi visited Singapore and proposed to establish EPA between Japan and ASEAN. Unlike the Chinese proposal, which is FTA (goods-centric), the Japanese proposal intends to be comprehensive covering trade in services, investment and intellectual property, which applied to both Japan–Singapore and Japan–ASEAN agreements.

Japan had a concern that the negotiations for EAFTA would be dominated by China. It therefore made a counterproposal on CEPEA in 2006 (Teh 2011). An emphasis of CEPEA was placed on its comprehensiveness, going beyond traditional goods trade, which is the focus of EAFTA. Trade in services, investment and intellectual property are the core components of the Japanese proposal. Japan's idea was that it could dominate the discussions in regional negotiation that would even include China, if the core issue areas are services and investment. With regard to the membership formulation, CEPEA included not only ASEAN+3 but also Australia, New Zealand and India. Japan considered that the involvement of Australia, New Zealand and India would contribute to its bargaining power *vis-à-vis* China. Moreover, it seems that the CEPEA does not rule out the possibility of US participation in future, provided that it joins East Asia Summit. The first experts' meeting for CEPEA was held in Tokyo in June 2007. Japan sped up the study so that it would not fall behind the EAFTA study led by China. The CEPEA study was finalised in July 2009, only one month after the completion of study on EAFTA. While the study result of EAFTA study was reported to ASEAN+3 Economic Ministers Meeting (EMM) in August 2009, that of CEPEA was reported to EMM among ASEAN+6, which were held back-to-back to each other.

In August 2011, Japan and China agreed to establish Working Groups where both EAFTA and CEPEA could be discussed, and this movement implies that China accepted CEPEA, as already discussed, although the prospective agreement obtained a new name — RCEP. This, however, did not lead to the situation wherein Japan could achieve its original goal of realising CEPEA, using the platform of RCEP. Rather, by 2011, Japan became very cautious to CEPEA/RCEP because it could lead to the creation of a regional FTA dominated by China. This is ironical because Japan was keen to establish CEPEA when China was reluctant, but it became disinterested in its own proposal when China became receptive to it. It is perhaps more accurate to argue that Japan became cautious to CEPEA *because* China became receptive to it. This clearly shows who leads and who dominates is critical in understanding Asian trade diplomacy (Hamanaka 2014, Teh 2011: 353).

But then, the question is why Japan agreed to make an announcement on East Asian cooperation with China, which resulted in the creation of the three Working Groups, despite the fact that it started to fear any regional trade agreements that are likely to be dominated by China? The only critical reason why Japan agreed to launch RCEP is that Japan wanted to obtain "China card" in order to make its TPP negotiations easier (Hamanaka 2014). Japan and China agreed to establish working groups in August 2011, but three months later in November 2011, at Honolulu where the APEC Leaders' meeting was held, Japan formally expressed the interest in participating the TPP negotiations. While Mexico and Canada expressed the interest at the same time as Japan, and their applications were approved in June 2012, the approval for Japan's participation was delayed, which made Japan frustrated. On 20th November 2012, Japanese Prime Minister Yoshihiko Noda met US President Barack Obama and requested the US support to Japan's participation in TPP; exactly on the same day, the RCEP negotiation was formally launched. The Japanese message was very clear: "if you (the US) do not treat us (Japan) in a friendly manner, there is a possibility that we would go to the Chinese camp". Partly because of the China card, Japan's participation in TPP negotiations was finally approved in March 2013.

After Japan secured a seat at the TPP negotiation table, it concentrated its negotiation resource onto TPP negotiations.

Once TPP was concluded, Japan started to think that China should join TPP and accept rules that are crafted by TPP members and does not seem to be keen to facilitate RCEP negotiations any longer.

4. Regional Financial Institution

4.1. *Japanese Approach to Regional Financial Cooperation: ADB and AMF*

Since the end of World War II, Japan has been a strong proponent of Asia-only financial cooperation. While it is true that Japan supported the US international financial hegemony namely, the Bretton Woods system, it had a strong desire to lead Asian financial cooperation, excluding the US. It is totally wrong if one argues that Japan was an obedient follower to the US, as long as regional finance is concerned (Hamanaka 2011a, 2011b).

The Asian Development Bank (ADB) established in 1966 included the US, but we should not overlook the fact that it is treated as a non-regional member. One cannot simply argue that the US's non-regional membership is natural because it is not an Asian country. A regional development bank responsible for regional development in Latin America is called as Inter-American Development Bank (not Latin American Development Bank), which included the US as a regional member; its head office is in Washington, D.C. Hence, it is not surprising that the Asia-Pacific Development Bank that included the US as a regional member was established in the 1960s. The point here is that Japan successfully excluded the US from ADB's regional membership, while securing its financial contribution. In short, ADB established by Japan in the 1960s is a Japanese arrangement with a large US financial contribution and with little US management voice, according to Huang (1975). The US was not keen to support the Japan-led ADB project, but reluctantly decided not to make an objection, just because it feared that the opposition to the proposal simply fuelled the anti-US sentiment in Asia caused by its bombing in the Vietnam War (White 1970). At the same time, we should remember that the US made every effort so that the ADB headquarters is located in Manila, and not in Tokyo. In fact, Manila was chosen as a result of voting (Yasutomo 1983).

In February 1991, the first meeting of Executives Meeting of East Asian and Pacific Central Banks (EMEAP) was held in Tokyo. EMEAP is a regional central bank forum, established by Bank of Japan (BOJ), which can be regarded as the Asian version of Bank for International Settlement (BIS). It should be noted that the EMEAP project started even before Mahathir floated the idea of East Asia Economic Group (EAEG), which later came to be known as East Asia Economic Caucus (EAEC). While some argue that EAEG/EAEC triggered the regionalism in East Asia, which eventually lead to ASEAN+3 (Terada 2003), such an argument tells us only a part of the story. In the finance field, Asianism existed even before EAEG/EAEC. EMEAP is not an exception in this regard. The US was excluded from EMEAP, and despite the fact that the US Central Bank (Federal Research Board) strongly requested for the membership, BOJ refused to accept its request (Yokoi-Arai 2002). What is also very interesting is that China is also excluded from its original membership, although it joined in 1992, unlike the US. BOJ officials may be able to list up several plausible excuses why China was not ready to be a part of EMEAP in 1991, none of them seems to be convincing enough because China obtained EMEAP membership only one year later. This is especially true given the fact that Asia-Pacific Economic Cooperation (APEC) accepted the Chinese membership in 1991. So, a more convincing argument is that BOJ excluded China from the original membership of EMEAP, while there is a growing trend of "engaging China" in the early 1990s. The absence of China for one year was critical to realise that EMEAP was dominated by Japan (Hamanaka 2009: 101).

The Japanese Ministry of Finance (MOF) attempted to establish Asian Monetary Fund (AMF) soon after the Asian financial crisis in 1997. The US was not included as a prospective member of AMF. The Japanese proposal on the AMF membership only included the contributors to the Thai rescue package agreed at the Thai rescue meeting organised in Tokyo in August 1997. It can be said that Japan took advantage of the fact that the US did not contribute to the Thai package to justify the US exclusion from the AMF.[12] The US did not support AMF on the ground that it ruins the function of the International Monetary Fund (IMF) (Blustein 2001). However, the real reason why the US blocked the proposal was that AMF excluded the US from its membership. In fact, Fred Bergstein, who was the President of Peterson Institute for International Economics (PIIE) and close aide to the then Clinton Administration, argues that the establishment of the Asia-Pacific Monetary Fund that included the US was desirable (Bergsten 1998).

While AMF was not established, Asian countries agreed to create Chiang Mai Initiative (CMI) in May 2000, and the US was unable to make an objection to it. CMI is a network of swap arrangement among financial authorities in East Asia. This is a virtual AMF because countries hit by crises can borrow money from regional partners, although there was no formal organisational structure attached to CMI, unlike AMF. While the US was not a part of CMI, there was one important trick; only 10% of CMI money can be disbursed without the approval of IMF. In other words, when members disburse more than 10% of CMI, the approval of IMF, where the US has the dominant voice, was necessary. Hence, CMI is Asian money which virtually requires the US approval upon disbursement. Japan, of course, was unhappy with such an arrangement and its strategy was to reduce the US influence by increasing the total amount of the fund and delinked portion of CMI from IMF.[13]

After 2005, Japan was no longer the single dominant player in Asia in the field of international finance. As Figure 3 shows, the foreign reserves of China and Japan were already comparable in 2005. At the same time, China was not confident enough to assume leadership in international or regional finance partly because of the global financial crisis that culminated in Lehman shock in 2008. What is very interesting is that China and Japan agreed to accept "equal footing" in Asian financial arrangement when their financial

---

[12] The US participated in the Thai rescue meeting, but refused to financially contribute to the package.

[13] The delinked share was increased to 20% in 2009 and to 30% in 2014.

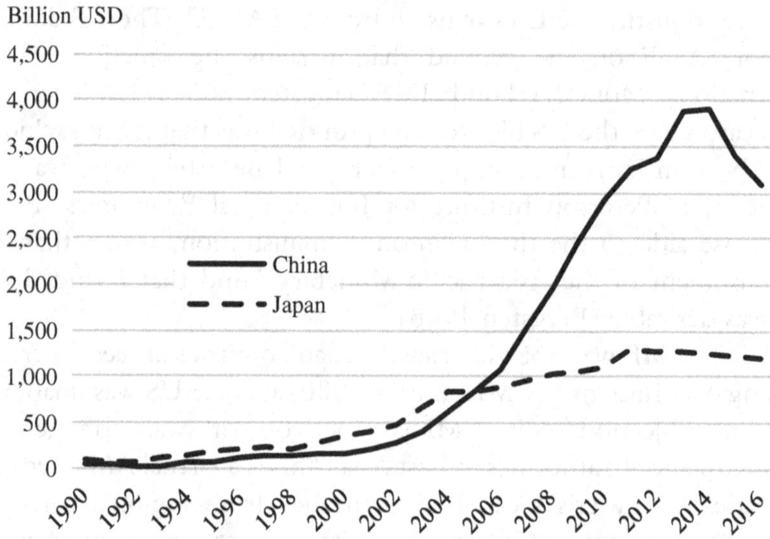

Figure 3. Foreign reserves of China and Japan

Source: Author's compilation based on IMF data.

power was comparable. CMI was multilateralised and started to introduce the voting mechanism in March 2010. The two parties agreed to hold the same voting power in multilateralised CMI. In May 2010, China and Japan agreed the basic modality of ASEAN+3 Macroeconomic Research Office (AMRO), a kind of secretariat for surveillance under multilateralised CMI.[14] The AMRO Office is located neither in Tokyo nor Beijing, but in a third country, Singapore. The head position of AMRO rotates between China and Japan.[15]

Japan became very cautious to the Asia-only financial arrangement after 2011. Japan has not been supportive to AIIB proposed by China in 2013 from the beginning. While some may argue that Japan is following the US with regard to the position to AIIB, in my view,

---

[14] AMRO was established in April 2011.

[15] The three-year term of the inaugural President was split into the first one year and the second two years because Japan and China were unable to agree on which country should send the inaugural President.

the reality is that it is Japan, not the US, that fundamentally dislikes AIIB. Any debate on AIIB in Japan always relates with ADB. The Japanese executives, officials and media always see AIIB in comparison with ADB. The tone of opinions expressed by any opinion leader is: "why do we need AIIB given the fact that there is ADB established by Japan a half century ago?" It is true that there are some cofinancing projects between ADB and AIIB. However, we should not overlook the fact that all of them are ADB projects cofinanced by AIIB; there is no AIIB project cofinanced by ADB.

4.2. *Chinese Approach to Regional Financial Cooperation: AIIB*

Beijing was not part of ADB when it was established. Taipei represented China. Beijing joined ADB as a latecomer in 1986, and Taipei continued to stay in ADB. ADB is one of the few international organisations wherein both Beijing and Taipei have membership. It was inevitable for China (Beijing) to join ADB in 1986 because it was a standing institution already for two decades. The options that China had was limited to whether or not to join ADB. The situation of the Chinese membership in EMEAP is similar to that of its ADB membership. Because EMEAP was secretly established in 1991 (EMEAP 2003), perhaps while Beijing did not notice, Beijing had no choice but to be a latecomer and so Beijing decided to join at least as a latecomer because it did not like to see Hong Kong Monetary Authority (HKMA) joining EMEAP before it. In short, because ADB and EMEAP already existed, all China can do is to join them before problematic competitors (such as Taiwan and Hong Kong) could join and block the Chinese membership.

When Japan proposed AMF in 1997, all Asian countries supported the Japanese idea, with a notable exception of China. It is very interesting to find that the Chinese position to the AMF proposal was very similar to the US's; the Japanese-led regional financial cooperation in Asia was undesirable. China did not speak at all at the meeting to discuss the AMF establishment held in Hong Kong in September 1997, despite the fact that Korean and ASEAN members supported the Japanese idea. Japanese MOF officials involved in AMF negotiations recall that China did not support the AMF proposal because silence means objection in international meetings (Blustein 2001: 167).

As discussed, the critical question regarding the institutional design of CMI established in May 2000 was its IMF linkage. Japan wanted an independent CMI wherein the money can be disbursed without IMF approval. The US insisted upon high portion of IMF linkage. A compromise was made to set the portion of IMF linkage as 90% (only 10% can be disbursed without IMF approval). Then, what was the Chinese position on this critical question? China's position was that CMI should be fully linked with IMF, meaning 100% linkage of CMI money to IMF conditionality (Amyx 2004). In other words, China was of the view that IMF and the US should be fully involved in the CMI decision-making via its IMF linkage. Because China did not like a Japan-dominated CMI, it chose CMI to be dominated by the US/IMF, which was "the second-worst scenario".

China announced the proposal on AIIB in October 2013. During the ADB annual meeting in May 2014, China arranged a dinner meeting and invited 16 countries to discuss AIIB; the US and Japan were not invited. In October 2014, MOU for AIIB was signed by 21 countries in which the headquarters in Beijing was mentioned. We can say that China learnt from the mistake committed by Japan during the ADB establishment process. Because the location of ADB headquarters was decided by voting, Japan failed to host it. China's strategy was that the MOU, which stipulates the location of headquarters as Beijing, to be quickly signed by the invited guests to avoid any complicated negotiations.

China set the deadline of expressing the interest in AIIB membership by March 2015. While more than 50 countries, including UK, France, Germany, Korea and Australia, expressed the interests, Japan and the US decided not to do so. Any country that wanted to participate in negotiations including Japan and the US needed to submit applications to Beijing. Both Japan and the US were of the view that the lack of transparency of AIIB governance made it difficult for them to join the organisation. It is possible to argue that China took advantage of such statements made by Japan and the US — as long as transparency is not guaranteed, the US and Japan will not request membership. In AIIB, there are two types of distinctions in terms of membership: (i) regional member and non-regional member; and (ii) original member and latecomers. Hence, neither Japan nor the US could satisfy the two conditions, which means that China is the legitimate leader of AIIB as far as its membership rules are concerned.[16]

5. Conclusion: Is China–Japan Cooperation Possible?

In general, we confirmed that Sino-Japan rivalries over the meta-level institutionalisation of negotiation modalities have been so intense. The launch of negotiations that comfortably involve both China and Japan is extremely difficult to exist. The meta-level power struggle concentrates on three negotiation modalities: membership (who should participate in the negotiations); prior agenda-setting (what should be discussed in the negotiations); and sponsorship (who can claim the credit, who chair the negotiations). They spend a huge amount of resources in order to launch negotiations favourable to themselves. The launch of negotiations sometimes becomes very difficult because of the intense struggle before the launch of negotiations.

The behaviour patterns of the two countries are very similar. First, on membership, both tried to assume leadership by excluding the other, as well as the US. Holding the predominant leadership position in regional projects excluding the US is the best scenario for both China and Japan. The worst scenario for them is the leadership assumed by the other, excluding the US. China/Japan often objects to the other's regionalism project. As a result, they tend to exclude not only the US but also the other. Regionalism including the US, wherein the US naturally assumes leadership, is between the two

[16] If the US and Japan had jointly made a counterproposal in the Asia-Pacific Infrastructure Investment Bank that is located in Beijing, but had a non-Chinese president at an early stage, the course of negotiations would have been totally different.

extreme scenarios — could be the second-best or the second-worst scenario, depending on the context. For China, Japan-led AMF and Japan-led CEPEA were the worst scenarios. Hence, it sometimes chose the second-worst option, i.e. US-led regionalism. In fact, China attempted to include US in CMI via its IMF linkage. Likewise, for Japan, China-led projects such as RCEP were the worst scenario. Japan is supporting the TPP led by the US. Similarly, in the field of finance, AIIB is the worst scenario for Japan.

Second, agenda-setting is also important for the two countries. While the two countries proposed FTA, the Chinese one was goods agreement, while what Japan attempted to establish was investment agreement in essence. The rivalry between trade-centric EAFTA among the 13 countries proposed by China and investment-centric CEPEA among the 16 countries proposed by Japan are some of the illustrative examples.

Third, sponsorship is critical. Perhaps, the most intense rivalry can be observed in the claim of sponsorship of negotiations. The two countries try to chair a meeting and host the secretariat or head office. Moreover, which country initially proposed a new institution is important; they stick to the project which they initiated and seldom support a project sponsored by the other rival country, even if its contents are agreeable. China wanted to launch a new negotiation for RCEP, though the content of RCEP was almost the same as that of CEPEA because the latter is originally a Japanese proposal, wherein Japan naturally has a larger voice. The fact that RCEP was regarded as a Chinese initiative simply reduced the Japanese appetite to it, even though the content of RCEP and CEPEA were similar. While Japan thought of AIIB as a redundant body which was a simple duplication of Japan-sponsored ADB, China just wanted an institution sponsored by itself. The fact that China proposed AIIB and hosted the negotiation meeting and the head office is important to China. Those are exactly the reasons why Japan is indifferent to AIIB, though what China is doing is almost the same as what Japan did a half century ago.

Now, we can have a relatively clear idea about what is likely to happen in the near future regarding Sino–Japan rivalry in economic cooperation in Asia. In the field of finance, the worst scenario for Japan is that Japan joins AIIB and the US does not because that would result in Asia-only cooperation dominated by China. The only scenario of Japanese participation in AIIB is that it joins together with the US. Here, the question is whether the US can be a dominant player in AIIB. The US may try to compete with China in AIIB by requesting a large voting power and executive positions such as vice president, but the important point here is that China already won *vis-à-vis* the US at the meta level. First, the US and Japan are treated as non-original members. Agenda of AIIB is already decided. Moreover, AIIB is under Chinese sponsorship. If Chinese dominance is clear even after the participation of the US and Japan, they are unlikely to join. In the field of trade because Japan does not have a desire to lead the region by establishing Asia-only FTA, it decided to join TPP led by the US, which is much better than its participation in RCEP dominated by China. While some argue that TPP and RCEP are the two wheels of trade liberalisation in Asia-Pacific, it is more likely that Japan will try to involve China into TPP without concluding RCEP negotiations. At least, until the US returns to TPP, it will try to delay the conclusion of RCEP negotiations. For Japan, having TPP that involves the US is a necessary condition to finalise RCEP negotiations.

References

Acharya, A. (1997). Ideas, identity, and institution-building: From the "ASEAN way" to the "Asia-Pacific way"? *The Pacific Review* 10(3), 319–346.

Amyx, J. (2004). Japan and the evolution of regional financial arrangements in East Asia. In Krauss, E. and Pempel, T.J. (eds) *Beyond Bilateralism: U.S.–Japan Relations in the New Asia-Pacific*. Stanford University Press, Stanford.

Aslam, M. (2012). The impact of ASEAN-China free trade area agreement on ASEAN's manufacturing industry. *International Journal of China Studies* 3(1), 43–78.

Bergsten, C.F. (1998). Reviving the "Asian Monetary Fund". *International Economic Policy Briefs* 98(8).

Blustein, P. (2001). *The Chastening: Inside the Crisis That Rocked the Global Financial System and Humbled the IMF*, Public Affairs, New York.

EMEAP (2003). What is EMEAP?: Its past, present, and future. Available at: www.emeap.org.

Hamanaka, S. (2008). Comparing summitry, financial and trade regionalism in East Asia: From the Japanese perspective. In Dent, C. (ed), *China, Japan and Regional Leadership in East Asia*, Edward Elgar.

Hamanaka, S. (2009). *Asian Regionalism and Japan: The Politics of Membership in Regional Diplomatic, Financial and Trade Groups*, Routledge, London.

Hamanaka, S. (2011a). Asian financial cooperation in the 1990s: The politics of membership. *Journal of East Asian Studies* 11(1), 75–103.

Hamanaka, S. (2011b). Asia-only versus Asia-Pacific regionalism: Regionalism cycle in summits and financial cooperation. *Pacific Focus* 26(2), 236–259.

Hamanaka, S. (2014). TPP versus RCEP: Control of membership and agenda setting. *Journal of East Asian Economic Integration* 18(2), 163–186.

Hamanaka, S. (2016). Insights to great powers' desire to establish institutions: Comparison of ADB, AMF, AMRO and AIIB. *Global Policy* 7(2), 288–292.

Hamanaka, S. (2017). China-Japan-Korea trilateral investment treaty: Implications for future investment negotiations in Asia. In Chaisse, J., Ishikawa, T. and Jusoh, S. (eds), *Asia's Changing International Investment Regime Sustainability, Regionalization, and Arbitration*, Springer.

Huang, P.-W. (1975). *The Asian Development Bank: Diplomacy and Development in Asia*, Vantage Press, New York.

Lukes, S. (1974). *Power: A Radical View*, Macmillan, London and New York.

Manger, M. (2005). Competition and bilateralism in trade policy: The case of Japan's free trade agreements. *Review of International Political Economy* 12(5), 804–828.

Pempel, T.J. and Urata, S. (2013). Japan: A new move toward bilateral trade agreements. In Aggarwal, V. and Urata S. (eds), *Bilateral Trade Agreements in the Asia-Pacific: Origins, Evolutions, and Implications*, Routledge.

Teh, B.C.G. (2011). Japan–China rivalry: What role does the East Asia Summit play? *Asia Pacific Viewpoint* 52(3): 347–360.

Terada, T. (2003). Constructing an 'East Asian' concept and growing regional identity: From EAEC to ASEAN+3. *The Pacific Review* 16(2), 251–277.

White, J. (1970). *Regional Development Banks: The Asian, African and Inter-American Development Banks*, Overseas Development Institute, London.

Yasutomo, D.T. (1983). *Japan and the Asian Development Bank*, Praeger, New York.

Yokoi-Arai, M. (2002). *Financial Stability Issues — The Case of East Asia*, Springer.

Young, O.R. (1991). Political leadership and regime formation: On the development of institutions in international society. *International Organization* 45(3), 281–308.

Chapter 7

The Belt and Road Initiative: Progress and Prospect in Southeast Asia

Xue Gong and Li Mingjiang

1. Introduction

The Belt and Road Initiative (BRI) is perhaps one of the rare mega foreign policy proposals made by China in decades. It is a clear indication of the transition in Chinese foreign policy from "low profile" to growing proactivism in international affairs. Many analysts believe that the BRI will play a significant role in pushing for economic integration in the Eurasian continent, sustaining the momentum of globalisation, modifying the geopolitical order in Asia and dramatically increasing Beijing's influence regionally and globally.

This chapter attempts to examine the prospects of the BRI in Southeast Asia. We select three countries that are broadly representative of the region and seek to analyse their responses to the BRI and possible areas of cooperation between these countries and China under the BRI framework. The three countries include Lao People's Democratic Republic (Lao PDR), Malaysia and Vietnam. Lao PDR is representative of a few countries in Southeast Asia that have developed close ties with China and are generally interested in strengthening economic ties with China without any notable concerns about domestic political repercussions and regional geopolitical consequences. Other similar countries include Cambodia, Brunei, Thailand and Singapore. Singapore may be slightly different when it comes to its views on the BRI's regional geopolitical impact as compared to the other four countries in this group. But Singapore's concerns about the regional geopolitical impact of China's growing economic influence has had almost no effect on the city state's actual policy response to the BRI. This group of countries evaluates the BRI mainly from an economic perspective and believes that the BRI will provide good opportunities for their own economic development.

The second group of regional states includes Malaysia, Indonesia and the Philippines. In general, these states are interested in expanding their economic ties with China under the BRI, but a few factors undermined their full acceptance of Chinese economic influence. First, these three countries have territorial and/or maritime disputes with China in the South China Sea. These disputes make maritime cooperation between these countries and China very difficult, if not entirely impossible. This means that cooperation in a significant part of the 21st century Maritime Silk Road (MSR) scheme is unlikely to take place. Second, because of the South China Sea disputes, these countries, to varying degrees, have national security concerns when engaging with China economically. This is particularly the case when it comes to infrastructure. Some regional countries worry that they cannot entirely trust China to build their major infrastructure projects. Third, Chinese investments and other economic activities in these countries have triggered domestic political contestations among different forces. This further complicates these states' interactions with China under the BRI. For this group of regional states, the BRI is acceptable, but the actual implementation of some BRI projects will not be without risks, challenges and even complications.

The third group of countries includes Vietnam and Myanmar. Officially, these two states proclaim that they welcome BRI and are willing to cooperate with China under the BRI framework. But in reality, actual cooperation pertaining to resources and major infrastructure or too much expansion of Chinese economic presence in the two countries have proven to be problematic in the past few years. Vietnam's reluctance in wholeheartedly accepting the BRI stems from a few factors: the dispute with China in the South China Sea, historical animosities and concerns about being financially indebted to Beijing. Myanmar's lacklustre response to BRI reflects significant negative views in the Myanmar society towards Chinese infrastructure investments, largely because of the predatory economic activities of some Chinese businesses during the junta rule in this country. Civil society groups and non-governmental organisations (NGOs) in Myanmar continue to distrust Chinese investments in the resource and infrastructure sectors. Societal suspicions towards Chinese infrastructure proposals will remain a major obstacle for the BRI's implementation in Myanmar.

We hope that the three cases will shed some light on how Southeast Asia has responded to the BRI and how the BRI may actually make progress in the region. The cases, at the aggregate level, suggest that the BRI is generally welcome in the region, but at the same time, there will be significant limitations as to how much the regional states and China can accomplish under the BRI framework.

2. Lao PDR: Embracing the BRI

The Lao PDR is one of the least-developed countries in Southeast Asia. Its landlocked location poses three main obstacles to its development: (1) isolation to foreign markets; (2) poor logistics services; and (3) underdeveloped domestic and cross-border transportation infrastructure.

Among the five countries of the Indo-China Peninsula, Lao PDR is the only country without a rail system. The existing 3.5-kilometre rail road, an extension of the Thai railway network, began operations in 2009. It was reported that the cost of a 40-foot equivalent unit (FEU) container transport from Vientiane, the capital city of Lao PDR, to Yokohama port in Japan is the most expensive route when compared to the transporting of the same unit from other main cities in Asia.[1] This cost disadvantage not only constitutes a major constraint

---

[1] Japan External Trade Organization (JETRO) (2015); Conference presentation shared by a Lao scholar, March 2017.

on Lao PDR's external trade relations but also reduces foreign investors' motivation. Hence, the poor logistical services and insufficient infrastructure are key factors which hinder Lao PDR's economic development. Lao PDR's underdeveloped economy and extremely insufficient infrastructure are key reasons for its keen support for the BRI.

2.1. *The BRI and Lao PDR's Development Vision, Strategy and Agenda*

In 1986, Lao PDR began to shift its centrally planned economy to an open market-oriented system known as "Chintanakarnmai" or New Economic Mechanism (NEM). To enhance socio-economic development, the government of Lao PDR (GOL) gradually expanded its economic cooperation with other countries and organisations in the world. In 1992, Lao PDR joined the Greater Mekong Subregion (GMS) and, in 1997, it was admitted into the Association of Southeast Asian Nations (ASEAN). In 2013, it was accepted by the World Trade Organization (WTO).

The first long-term national development vision of the country was introduced in 1996 at the Sixth Congress of the Lao People's Revolutionary Party (LPRP) with the objective of "graduating the country from the list of least-developed countries status by 2020".[2] The aim of this national vision is to gradually improve the living standards of the Lao people to the level that is seen in many other countries in the region and in the world. In 2001, the GOL came up with the Industrialization and Modernization Strategy.[3] An important part of this strategy was the Land-linked Strategy, which aimed at transforming the country's landlocked obstacle into an opportunity by building the country as a regional land transit in the GMS. For this purpose, a few Long-term Development Master Plans, the Mid-term Socio-economic Development Plans (five-year plan) and Annual Socio-economic Development Plans were drafted.

[2] Lao People's Revolutionary Party (LPRP) (1996).
[3] Government of Lao PDR (GOL) (2001).

To ensure that the country is able to materialise the benefits of integrating into the ASEAN Economic Community (AEC), the 2030 Vision and the 2025 Strategy were introduced in 2016.[4] With the Vision and Strategy, the GOL aims to revitalise the 2020 Vision and ensure continuous development beyond 2020. The main goal of the 2030 Vision is to ensure that Lao PDR elevates its status to an upper-middle-income country by 2030, avoiding the middle-income trap and reaching higher income level in the next few decades. The 2025 Strategy is a 10-year socio-economic development plan for moving out from the least-developed country (LDC) status, smoothly transitioning in the post-LDC and stepping up to the upper-middle-income country by 2030.

In Lao PDR, the Five-Year National Socio-Economic Development Plan (NSEDP) has been the main development tool to implement the long-term strategy and to achieve national visions. Currently, the country is implementing its 8th NSEDP (2016–2020). The 8th NSEDP is the first half of the 2025 Strategy, which plays the most important role to materialise the 2020 and 2030 Visions. In order to achieve the overall goals of national agenda towards 2030, the 8th NSEDP aims for economic growth of not less than 7% per annum on average between 2016 and 2020 in a sustainable manner.[5] To achieve the target, the Plan set the required investment capital of not less than US$22 billion between 2016 and 2020. It is expected that the government budget will be able to finance approximately 10% of the total investment, with the rest of the funds coming from the private sector (55%), official assistance (15%) and bank loan (20%).[6]

The GOL understands that these development goals are ambitious given their current economic base and significant shortage of capital. The Lao leaders believe that China's BRI could be leveraged to assist their country in achieving all those short-term and long-term objectives.

[4] Government of Lao PDR (GOL) (2016).

[5] Ministry of Planning and Investment (MPI) (2016).

[6] *ibid.*

2.2. *The BRI and Lao PDR's Infrastructure and Industrial Plans*

The Lao elites understand very well that infrastructure development is important for the country's development, including poverty eradication, livelihood stabilisation, private sector development as well as equality issues. The GOL has taken steps to improve its infrastructure connectivity with the neighbouring countries. Immediately after the country joined the Greater Mekong Subregion economic cooperation (GMS) in 1992, the First Lao–Thai Friendship Bridge connecting Vientiane with Thailand, which has been Lao PDR's major trading country, was introduced. Under the Australian soft-loan programme, the bridge was completed and open to traffic in 1994. As the first friendship bridge brought the socio-economic benefit of facilitating international trade and foreign direct investment, the GOL decided to build a few more bridges over the Mekong River to connect the country to Thailand and Myanmar. The first Lao–Myanmar Bridge to connect Louang Namtha province of Lao PDR with Thacilek of Myanmar was completed and open to traffic in 2015. This project was touted as a milestone cooperation between the two countries.[7] In early 2015, the GOL discussed the possibility of constructing a Lao–Cambodian Friendship Bridge with the Cambodian government and both sides agreed to launch it soon.

The bridge construction projects along Mekong River are not only for connecting with neighbouring countries. In fact, several domestic Mekong bridges have been designed and constructed for improving connectivity within the country. Pakse Bridge, for instance, was the first Mekong bridge connecting two regions in the southern part of the country. Another Mekong bridge is in the Xayaboury province in the northern part and it is currently under construction to improve connectivity of the northern provinces especially the Xayaboury and Louang Prabnag provinces. Currently nine Mekong bridges are already in place including both the international and domestic ones. Out of the nine, six of them are open to traffic; one is under construction, one is under feasibility study and one is in the initial agreement stage.

[7] Myanmar, Laos open first friendship bridge (2015).

Since the northern part is the least-developed region in the country, the GOL has made it a priority to develop this region to eradicate poverty.[8] This region is largely mountainous with poor infrastructure development and undeveloped agricultural base. In 2005, the GOL formulated a strategic master plan for the nine northern provinces to enhance and accelerate the development process in the region. The most important policy introduced in the plan was the industrial layout that connects the region with border cities of neighbouring countries including China, Thailand and Vietnam. For this purpose, the 1334 Model (comprising one economic centre, three economic corridors, three focal industrial zones and four large border economic cooperation zones) was introduced in the northern region.

In order to implement the 1334 Model, a comprehensive highway infrastructure design has been introduced. This includes three vertical routes, five horizontal routes and eight connecting routes. Furthermore, railway transportation has also been mapped out as one vertical route and three horizontal routes. Besides the surface mode of transportation, airports and flight routes have also been planned (both domestic and overseas). Other infrastructure projects, including hydropower and connecting power grids, telecommunications, among others, have also been designed.

The Lao policy-makers recognise that these infrastructure projects and the northern region's development plans would need significant Chinese participation. The BRI fits very well with Lao PDR's infrastructure and regional development plans.

2.3. *Development of Special Economic Zones (SEZ)*

In Lao PDR, the concept of special economic zone (SEZ) emerged in the late 1990s when the country sought to attract more foreign direct investment. To provide incentives to foreign investors, these SEZs were gradually developed, with the provision of tax incentives as well as other necessary policy incentives for foreign investors. At present, 11 SEZs have been approved and some of them are already

[8] Ministry of Planning and Investment (MPI) (2008).

in operation, such as the Savan–Seno SEZ and the Golden Triangle SEZ. The 11 SEZs are spread out from the northern to the southern parts of the country. More SEZs are currently under feasibility study.

The 11 SEZ projects cover more than 13,760 hectares of land and have attracted an accumulated total investment of more than US$4.2 billion.[9] These SEZ projects cover various sectors of the country, such as agriculture, trade, logistic, tourism and finance. The projects aim to strengthen the business and economic environment of the country as well as bring in employment opportunities to local people and contribute to the socio-economic development of the country. As most FDIs in the SEZs are export-oriented, improvement of connectivity (not only within Lao PDR but also between Lao PDR and its neighbouring countries) is necessary for the success and growth of these SEZs. Again, the Lao people acknowledge that China can play a very important role in the development of these SEZs as many low-end manufacturing facilities in China need to relocate to countries that offer cheap labour.

2.4. *Some Obstacles and Risks*

Although Lao PDR eagerly expects China to play a positive role in the country's development, Lao–China smooth cooperation under the BRI may face several challenges.

First, the maritime segment or the 21st century MSR may seem irrelevant to Lao PDR, a landlocked country. However, Lao PDR is strongly interested in gaining access to seaports and making sure that maritime transport is not interrupted because of territorial and maritime disputes in the South China Sea. Although Lao PDR maintains good relations with other countries, the tensions arising from the disputes in the South China Sea inevitably becomes a problem because Lao PDR is a member of ASEAN. As Lao PDR has very close relations with other ASEAN countries, it has to abide by the consensus principle in ASEAN-related matters. Although Lao PDR has no

---

[9] Investment Promotion Department, Vientiane Capital, Laos PDR (n.d.).

claim in the South China Sea, it is constantly under pressure to support other members who are claimant parties. Lao PDR's partial support to other ASEAN member states may not be well understood and accepted by China.

Second, China may face competition from other powers' economic activities in Lao PDR. Although most investors come from neighbouring countries such as Thailand, China and Vietnam, the investment from Japan, Korea, the United States and European countries has also increased dramatically in the past decades. Major powers' competition for market and influence in Lao PDR is obvious. For example, aside from the GMS cooperation initiated by Japan, the Lower Mekong Initiative (LMI) proposed by the United States emerged in 2009. The LMI involves countries in the Lower Mekong Region: Cambodia, Lao PDR, Myanmar, Thailand and Vietnam but excluding China. Under the LMI, the United States is the key actor from outside the region, but through this initiative, the United States has gained direct involvement in this region. As China and the United States have been entangled in conflicts in the South China Sea and other issues, competition between China's BRI and similar initiatives may arise and even intensify.

Third, the general perception of Chinese investment projects may influence BRI cooperation between Lao PDR and China. The inflow of FDI is important for the socio-economic development of the country. It creates jobs and ensures stable income for the local Lao people. However, some Chinese investment projects have been criticised for damaging the environment, health and livelihood of the local people. For example, China was involved in the project to improve Mekong River navigation. Although the removal of rocks along Mekong River would improve the navigation of larger commercial vessels on the river and enhance trade among Mekong River Basin countries, the project has encountered protests from many grassroots civil society organisations due to the negative impact of rock removal on the ecological system of the Mekong River. Should the negative views of Chinese investments continue to exist and even intensify, BRI cooperation between Lao PDR and China will be hampered.

3. Malaysia: Supporting and Participating in the BRI with Concerns

Malaysia is one of the strategic partners that China may be able to work with under the BRI. Situated in the centre of Southeast Asia and well-positioned in the Straits of Malacca, Malaysia is right next to one of the busiest trade routes in the world. With relatively well-functioning socio-economic and political systems and close ties with China, Malaysia has an outstanding advantage in the implementation of the BRI as compared to most of the Southeast Asian countries.

3.1. *Malaysia's Response to the Maritime Silk Road (MSR)*

Malaysia was one of the active BRI supporters in the region during the Najib administration, as evidenced by positive official statements, scholarly papers, news articles and public opinion polls. In the early years, Malaysia was somewhat sceptical of China's BRI as it did not know China's exact intention and the details of the BRI. But through active engagement over time, Malaysia has become more positive. Overall, the Malaysian government officials (from the former prime minister, ministers, political party leaders, Sultans and local Members of Parliament) have all expressed support for China's MSR. For instance, former Prime Minister Najib Razak welcomed the BRI, saying that there are "clear synergies" between the BRI and Malaysia's national transformation plan. UMNO information chief Tan Sri Annuar Musa said that Malaysia is the first to participate in the BRI due to the enormous potential for global economy and trade.[10] Among the senior officials, former Transport Minister Datuk Seri Liow Tiong Lai was one of the strongest supporters of China's MSR. He said that Malaysia is willing to support and cooperate in the construction of the MSR initiated by China because Malaysia believes that the New MSR and the Trans-Asian Railway will be instrumental in expanding the economy in Asia.

Similarly, Y.Bhg. Tan Sri Kong Cho Ha, Chairman of Port Klang Authority and the former Prime Minister's Special Envoy for the

[10] Najib creates history in diplomatic ties with China–Annuar (2016).

MSR, considered the MSR as a huge opportunity for Malaysia's port sector in particular.[11] In an open letter, Tan Sri Annuar Musa, former Member of Parliament praised Najib for making the bold and unprecedented effort to integrate several states on the east coast with China's newly launched BRI and MSR. He expressed that these coastal states will be the greatest beneficiaries of China's unstoppable economic boom.[12] In December 2016, the Malaysian Chinese Association (MCA) set up the Belt and Road Centre to help the country's small and medium-sized enterprises (SMEs) to participate in the China-proposed BRI. In the past few years, various MSR conferences and forums were organised by different Malaysian organisations and institutes.

Majority of the Malaysian media reports on the BRI are positive. The Chinese business community, along with the Chinese and English media, is supportive of China's BRI. Although few in Malaysia fully understand China's BRI, the majority of the population thinks positively of China and Chinese investment in Malaysia. Nonetheless, it should be noted that the opinion on China is divided across ethnic groups: Malaysian Chinese generally favour China, Malaysian Malays tend to be wary of China and Malaysian Indians tend to be averse to China.[13]

3.2. *The MSR and Malaysia*

Like the Lao PDR, Malaysia's positive attitude towards the BRI stems from the compatibility between its development plan and the BRI. Malaysia has an ambitious plan to raise its per capita income above US$15,000 to become a high-income country by 2020.[14] To achieve this goal, the Malaysian government launched the 11th Malaysia Plan (2016–2020) to raise the living standards of the bottom 40% of the population by reducing the income and infrastructural gaps between

[11] Welcome Message (2015).

[12] Heartfelt gratitude from the east coast.

[13] Interviews with researchers at Malaysian Institute of Maritime Affairs, April 2017.

[14] Malaysia hopes to become a high-income country by 2020.

Table 1. Major projects in the 11th Malaysian Plan

	Name of project	RM million
1	Malaysia Youth City	100
2	Water projects — Rural areas	>10,000
3	Electrical supply projects — Rural areas	>3,000
4	Affordable houses	
5	Flood mitigation	
6	Pan-Borneo Expressway	27,000
7	Central Spine Road (Kuala Krai–Simpang Pelangai Pahang)	8,000
8	Kota Bharu–Kuala Krai Expressway	
9	West Coast Highway	5,000
10	Double Tracking Gemas–Johor Bahru	
11	KVMRT 2 (Sg. Buloh–Serdang–Putrajaya)	25,000
12	LRT	39,000
13	High Speed Rail (HSR) (Bandar Malaysia, KL to Jurong East, Singapore)	650,000[a]
14	Five power plants (7,626 MW)	28,000
15	Langat 2 Water Treatment Plant	
16	Petroleum Integrated Complex, Pengerang	53,000
17	Regassification Terminal 2 — Pengerang	
18	Airports Mukah & Lawas, Sarawak	
19	Airport expansion — Kota Bahru	
20	Kuantan Port refurbishment	
21	Padang Besar Terminal upgrading	

Note: [a]Kuala Lumpur–Singapore high-speed rail tender to be called 'within a year' (2016).

Source: Bank Islam 2015.[15]

richer and poorer states. Table 1 summarises the major projects in the 11th Malaysian Plan.

The MSR had a good start in Malaysia. Malaysia and China commenced numerous joint MSR projects that cover a wide range of sectors. Since 2009, China has been Malaysia's biggest trading partner

[15] Economic Planning Unit, Prime Minister's Department (n.d.).

while Malaysia has been China's top trading partner in ASEAN. The two countries have plans to raise bilateral trade to US$160 billion in the coming years. In 2015, China's investment in the Malaysian manufacturing sector reached US$500 million, making China the second largest investor in the Malaysian manufacturing sector.[16] With more than US$2.1 billion Chinese investment in Malaysian real estate in the three years before 2017, China has become Malaysia's largest property investor.[17]

China is Malaysia's key partner in infrastructure construction. Among the flagship projects that China is participating, a few have taken off well. One example is Bandar Malaysia, an integrated underground city jointly developed by China Railway Group Limited (CREC) and Iskandar Waterfront Holdings. Another example is Melaka Gateway, a mega development project of PowerChina International Group and KAJ Development. So far, projects valued over US$30 billion have been awarded to the Chinese companies. Examples include the US$2 billion Southern Railway project and US$15 billion East Coast Railway project. China was also hopeful of receiving the contract for the Kuala Lumpur–Singapore HSR, a project whose destiny now seems uncertain.

Two industrial parks are expanding as well. The Malaysia–China Kuantan Industrial Park in Pahang, jointly owned by Chinese and Malaysian private and public sector entities, has a fund of RM 5.6 billion for building a steel mill and for upgrading port infrastructure. Guangdong province is teaming up with the Melaka government to promote tourism and manufacturing opportunities. Private Chinese firms have also shown interest in participating in the Melaka Gateway project.

People-to-people exchange is flourishing as well. A total of 2.2 million Chinese tourists visited Malaysia in 2016, as compared to 1.6 million in 2015.[18] Over 3 million Chinese tourists are expected to

---

[16] China emerged as Malaysia's second largest investor in the manufacturing sector (2016).

[17] China overtakes Singapore as Malaysia's largest property investor (2017).

[18] Malaysia's Jan–June 2016 tourist arrivals grow 3.7% (2016).

visit Malaysia in 2017.[19] In 2015, Xiamen University launched China's first overseas university in the Sepang district of Selangor, Malaysia. Its current enrolment of 2,300 students is expected to expand to 5,000 by 2020 and eventually reach 10,000.[20]

New areas of cooperation are also being explored. China's major banks including China Construction Bank, Bank of China, and Industrial and Commercial Bank of China have established branches in Malaysia. In 2015, the RMB clearing centre was established in Malaysia.[21] In 2017, the Chinese e-commerce giant Alibaba Group Holding Limited announced its plan to set up a regional distribution hub in Malaysia to cater to its fast-growing business in the region.[22]

3.3. *Problems and Challenges of the MSR in Malaysia*

In general, many people in Malaysia still do not fully understand the MSR.[23] Dato Baharin, a senior official from Malaysia's Ministry of Transport, the most supportive Malaysian ministry towards China's MSR, admitted that government officials, himself included, do not know much about China's BRI. Malaysian researchers are no better off. For instance, according to a senior researcher from the Maritime Institute of Malaysia (MIMA), which plays the leading role in studying China's BRI and introducing it to other ministries and departments, "While Malaysia is supportive of China's Belt and Road Initiative, the country primarily supports the land-based Silk Road Economic Belt and not so much the 21st Century Maritime Silk Road." Chinese investment on land, in her opinion, is not a problem, but the marine-based investment could be quite problematic. Clearly, she perceives the Silk Road Economic Belt as China's land investment and MSR as marine investment. Her perception certainly does not

---

[19] Malaysia China tourism up 72pct after Korea row: Maybank (2017).

[20] Wang (2017).

[21] Bank of China (Malaysia) appointed clearing bank for RMB business in Malaysia (2015).

[22] Lee (2017).

[23] Lockman (2017).

match China's BRI concept.[24] This is in part due to changes in the acronyms from the commonly known OBOR to BRI. Some researchers in Malaysia indicated that the terms (either OBOR or BRI) are problematic because they bring back the old memories of China dominating the region and China's ambition of re-establishing the old tributary system.

Some researchers were also concerned about the long-term impact of the MSR on Malaysia. They view the MSR as China's strategy for exporting its overcapacity to other countries and doubt Malaysia's capacity to absorb the overcapacity. The Malaysian business community and foreign investors are eager to know more about the BRI, but information is not easily available.

Public attitude towards China could also hinder the development of MSR in Malaysia. Already, the government has been criticised for being too close to China and for selling Malaysia to China. More engagement and public awareness campaigns are needed to address this problem. Although the Malaysian government has already taken steps to counter the negative publicity on China, MSR development can be limited by the fluid nature of domestic politics. A politician's stance on a certain issue can change very fast and it all depends on whether this politician personally benefits from the issue. During the Najib administration, the opposition parties opposed the MSR because they had not benefited much from it. And sometimes, they simply played the China card to attack the ruling party. The new Malaysian Prime Minister Mahathir Mohamad has decided to suspend a few major Chinese investments, including the East Coast Rail project, arguing that Malaysia needed to curb and reduce its rising foreign debts. Mahathir's decision has posed a significant challenge for

---

[24] The BRI aims to connect Asia, Europe and Africa via five routes. The Silk Road Economic Belt focuses on three routes: (1) link between China and Europe through Central Asia and Russia; (2) link between China and the Middle East through Central Asia and (3) link between China and Southeast Asia, South Asia and the Indian Ocean. The 21st century MSR focuses on using Chinese coastal ports along two routes: (1) link between China and Europe through the South China Sea and Indian Ocean and (2) link between China and the South Pacific Ocean through the South China Sea.

Malaysia–China relations. The issue of financial burdens that the China-backed infrastructure projects may have led to appears to be a genuine concern for Malaysia. It raises the whole question of what impacts China's MSR megaprojects will have on the host country's long-term economic development.

Of all the potential challenges to China's MSR in Malaysia, the South China Sea issue is the most significant one. The Malaysian government, particularly the National Security Council, is concerned about the potential impact of the MSR on the outcome of the South China Sea dispute. Malaysia is concerned about the illegal, unreported and unregulated (IUU) fishing issue (referring to the large Chinese fishing fleet accompanied by Chinese coast guards in the waters off the coasts of Sarawak and Sabah). Local fishermen's discontent will eventually put pressure on the local and federal governments to act against China. For some Malaysian researchers, the fundamental issue lies in unresolved competing claims. Some have even urged China to follow the arbitral tribunal's ruling on the South China Sea issue brought by the Philippines.

As for port projects, the Ministry of Transport is very supportive of the Port Alliance initiative proposed by China whereas some government officials, scholars and security analysts have raised alarm. Owing to the strategic importance of the Straits of Malacca to Malaysia, some who fear that China will eventually use the ports for military purposes stress that it would not be wise to accept Chinese port-related investments. Others fear that the Melaka Gateway project could become a competitor to Port Klang. Many researchers doubt that there will be enough cargo to meet the handling capacities of the new ports.

China's approach to the local Chinese community and the influx of Chinese laborers is also a major concern. To many, it is quite natural for Malaysian Chinese or Malaysian Indians to play a major role in attracting investment and business opportunities. The local Chinese community in Malaysia certainly plays a positive role in attracting Chinese investors. But there are several problems and risks associated with China's current approach to engage the local Chinese business community. First, the local SMEs are not so enthusiastic, and are sometimes even against Chinese investments because business opportunities are only granted to the elites, big local Malaysian Chinese companies and large interest groups. Many ethnic Chinese claim that the MCA cannot represent the Chinese community in Malaysia and some even believe that the MCA is just the puppet of the former ruling party. There are also conflicts of interest among local Chinese business groups and even among the big companies in Malaysia. For example, some key local developers are unhappy with the China Railway Engineering Corp (CREC)'s involvement in the investment of Bandar Malaysia. Chinese investment in infrastructure is often believed to harm the local construction industry because few Chinese projects are subcontracted to local companies.

Second, Chinese investments are also vulnerable to the outcome of domestic ethnic conflicts in Malaysia.[25] As the Malays believe that the ethnic Chinese are dominating the economy and large businesses, the Malaysian government has long been implementing affirmative action policies that favour Malays. Such affirmative action further entrenches the ethnic divide, which is in the interest of the United Malays National Organisation (UMNO).[26] The growing presence of Chinese in Malaysia and the ever closer economic and political ties between China and the local Chinese community would inevitably deepen suspicion and resentment between the Malaysian Malays (and other non-Chinese ethnic groups) and the local Malaysian Chinese. Anti-Chinese sentiment could be utilised by the politicians.

Third, the influx of Chinese labourers remains a pressing issue. It deprives the local people of job opportunities and aggravates social-cultural conflicts. Social media reports and rumours are rife that Chinese investment mainly benefits Chinese workers. There were even stories that some Chinese restaurants would only admit Chinese. As a result, the influx of Chinese workers (and even tourists) has become a controversial issue. Large-scale government-to-government projects are not a problem due to official labour rules and regulations which protect the rights of local workers; however, private business deals do

---

[25] Economic Malays: A guide to Malaysia's politics and economics in graphics (2015).
[26] Su (2017).

not come under such control. As a result, private investment from China, sometimes at the invitation by local Chinese communities, has limited employment and economic benefits for the local economy.

Finally, compared to other ASEAN countries, particularly Indonesia and the Philippines, land acquisition for infrastructure projects is much easier in Malaysia. The law of land acquisition is mainly related to compulsory procedures for land acquisition and compensation to the dispossessed landowner. Property is acquired by the state against the will of the landowner, but this is done in the public interest.[27] In most cases, federal government has the power to address land acquisition issues because land is controlled by the state. But in some states, particularly Johor, the Sultan is the most powerful person with strong influence on local affairs, including land issues. Nevertheless, problems of corruption and transparency continue to afflict foreign investors.

4. Vietnam: Supportive with Limited Action

4.1. *Vietnam's Perception and Response to the BRI*

Compared to other Southeast Asian countries, Vietnam has a better understanding of China's policy papers on the BRI and hence the political purposes for the BRI. This is because Vietnam has invested substantial efforts in studying China.[28] In the past few years, the Vietnamese leaders have occasionally expressed support for the BRI. Apparently, the Vietnamese government has responded to the BRI more positively and actively after the United States decided to leave the Trans-Pacific Partnership (TPP). However, domestic economic problems in the past few years have driven Vietnam to change its attitude towards the BRI lest it becomes marginalised for not participating in the BRI. Serious security concerns also limited Vietnam's support for the BRI.

In fact, the South China Sea disputes and activities of Chinese businesses have tarnished China's image in Vietnam. Vietnamese interlocutors admitted that the South China Sea disputes have limited

[27] Alias and Daud (2015).

[28] Interviews with scholars at Vietnam Academy of Social Sciences, April 2017.

the scope for China–Vietnam cooperation under the BRI. Chinese investment in the Vietnamese port sector and infrastructure in general has also been greatly hindered.

Apart from the South China Sea disputes, Vietnam's concerns and reservations about the BRI are also due to some other factors. First, to many Vietnamese officials and scholars, the BRI and MSR are not new. In the past, many investment memorandums of understanding (MoUs) were signed by the two countries, though not under the framework of the BRI. However, very little progress has been made after these MoUs were signed. Second, in Indochina, the Asian Development Bank (ADB) led the regional integration effort for many years and has made notable progress in enhancing regional connectivity and cooperation. In comparison to its attitudes towards the ADB, Vietnam is wary of the impact of China's BRI on regional integration. Third, Vietnam is concerned about the risks of being heavily indebted to China. If Vietnam continues to seek loans from China, its economy will be more vulnerable to China's possible economic sanctions and its maritime claims will be harder to defend in the future.[29]

4.2. *Opportunities and Areas for MSR Implementation in Vietnam*

Vietnam's socio-economic development programme (2011–2020) lays out a vision for environmentally sustainable and socially equitable economic development with the goal of transitioning Vietnam to upper-middle-income status. It has entered its second phase (2016–2020) which focuses on the following: (1) supporting private sector development, industrial restructuring and service sector development; (2) developing SEZs and regions; (3) integrating urban infrastructure, including improving urban planning and linking major urban centres; (4) enhancing education and human resource quality, with a focus on innovation and technology development; (5) mitigating and preventing the adverse impact of climate change and environmental degradation and (6) increasing public sector efficiency and reducing

[29] Interviews with scholars at Vietnam Diplomatic Academy, April 2017.

corruption. With this development plan, Vietnam is motivated to strengthen cooperation with China in the following areas: solar energy technology, agriculture, environmental protection, education, poverty reduction, infrastructure and border trade. Meanwhile, Vietnam welcomes investments to boost its export trade.

In the past decade or so, Vietnam has increased its investment in infrastructure despite fiscal difficulties. The Vietnamese government plans to invest US$130 billion by 2020 to improve infrastructure, with an average annual investment of nearly US$10.2 billion. The breakdown is as follows: US$1.99 billion for road construction, US$2.13 billion for railway building, US$300 million for maritime transport expansion, US$190 million for civil aviation upgrading, US$2.15 billion for urban transport development of Hanoi and Ho Chi Minh City and US$570 million for rural transport construction. With the rapid growth of investment in industrial and civil construction sectors, the future of Vietnam infrastructure market will present plenty of opportunities for Chinese investors.

Between 2016 and 2021, the Vietnamese government plans to build 4,145 bridges. Among them, three major bridges (namely, the 3.26-kilometre Chau Doc Bridge, the 0.86-kilometre Dai Nghia Bridge No 1 and the 2.24-kilometre Dai Nghia Bridge No 2) will be completed by 2018. In the meantime, the Vietnamese government will undertake some small road and bridge projects worth US$408.9 million. Vietnamese senior official Nguyen Van Huyen pointed out that the country will build 2,200 small bridges in 50 remote mountainous areas. The government needs a loan of US$385 million from the World Bank to finance these projects, which are potential areas for the two countries to cooperate under the BRI.

In addition to infrastructure, a serious lack of energy transportation and distribution systems has stalled the economic development of Vietnam. Some remote areas still do not have access to electricity. Vietnam is overly dependent on hydroelectric power, and because hydropower is dependent on climate conditions, especially precipitation, Vietnam is facing severe power shortage. At the same time, coal-power generation is gradually replacing hydropower as the main source of Vietnamese electricity. In response to the growing demand for electricity, Vietnam is building more coal-fired thermal power plants and importing electricity from China. Vietnam's electricity supply will grow at an annual rate of 14% from 2015 to 2030. Vietnam plans to build a competitive electricity market by 2030 to restructure its power industry.[30]

Vietnam encourages Chinese companies with advanced technology and expertise to invest in Vietnam. Chinese enterprises, especially advanced manufacturing enterprises, can transfer new technology and create employment opportunities for Vietnam. For instance, Everbright International invested in Vietnam's first high-standard waste-to-energy project. The project has become the flagship project for Vietnam's waste disposal sector. It fully utilises China's capital, equipment and standards for investment development and construction management. This represents a new breakthrough in environmental protection for Vietnam.

Vietnamese business community and social organisations are actively promoting clean energy sectors. For instance, Vietnamese NGO Towards Transparency (TT) is working with foreign companies to share state-of-the-art international standards. At the same time, the Governance and Integrity Working Group (GIWG) of the Vietnam Business Forum (VBF), together with other foreign governments such as the United Kingdom and other international organisations, concentrates on promoting business ethics and good business practices in the clean energy sector. In general, some of the potential areas for cooperation include logistics and transportation; "two corridors and one economic circle"; SEZs; renewable energy; infrastructure; agricultural development; human resources and education; border socio-economic cooperation and law enforcement; bilateral trade; marine products and tourism.

4.3. *Possible Hindrances and Risks*

There are many challenges in Sino–Vietnamese cooperation under the BRI. First, the lack of political trust is perhaps the most significant

[30] Vietnam's Ministry of Electric Power reduces purchase of electricity from China (2016).

obstacle. Owing to maritime territorial disputes in the South China Sea and historical animosities, the degree of MSR cooperation between two countries in the maritime area is low. At present, there are more opportunities for two countries to cooperate on land.

Second, the Vietnamese public perception of China is extremely negative. The territorial and maritime disputes in the South China Sea, historical conflicts and negative impressions of Chinese investments due to previous experience suggest that nationalism in Vietnam is unlikely to drop significantly soon and will continue to undermine bilateral economic cooperation. The Haiyang Shiyou 981 oil rig incident triggered a series of protests and even attacks on Chinese companies and Chinese workers in Vietnam, resulting in property damage and several casualties. Subsequently, Vietnam's anti-China sentiment led to the suspension of several cooperation projects between the two countries. For example, the Van Don–Mong Cai project, a 96-kilometre highway that connects Van Don district and Mong Cai City of Quang Ninh province, was suspended because of strong public opposition against loans from China.

Finally, although the Vietnamese business and legal environments have improved, there are still many problems in the Vietnamese judicial system due to the absence of sound laws and regulations, and the lack of transparency. The conflicts of interest and contradictions in policies between local governments and central government are common. Corruption penetrates all levels of Vietnam. Some scholars pointed out that even though the Vietnam society has negative views towards China, and Vietnam is trying hard to reduce its dependence on the Chinese economy, many large projects have been quietly granted to Chinese enterprises.

Owing to changes in regional geopolitics and overall economic trends, Vietnam has actively strengthened its relations with other major powers including the United States, Japan, Australia, India and European countries. Since the late 2000s, especially amid the rising tension in the South China Sea, Vietnam has reinforced maritime cooperation with Japan. Japan provided ships to Vietnam to strengthen the latter's maritime law enforcement capabilities. In addition to maritime security cooperation, Vietnam's infrastructure development received a boost from Japan's infrastructure loan of more than ¥21 billion (approximately US$190 million). Funding in the form of official development assistance (ODA) was channelled to the upgrading of Ho Chi Minh City's sewage system. Japan also provided a total of about ¥890 million (approximately US$8.14 million) for training Vietnamese officials. According to the Vietnamese government data, Japan is second largest source of investment in Vietnam, only after South Korea. As of April 2016, Japan's investment in Vietnam amounted to about US$39 billion. For decades, the Japan-dominated ADB has led the investment and development in the Indochina Peninsula (Vietnam included). Through the GMS framework, the ADB has developed cross-border logistics infrastructure, facilitated regional trade and improved health and education.[31] Obviously, China will have to face a lot of competition from other major players, especially Japan, when it comes to developing infrastructure and industrial projects in Vietnam.

5. Conclusion

China appears to be quite serious about the implementation of the BRI, particularly in Southeast Asia. The region is naturally important for the BRI because of the geographic proximity with China. China's focus is on improving connectivity between Yunnan and Guangxi with Southeast Asian regional states in order to ensure steady economic growth in the region, maintain access to abundant resources in many regional states and further its geopolitical ambitions in the region.

Almost all Southeast Asian countries' official positions on the BRI have been positive because of the potential economic benefits of cooperating with China under the BRI. Regional countries understand that the BRI could facilitate their own short-term and long-term economic development plans. From this perspective, we can confidently conclude that the BRI will proceed in Southeast Asia in the coming years and even decades. There will be many more China-led major infrastructure projects in regional states and further improvement of connectivity within the region and between the region and China.

---

[31] Asian Development Bank (ADB) (2016).

However, we should recognise that different regional states have different interests and concerns regarding the BRI. Some countries, such as Cambodia, Lao PDR, Thailand and Singapore, are very enthusiastic about the initiative. A few countries (such as Malaysia, Indonesia and the Philippines) are supportive of the BRI but have reservations due to constraints arising from domestic politics, the South China Sea dispute and geopolitical concerns on the expansion of Chinese influence. The other two ASEAN countries, Vietnam and Myanmar, are officially supportive of the BRI but are limited by many significant challenges arising from cooperation with China in new major projects on infrastructure or regional connectivity. Anti-China sentiment in both countries towards China significantly impedes China's expanding role in these countries' mega socio-economic development plans. Both countries are concerned about the increase of debts to China as a result of accepting Chinese loans.

Throughout the region, many socio-political elites believe that China has been too assertive and even aggressive in handling the South China Sea dispute. This perception has affected many regional countries' attitudes towards the BRI and towards China's economic progress in general. The diverse interests and slightly diverse views in the region explain why ASEAN as a grouping has not provided clear and strong support towards the BRI. It is likely that the BRI will only be implemented at the bilateral level between China and each regional state in the foreseeable future.

References

Alias, A. and Daud, M.D. (2015). Payment of adequate compensation for land acquisition in Malaysia. *Pacific Rim Property Research Journal* 12(3), 326–349. doi: 12. 10.1080/14445921.2006.11104213.

Asian Development Bank (ADB) (2016). Vietnam, 2016–2020. Fostering more inclusive and environmentally sustainable growth. *Country Partnership Strategy*. Available at: https://www.adb.org/sites/default/files/institutional-document/199661/cps-vie-2016-2020.pdf.

Bank of China (Malaysia) appointed clearing bank for RMB business in Malaysia (2015). *Borneo Post Online*, 6 January. Available at: http://

www.theborneopost.com/2015/01/06/bank-of-china-malaysia-appointed-clearing-bank-for-rmb-business-in-malaysia/.

China emerged as Malaysia's second largest investor in the manufacturing sector (2016). *The Star Online*, 1 November. Available at: http://www.thestar.com.my/business/business-news/2016/11/01/china-emerges-as-second-largest-investor-in-manufacturing-sector/#lQG0Fhkrt6zH6mPE.99.

China overtakes Singapore as Malaysia's largest property investor (2017). *CCTV News (English)*, 29 March. Available at: http://english.cctv.com/2017/03/29/ARTI7T1DODNv61ZfZuv8NioV170329.shtml.

Economic Malays: A guide to Malaysia's politics and economics in graphics (2015). *The Economist*, 25 September. Available at: http://www.economist.com/blogs/graphicdetail/2015/09/malaysia-graphics.

Economic Planning Unit, Prime Minister's Department. (n.d.). Eleventh Malaysia Plan (2016–2020). Available at: http://www.epu.gov.my/en/rmk/eleventh-malaysia-plan-2016-2020.

Government of Lao PDR (GOL) (2001). Industrialization and modernization strategy toward 2020 (CPI: Vientiane) (in Lao).

Government of Lao PDR (GOL) (2016). 2030 vision and 2025 strategy. MPI (in Lao).

Investment Promotion Department, Vientiane Capital, Laos DPR (n.d.). Special Economic Zones (SEZ). Available at: http://www.investlaos.gov.la/index.php/where-to-invest/special-economic-zone?limitstart=0.

Japan External Trade Organization (JETRO) (2015). Proposal for improving business environment in Lao PDR. Available at: http://businessdocbox.com/Logistics/69527190-Proposal-for-improving-the-business-environment-in-lao-pdr-based-on-a-jetro-survey-on-business-needs.html.

Kuala Lumpur–Singapore high-speed rail tender to be called 'within a year' (2016). *The Straits Times*, 18 July. Available at: http://www.straitstimes.com/asia/kl-spore-high-speed-rail-tender-to-be-called-within-a-year.

Lao People's Revolutionary Party (LPRP) (1996). The resolution of the sixth congress of LPRP.

Lee, L. (2017). Jack Ma to launch Alibaba's regional distribution hub in Malaysia: Sources. *Reuters*, 18 March. Available at: http://www.reuters.com/article/us-malaysia-alibaba-idUSKBN16P041.

Lockman, S. (2017). The 21st century Maritime Silk Road and China–Malaysia relations. Guangdong Institute for International Strategies, 11 March. Available at: http://giis.gdufs.edu.cn/info/1356/7413.htm.

Malaysia China tourism up 72pct after Korea row: Maybank. *GGRAsia*, 11 April. Available at: http://www.ggrasia.com/malaysia-china-tourism-up-72pct-after-korea-row-maybank/.

Malaysia's Jan–June 2016 tourist arrivals grow 3.7% (2016). *Tourism Malaysia*, 9 September. Available at: http://www.tourism.gov.my/media/view/malaysia-s-jan-june-2016-tourist-arrivals-grow-3-7.

Ministry of Planning and Investment (MPI) (2008). Development master plan for 9 northern provinces.

Ministry of Planning and Investment (MPI) (2016). The eighth SNEDP 2016–2020.

Myanmar, Laos open first friendship bridge (2015). *Xinhuanet*, 9 May. Available at: http://news.xinhuanet.com/english/2015-05/09/c_134224520.htm.

Najib creates history in diplomatic ties with China–Annuar (2016). *New Straits Times*, 5 November. Available at: http://www.nst.com.my/news/2016/11/186065/najib-creates-history-diplomatic-ties-china-annuar.

Su, J. (2017). Najib's 1MDB scandal: Understanding Malaysia's ethnic divide. *Fox and Hedgehog*, 3 March. Available at: http://www.foxhedgehog.com/2017/03/najibs-1mdb-scandal-understanding-malaysias-ethnic-divide/.

Vietnam's Ministry of Electric Power reduces purchase of electricity from China (2016). *China International Contractors Association*, 6 September. Available at: http://obor.chinca.org/scdt/57076.jhtml?country=536 (in Chinese).

Vietnam to construct more than 4,000 bridges by 2021 (2016). *Road Traffic Technology*, 3 January. Available at: https://www.roadtraffic-technology.com/uncategorised/newsvietnam-to-construct-more-than-4000-bridges-by-2021-4766583/

Wang, Z. (2017). Xiamen University opens branch campus in Malaysia to promote China's soft power to the world. *Chinese Internet News Center*, 7 July. Available at: http://news.china.com.cn/world/2017-07/07/content_41172790.htm (in Chinese).

Welcome Message (2015). Forum enhancing the 21st century Maritime Silk Road through Malaysia, 14–16 December 2015, Dorsett Grand, Subang. *Port Klang Authority, Malaysia*. Available at: http://pkapp.pka.gov.my/silk_road/index.php.

Chapter

8

The Impact of Chinese Maritime Policy on Malaysia: A Long-term Geopolitical Scenario

Hans-Dieter Evers, Abdul Rahman Embong and Rashila Ramli

1. Maritime Policy: OBOR/BRI and the Maritime Silk Road (MSR)

The geopolitics of Asia is changing fast. While after World War II, the "Asia Pacific region" captured the attention of political analysts, the land and maritime silk road connection from East Asia to South Asia, Europe and the Middle East gained in importance and gave rise to the geopolitical concept of a continent "Eurasia" (Evers and Kaiser 2001).

The term "silk road" was coined by the German geographer Ferdinand Freiherr von Richthofen (1833–1905) (see Figure 1), who after travelling around China for five years (Wu 2014: 339) started his academic career as a professor of geology at the University of Bonn, where he produced a massive five-volume work on China and

Figure 1. Ferdinand Freiherr von Richthofen

outlined his idea of the *Seidenstraße* in a widely read journal article (von Richthofen 1877).

This article concludes that after the 7th century, when silk production became known in Europe, the silk roads stopped functioning. "Der Begriff transcontinentaler Seidenstrassen hat für die fernere Zeit seine Bedeutung verloren" (The concept of transcontinental silk roads has lost its significance for the distant future.). This "distant future", which Ferdinand Freiherr von Richthofen talked about in his lecture in 1877, has arrived now.

In a departure from earlier policies of maintaining a coastal line of defence, militarily and economically, along China's long coast, the Chinese-claimed territory now extended across the South China Sea within the so-called nine-dotted line. The sea, however, is protected by the United Nations Convention of the Law of the Sea (UNCLOS), which grants free passage to all shipping and air traffic beyond a narrow 12 miles' strip from the coast. Free passage is guaranteed even within the 200 miles of the Exclusive Economic Zone (EEZ) that grants exclusive rights to a coastal state for the exploitation of maritime resources. To extend its territory, the Chinese government has turned rocks in the South China Sea into small islands, apparently treating them as extended territory, within an imaginary roughly drawn red-dotted line on official maps.

Extending its territorial boundaries into the South China Sea is one move, but proclaiming a new maritime policy is another. China has embarked on a large-scale development programme under the name "Maritime Silk Road" or "One Belt, One Road (OBOR)", where the "road" is the MSR. Massive investments are planned and construction has started on several megaprojects: deep water harbour construction, land traffic infrastructure projects like roads and railroads, and large-scale urban development projects.

In greater detail, this policy can be described as follows: In 2013, Chinese premier Xi Jinping announced a pair of new development and trade initiatives for China and the surrounding region: the "Silk Road Economic Belt" and the "Twenty-first-century Maritime Silk Road," together known as "One Belt, One Road"(OBOR). "Along with the Asian Infrastructure Investment Bank (AIIB), the OBOR policies represent an ambitious spatial expansion of Chinese state capitalism, driven by an excess of industrial production capacity, as well as by emerging financial capital interests" (China–British Business Council 2017: 1).

From a Chinese perspective "the official ideology behind OBOR ... is peaceful development — to sponsor infrastructure investments and facilitate economic development, promoting cooperation and minimising conflict. There is no doubt that peaceful development is more sensible and sustainable than American-style militarised 'security'; poverty and injustice are hotbeds for extremism" (Wong *et al.* 2017).

Economists by and large welcome the plans for massive investments in maritime and land transport, but also caution the possible increase of differences of economic development between maritime countries and the rest of ASEAN (Jetin 2017). As the China–British Business Council observes in their recent report (China–British Business Council 2017: 11), the land route along the Northern Silk Road is days shorter than the sea route and cheaper than the air route. Several "corridors" will link specific Chinese regions with countries throughout Asia. A massive "Silk Road Fund" will finance infrastructure projects, like deep water harbour construction, satellite towns and fast railroads. Financial and business circles are by and large enthusiastic about the OBOR project and expect high profits for banks and the construction industry.

The MSR (the Belt in OBOR) runs all the way from major Chinese port cities through the South China Sea and the Straits of Malacca to the Arabian Peninsula, Eastern Africa and through the Suez Canal to the Mediterranean and the North Sea. In Hamburg, Rotterdam and London, the northern and the southern silk roads will meet again.

Along the MSR, several major projects stand out. Deep water harbours are constructed in Kuantan and Melaka and are under construction in Sri Lanka, Yemen and Greece in the Mediterranean. In addition to these harbours that will be mostly owned and/or operated by Chinese companies there will be other infrastructure developments, like the new fast railroad line from Malaysia's East to the West Coast, enabling Chinese goods to bypass Singapore and parts of the Straits of Malacca.

The OBOR initiative is seen differently by other regional powers. Russia has been indifferent so far, but business interests and business friendly governments in the European Union have seen merits in the OBOR initiatives. Eventually transaction costs in trade between Europe and China (and the rest of Asia) would be reduced and trade facilitated. In Malaysia, "Prime Minister Datuk Seri Najib Razak, at a press conference at the end of the two-day Belt and Road Forum for International Cooperation here, described developments following Malaysia's support for OBOR and its close ties with China as 'very exciting', not just for businessmen but also the people through the creation of more jobs" (New Straits Times 2017).

The United States has reacted first cautiously under Barack Obama and now more aggressively under Donald Trump's "America First" policy, which seeks to reduce the trade imbalance between China and the United States. No clear position on OBOR has so far emerged from the White House. Whether peaceful development is maintained in the long run will have to be seen. So far China is not (yet) a strong naval power, but expanding its naval presence in the South China Sea. Building military bases on artificial islands can no longer be seen as "coastal defence". The increasing dominance of the Chinese economy throughout ASEAN and beyond is, however, clearly visible. A cartoonist has forcefully depicted the situation.

Most harbour projects will be combined with the creation of massive satellite towns in Johore and Malacca, like Iskandar Malaysia in Johor and Melaka Gateway including a newly constructed port. In Malacca, there will be four artificial islands of reclaimed land, devoted to (1) tourism, entertainment and property development island, (2) free trade economic zone island, (3) Melaka Gateway port island and (4) maritime industrial park.

In Kuala Lumpur, at one end of the proposed Singapore–KL fast railway line, the construction of Bandar Malaysia, a multibillion-dollar city is already in the planning stage. The China Railway Engineering Corporation (CREC) will invest US$2 billion in the 1MDB project and own a majority (60%) of the shares. The properties will be mostly owned and managed by Chinese property companies, though low-cost housing for Malaysians will also be included. In 2017, deals to let buyers of two flats in Shenzhen have one flat for free in Malaysia were said to be advertised in China already. The satellite cities are likely to create Chinese-occupied special diasporas, catering to Chinese needs and following a distinct modern Chinese conception of space (Evers 2015). As of today, Chinese nationals are already the largest group under the Malaysia My Second Home (MM2H) scheme, which entails privileges for buyers of residential property. Many flats in residential condominiums in Penang or Selangor have been bought by Chinese nationals, but remain unoccupied. This trend is likely to continue with property development under the OBOR umbrella.

Another part of the infrastructure development plan concerns the building of a network of fast railway lines, connecting China with Central Asia, Southeast Asia, India and eventually Europe. Deutsche Bahn, the German government-owned railway company, already runs a cargo service from China to Duisburg, Rotterdam and London, but still on the old and slow lines that have been in existence for a long time. As soon as this line is modernised, China will have completed another part of the Northern Silk Road under its OBOR scheme.

In Malaysia, two contracts for fast rail connections have already been signed and the construction was to begin in 2017. One fast line connects Singapore with Kuala Lumpur, the other line is a fast line connecting new deep-water ports in Kuantan and Malacca. Transhipment across this line will allow Chinese shippers to avoid passing Singapore with its US naval base as well as the narrow eastern part of the Straits of Malacca.

Construction of ports and railroads is largely financed by loans of Chinese banks. These loans will eventually have to be repaid by the Malaysian government. Majority ownership of the new ports and railway lines will stay with Chinese (mainly state-owned) companies. As reported in the *Straits Times* daily newspaper, in December 2016 in Beijing, "Mr Najib's government signed an agreement to award the construction of the East Coast Railway Line (ECRL) to state owned China Communication and Construction Company, in a deal to be financed by a soft loan from the Export-Import Bank of China. Kuantan port is owned by IJM (a Malaysian construction company) and Beibu Gulf Port Group (a Chinese company). The nearby industrial zones are earmarked specially for Chinese manufacturing companies" (Straits Times 2016).

The deal struck with China is obviously seen positively by the Prime Minister's office, but criticised harshly by independent observers. As Wan Saiful, a journalist with the business weekly *The Edge* pointed out, "the deal is very good for China. It came with the understanding that the Malaysian government will contract out the job to another Chinese state-owned enterprise, the China Communication Construction Company (CCCC). There are conditions that they must subcontract to local firms but they remain as the tier one contractor.

"This means we borrowed money from China in order to pay a Chinese company to do the job, and, after seven years, we still need to pay back the loan plus interest, again, to China. Not only does China get back their money immediately in the form of payment for work done by CCCC, they will get more money from us when we repay the loan. We shoulder all the risk while China gets guaranteed profit" (Jan 2017). Prime Minister Mahathir, who replaced Najib after a resounding election victory in 2018, has also been critical of unfavourable conditions for the financing of the railway lines and port developments and promised to renegotiate the agreements.

There will probably be short-term profits for Malaysian companies. Malaysian employment will rise, even if foreign workers will be imported to complete the project. The railway line will not only get local freight from the East to the West coast, but will also profit from container through traffic on the way from East Asia to the West, thus impacting Singapore's position, a problem noted in Singapore, especially as Singapore was not invited to attend the OBOR meeting in May 2017. Adopting a view along the *longue durée* of history, a different picture may emerge. There will be long-term predictable and unpredictable outcomes for Malaysia as a maritime nation, for Malaysia's political system and Malaysia's multi-ethnic population.

2. Port Cities and Maritime Connectivity

The maritime economy is divided into four major sectors: food production (fishing), transport (shipping), industrial production (ship yards and related industries, harbour construction, sea lane maintenance, etc.) and maritime services (like stevedoring, ship supplies, shipping agencies, insurance companies, maritime research and other services). Most of these economic activities by one way or another enhance "connectivity" by connecting harbours, countries and regions. Moreover, enhanced connectivity is essential for ASEAN's way towards a true community (Zen and Anandhika 2016). ASEAN has therefore announced a Master Plan of ASEAN Connectivity that also includes (but does not emphasise) maritime connectivity. An ASEAN single shipping market is planned, along with the integration of land and maritime transport.

The Malaysian long-term development plan is also concerned with the maritime sector and focuses on the development of selected ports and port facilities. Both plans, the ASEAN and the national Malaysian plan are not integrated. The maritime sector is lagging behind land-based planning in the agricultural, urban and land-transport sectors. This is surprising, as especially container shipping is growing worldwide. Malaysian and Singapore ports have become the central hubs in the ASEAN region, with an ever-increasing throughput of containers mainly filled with manufactured goods. Malaysia in particular has outgrown most other ASEAN countries and has matched Singapore's growth rates. Singapore and Malaysia dominate the ASEAN container shipping market (see Figure 2).

Ports and port cities are, indeed, nodal points in maritime networks of differing rates of connectivity. The success of a maritime policy can therefore be assessed not only by measuring the contribution of the maritime sector to GNP, but also by the increase of connectivity. The concept "connectivity" requires some further explanation and definition. In general terms, "connectivity" refers to the number and strength of connections between points of a surface. In an earlier publication, we used an indicator on scientific cooperation to show changing connectivity between universities in the ASEAN region (Evers 2016a: 22, Evers and Gerke 2012).

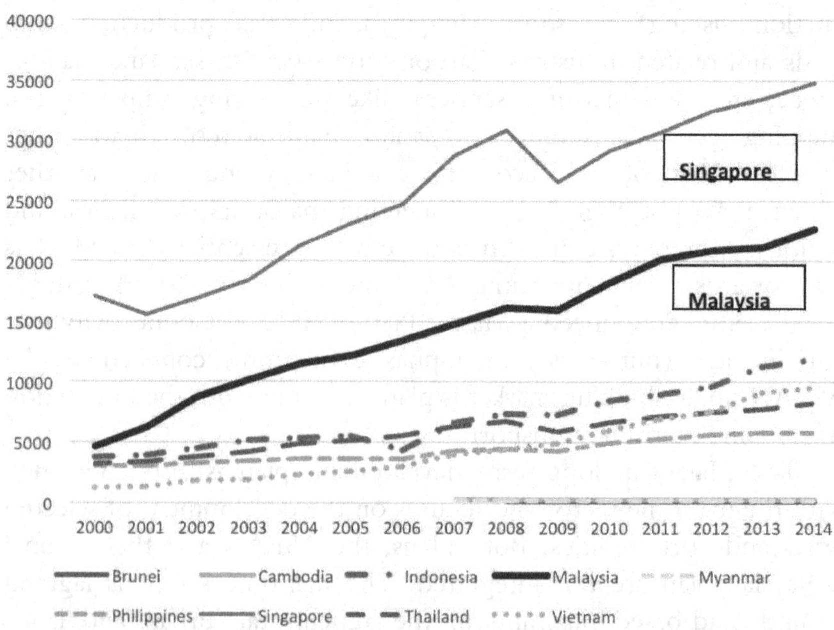

Figure 2. Container shipping, ASEAN 2000–2014, 1000 t TEU

Source: ASEAN.

In this paper, "Maritime Connectivity" refers to the number of ports connected by shipping services. The strength of the maritime connectivity is measured by the amount of cargo (in tons or TEU) transported between ports or alternatively by the number of sailings between ports, measured by the number of ships or the combined DWT of ships.

What is the position of each of the Malaysia's official ports within the network of ports in ASEAN and how do these positions change over time? In other words, which Malaysian ports improve their relevance to Malaysia as a maritime nation or which are surpassed by their competitors like Singapore or Surabaya?

Port cities have a long history in the Nusantara. Before and after the advent of European traders and their companies, three well-documented "Malay" port cities stand out: Malacca, Aceh and Banten (Guillot 2005). They were nodal points in a widespread commercial trading network with a high degree of "connectivity".

"Formerly, as far as we know, old trading cities were actually made up of two distinct towns built along the same river; such was clearly the case with Pasai, Banten, and Malacca, where royal compounds and harbour settlements were located several kilometres apart, each town sometimes bearing a different name. This physical split reflected a peculiar perception of society: the harbour population on the shore was turned towards the sea and the sea activities, whereas the king faced landward, indicating that he wanted to be considered as the necessary intermediary between inland and coastal populations. A neat boundary specified the different roles. The king had political power over the land and its populations. The harbour population, of foreign extraction, had the right to settle in the kingdom and to trade in exchange for taxes paid to the king. But as guests of the country, they had no say in political matters" (Guillot 2005: 44).

Modern Malaysia has many ports along its long coastline. Most are recognised as official ports, administered by a port authority or port management company. These ports differ greatly in their capacity of cargo handling and their function within the shipping networks (Jan 2017, Jeevana *et al.* 2015).

Only two ports, Tanjung Pelepas in Johore and Port Klang in Selangor qualify as the major nodal points of international sea traffic. Both serve as harbours for major transhipment throughout the Straits of Malacca and South China Sea areas.

Port cities also have inherited specific social characteristics from their historic past (Guillot 2005). The distinction between government offices, mainly staffed by Malay civil servants and a multitude of workers of different ethnic origin populate the port cities. As the result of their historic role and as points of entry for migrants (now largely replaced by airports) they have a greater ethnic diversity than surrounding areas. Their diasporas interact commercially and privately with other countries, thus enhancing the connectivity of port cities. An interesting side-aspect is also the fact that ports tend to have a higher rate of biodiversity than surrounding areas. Biologists talk about the "invasion of foreign species" through shipping, a term that should better not be applied to human immigration!

A high degree of diversity accounts for the high productivity of port cities and coastal areas. Not all, but most "silicon valleys" or high-tech hubs are found in coastal areas. Trying to create a Cyberjaya (Evers and Nordin 2012) far away from the coast has proven to be more difficult than locating high-tech industries and research labs in Butterworth, Penang island or Singapore. We are not advocating a geographical determinism, but rather the "value of diversity" for productivity and innovation.

The changing connectivity of Malaysian ports among themselves and ASEAN and the rest of the world will be an essential aspect of Malaysia's move towards a truly maritime nation. A glimpse of the current situation is shown in Figure 3 (screen shot from the density of shipping in the ASEAN region as of April 2017).

This density map shows the dominance of maritime connectivity of shipping across the South China Sea from and to China and through the Straits of Malacca. Another dense connectivity is seen on a N–S axis from the Gulf of Thailand along the Eastern coast of Peninsular Malaysia towards Indonesia's Java Sea (see Figure 4). A relative low density of shipping is visible between Peninsular and East Malaysia and the Philippines. Overall, the maritime connectivity

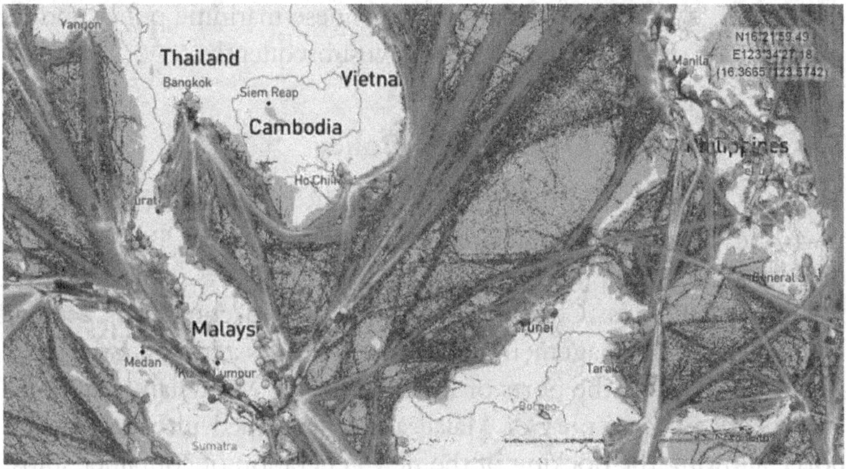

Figure 3. Density of shipping, Maritime ASEAN, May 2017
Source: Screenshot, emissions from shipping, April 2017.

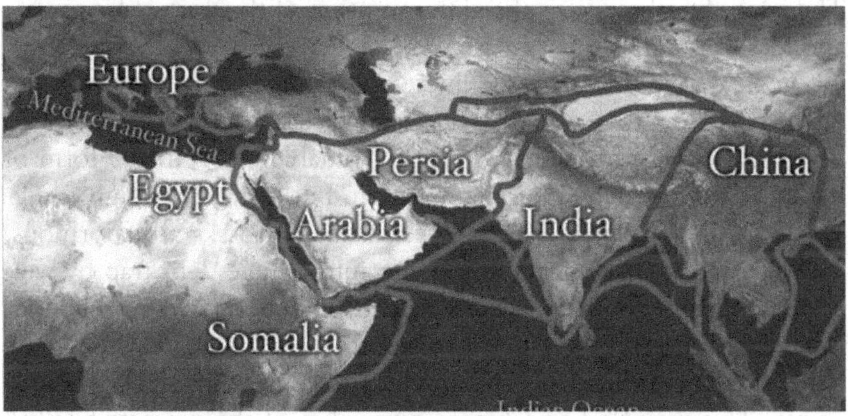

Figure 4. The Northern and Southern MSR

between ASEAN countries is not yet intense. This points to the necessity for a stronger ASEAN maritime policy. Indonesia with its Maritime Fulcrum and China with its OBOR policies are set to consolidate and strengthen their maritime connectivity.

More detailed research will be necessary to follow trends and open opportunities for a closer maritime cooperation and integration of ASEAN. A closer look at the new Chinese maritime policy and its possible impact on Malaysia will follow subsequently.

3. Outline of the OBOR/BRI Policy

The OBOR initiative of the Southern MSR can be described as follows: the Chinese government through its Investment Bank and the Silk Road Fund supports the construction of ports, port facilities, roads and railroads. Chinese government-linked companies acquire equities in port management companies, railways and estate development. In Malaysia, the ports of Kuantan on the Malaysian East Coast and the West coast port of Malacca are developed into deep-water ports, allowing the docking of the new generation of container ships. The two ports are connected through a fast-track railway line that would allow the trans-shipment of containers, thus avoiding the narrow Singapore Straits and the shallow part of the Straits of Malacca. The geopolitical aspect is the circumvention of the port of Singapore and its US American naval base.

Port development by Chinese government-linked companies from Sri Lanka to Gwadar in Pakistan to some gulf state ports to Piraeus in Greece provides a string of valuable pearls in the form of harbours from which adjoining areas can be serviced through feeder vessels or railway lines. The long-term financial risks are enormous. "It is no secret that Sri Lanka has run into a huge debt trap by welcoming Chinese funded projects. Sri Lankan debt exceeds $60 billion, more than 10 percent of that is owed to the Chinese. To resolve its debt crisis, the Sri Lankan government agreed to convert its debt into equity. This may lead to Chinese ownership of the projects finally." Malaysia may head into the same direction.

Another important aspect of the OBOR policy is the development of large property estates like Malaysia Gateway in Kuala Lumpur, which creates partly extraterritorial zones.

Chinese Ambassador Liu noted how the OBOR initiative is being misinterpreted by some as confirming Mackinder's (1904) heartland theory — that China is seeking to control the "pivot area" of Eurasia for geopolitical domination. Instead, he stressed the shared benefits of "development and prosperity" from China's ongoing foreign policy engagements, arguing that "the Chinese mind is never programmed around geopolitical or geoeconomic theory" (Liu 2015: 9, cited in Sidaway and Woon 2017: 3). This assertion has been met with some scepticism, as the geostrategic aim of the Chinese government is quite visible in its combined efforts to secure access to the European, Middle Eastern and African markets both in terms of importing energy supplies (oil and ore) and exporting manufactured goods. Going back to the age-old silk roads, the new OBOR strategy entices the vision of a mutually beneficial two-way trade and, in Western eyes, a romantic and mysterious East. Combining an emotional vision and romance of the East with the hard exigencies of access to markets is, indeed, a masterpiece of cultural policy, serving the national interest of China.

4. Backcasting into Malaysia's History

The MSR will be managed and economically, possibly also militarily, secured by a string of Chinese-controlled properties and harbour facilities. This policy brings up reminiscences of British imperial policies from the 18th century onwards. British commercial and later colonial bases were developed in Gibraltar, Malta, Suez, Colombo, Malacca, Singapore and Hong Kong. These strongholds securing and controlling the sea route from Britain to China follow the same geographical pattern as the new Chinese OBOR policy, only from East to West instead. Buying land from local rulers, heavy investment in harbours and roads and railroads secured commercial interests.

After the demise of the British East India Company, the British government eventually annexed the territories adjacent to the port cities and extended the British Empire (see Figure 5). While it created an improved infrastructure, and spured an economic boom from which also local business profited, it also impoverished the local peasantry and exploited local and immigrant labour. Local wars were fought and the new British colonies were militarily secured.

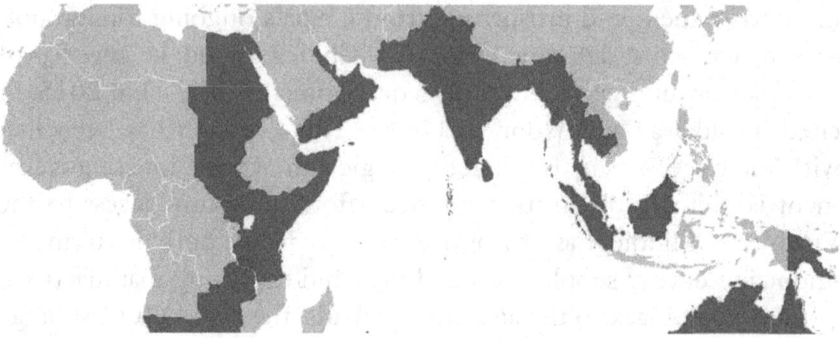

Figure 5. The British Empire around 1917

The Chinese government insists that their intentions are peaceful and directed at one aim only: economic prosperity for all countries along the Northern MSR. In a keynote speech in March 2015, "China's Foreign Minister Wang Yi said that OBOR is not a tool of geopolitics (地缘政治的工具)" (Godement and Kratz 2015: 6, cited in Sidaway and Woon 2017: 3), a statement regarded with some scepticism by political scientists. History will show what is going to be implemented and whether historical precedents will not be repeated.

This has been an experiment in backcasting, looking into the past, analysing the present and, somewhat vaguely, forecasting the future by looking back at the *longue durée* of history (Braudel 1993). There is reliable information on the past 100 years of world history, backed by thousands of carefully researched scholarly studies. The present history detail is visible as, even while evolving, it is made transparent by the flow of "big data" of our information society. Still forecasting is much trickier. Will history repeat itself? Do past developments predict the future or is "past performance no indication of future developments" (as declared on flyers of cautious stock brokers and banks)?

The Chinese-initiated OBOR (see Figure 6) may turn out to bring economic benefits, as promised by the initiators of this grand scheme. But the dangers are obvious if we engage in backcasting

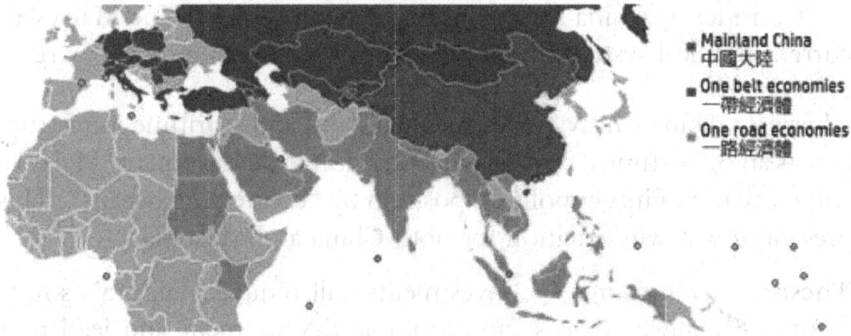

Figure 6. OBOR economies 2017 — Chinese map

(Miller 2017). The British Empire has brought advantages and prosperity, it has made some people very rich, it has elevated cooperating feudal elites to new heights, if not necessarily politically, but socially through added respectability. British rule and administration created Weberian-type bureaucracy, a reasonably well-off middle class of teachers and professionals, introduced English as a *lingua franca* (partly replacing Malay in Southeast Asia and beyond), provided education and healthcare, but also inflicted colonial violence, loss of political power and independence and led a large part of the population to poverty and suffering. Will OBOR have similar effects on states participating in the various economic programmes propagated by the Chinese government and supported by the financial sector of practically all countries along the Silk Roads? Even if one tends to accept in good faith the benign intentions of the current Chinese communist government, will the *longue durée* of history produce unintended consequences, like loss of sovereignty, loss of culture, loss of political and/or economic independence? To return to an earlier theme: will OBOR entail the demise of Nusantara culture, of diversity of languages and ways of life? The colonial system is not likely to recreate itself, and cultural assimilation and loss of ethnic identity are only remote possibilities, given the strength and flexibility of the Nusantara civilisation.

Considering China's maritime development strategy and Malaysia's current political system, the following *two contrasting theses* emerge:

Thesis 1: China's heavy investments in land and maritime infrastructure is an opportunity for Malaysia's economic development. Malaysia will make use of its geopolitical position by "connecting oceans". This presents a win-win situation for both China and Malaysia.

Thesis 2: China's massive investments will reduce Malaysia's sovereignty, strangle its own socio-economic development and lead to a "sinicisation" of Malay Nusantara culture. Malaysia's once powerful geopolitical position of "connecting oceans" will be reduced to just a link in China's production chain.

The *longue durée* of history is, as the term implies, a very long process. None of us, reading these lines will live long enough to see the outcome, but will probably experience some turbulences on the way for sure. The world order is changing, climate change will certainly have an impact, but the human mind appears to be the most unpredictable factor in human history. Cautiously weighing facts, carefully employing concepts and theories and showing alternative ways to achieve positive outcomes (by following Kant's moral imperative) appears to be the only viable "way forward" for the social scientist.

5. Outlook: Who Is Going to Benefit in the Long Run?

Looking at the long range (Braudel's *longue durée*) of history, the door is open for speculation. Are Peking and Tokyo equivalent to Rome and Carthage? Is Singapore the Venice of the South China Sea? Is Penang the Malta rather than the Pearl of the East? Will the US empire, controlling the Pacific Ocean, also try to govern the Mediterranean South China Sea, or will China take over this role? Has the tide now turned and is expansion now coming from the East, from China, which is investing heavily, as the East India Company and the British Colonial Office before, in infrastructures like ports and railroads? And what will happen, after the infrastructure projects have been completed? Will history repeat itself and will the domination over ports and port cities eventually be followed by colonising the hinterland as well? "Will China as the new global power behave the way western imperialist powers behaved in the 19th and 20th centuries, or will China behave differently?" (Embong 2018) These are speculations indeed. Much more detailed research would be necessary to answer these queries, before a comparative picture would emerge or political strategies could be formulated.

All Mediterranean seas experienced periods of intensive trade relations, exchange of knowledge, economic prosperity and the flowering of science, religion and innovation. A common Mediterranean culture emerged around the Mediterranean Sea, centred at times on Athens, Alexandria, Rome and much later Venice. The same cultural integration took place around the Java Sea and later the Straits of Malacca, known in Arab sources as the "Sea of Melayu" (Andaya 2000). This "Austronesian" and later "Nusantara culture" extended to the shores of the South China Sea. It did not encompass all the areas surrounding the South China Sea, which only hesitatingly are developing into a Mediterranean civilisation. Extensive trade, naval expeditions, like those of Srivijaya or much later the Bruneian thalassocracy (de Vivienne 2012) in the 16th century, or the short-lived Japanese Greater Co-Prosperity Sphere, massive migration and economic modernisation and ASEAN integration increasingly unified the Southeast Asian mediterranean seas, including the South China Sea to become a culturally mediterranean region and civilisation. What will be the impact of the Chinese OBOR initiative? Will Malaysia become part of yet another greater co-prosperity sphere (co-prosperity, an aspect of OBOR emphasised by Xi Jinping)? One of the ASEAN countries that has forged not only close political and diplomatic relations, but also economic relations with China is "Malaysia, a country which in the last several years seems to have been in the forefront in terms of aligning itself closer with China and obtaining massive investments and loans from the latter, especially since the launching of the New Maritime Silk Road" (Embong 2018).

The South China Sea and the Straits of Malacca have been important shipping lanes for the past 2,000 years. Its rich fish resources have provided livelihood for the surrounding countries for centuries. But the discovery of oil and gas reserves in the South China Sea "is producing a new geography of conflict in which resource flows rather than political divisions constitute the major fault lines" (Yee 2011). The positions of the governments of surrounding states have hardened, negotiations have largely failed and a solution is not in sight. Why has it not been possible to come to agreements between contending states as has been the case in the Baltic or Mediterranean seas? As we have argued in another paper (Evers 2014: 89, Evers 2016b), deep-seated cultural perceptions and core values ("arch-types") of Nusantara and Sinic civilisations may play a greater role than a short-term political science analysis is able to reveal.

Malaysia is a country that because of its geopolitical position is destined to "connect oceans" (Evers *et al.* 2018). Its political position in terms of relative power and of its economic position will depend on the strength of its connectivity across seas and oceans. The connections northwards may gain some importance with new railroad and road connections towards China, but the maritime connectivity appears to be more viable, now as in the past. Malaysia therefore needs a clear and forceful maritime policy to match those of Indonesia and China.

How could such a maritime policy look like? This question can only be answered by intensive comparative research on the maritime policies of other countries, especially Indonesia's "Maritime Fulcrum" and China's Southern Silk Road policies. Earlier studies have usually bemoaned the absence of a Malaysian maritime policy. "It can be seen that existing policies to develop comprehensive ocean governance have not received the full attention they deserve. Organizational structures governing the ocean for implementing national policies are well in place but in a fragmented and uncoordinated fashion. As a result, sectoral and intersectoral management problems were created such as multiple-use conflicts, overlapping of jurisdiction and duplication of efforts. Environmental problems have also not been properly addressed" (Saharuddin 2001: 427).

The development of a consistent Malaysian maritime policy is urgently required.

References

Andaya, L. (2000). A history of trade in the sea of Melayu. *Itinerario* 24, 87–110.

Aya, R. (1978). Norbert Elias and the civilizing process. *Theory and Society* 5(2), 219–228.

Braudel, F. (1966, 1993). *La Méditerranée et le Monde Méditerranéen a l'époque de Philippe II.* Paris: Poch. 2e e'd. Colin, Paris.

China–British Business Council (2017). Belt and Road Initiative. Available at: http://www.cbbc.org/resources/belt-and-road-initiative-southern-routes.

de Vivienne, M.-S. (2012). *Brunei de la Thalassocratie à la Rente.* CNRS Éditions, Paris.

Elias, N. (1978). *Über den Prozeß der Zivilisation. Soziogenetische und Psychogenetische Untersuchungen.* Suhrkamp, Aufl. Frankfurt am Main.

Embong, A.R. (2018). The charms of China's new silk road: Connecting the dots in Southeast Asia. In Evers, H.-D., Embong, A.R. and Ramli, R. (eds), *Connecting Oceans: Malaysia as a Nusantara Civilization.* UKM Press, Bangi.

Evers, H.-D. (2014). Understanding the South China Sea: An explorative cultural analysis. *International Journal of Asia Pacific Studies* 10(1), 80–95.

Evers, H.-D. (2015). Kampung air: Water settlements on the island of Borneo. *Journal Malaysian Branch of the Royal Asiatic Society* 88(1), 79–86.

Evers, H.-D. (2016a). Nusantara: Malaysia and the geopolitics of the South China Sea. The 11th Pok Rafeah Chair Public Lecture. Institute of Malaysian and International Studies, Penerbit Universiti Kebangsaan Malaysia, Bangi.

Evers, H.-D. (2016b). Nusantara: Malaysia and the governance of the South China sea. *Southeast Asian Social Science Review* 1(1), 7–23.

Evers, H.-D., Embong, A.R. and Ramli, R. (eds) (2018). *Connecting Oceans: Malaysia as a Nusantara Civilization*, UKM Press, Bangi.

Evers, H.-D. and Gerke, S. (2012). Globalisation of social science research on Southeast Asia. In Ibrahim, W.Z. (ed), *Knowledge and Social Science in a Globalising World*, Persatuan Sains Sosial Malaysia, Bangi, Selangor, pp. 103–116.

Evers, H.-D. and Kaiser, M. (2001). Two continents, one area: Eurasia. In Preston, P. and Gilson, J. (eds). *The European Union and East Asia: Interregional Linkages in a Changing Global System.* Edward Elgar Publishing House, Cheltenham, pp. 65–90.

Evers, H.-D. and Nordin, R. (2012). The symbolic universe of Cyberjaya, Malaysia. ZEF Working Paper Series 95.

Guillot, C. (2005). Urban patterns and polities in Malay trading cities, fifteenth through seventeenth centuries. *Indonesia* 80, 39–51.

Hall, K.R. (1985). *Maritime Trade and State Development in Early Southeast Asia*, University of Hawaii Press, Honolulu.

Jan, W.S.W. (2017). Ideas: Is China a good investor?. *The Edge Markets,* 4 April. Available at: https://www.theedgemarkets.com/article/ideas-china-good-investor.

Jeevana, J., Ghaderi, H., Bandara, Y.M., Saharuddin, A.H. and Othman, M.R. (2015). The implications of the growth of port throughput on the port capacity: The case of Malaysian major container seaports. *International Journal of e-Navigation and Maritime Economy* 3, 84–98.

Jetin, B. (2017). One Belt-One Road initiative and ASEAN connectivity: Synergy issues and potentialities. Working Paper No. 30. IAS – UBD, Gadong.

Kant, E. (1998). *Kritik der Reinen Vernunft.* Meiner Verlag, Hamburg (First Published 1781).

Miller, T. (2017). *China's Asian Dream: Empire Building along the New Silk Road.* ZED Books, London.

New Straits Times (2017). Najib: M'sia committed to help realise OBOR initiative, 15 May. Available at: https://www.nst.com.my/news/nation/2017/05/239540/najib-msia-committed-help-realise-obor-initiative.

Saharuddin, A.H. (2001). National ocean policy — New opportunities for Malaysian ocean development. *Marine Policy* 25(6), 427–443.

Sidaway, J.D. and Woon, C.Y. (2017). Chinese narratives on "One Belt, One Road". *The Professional Geographer* 69(4).

Straits Times (2016). Malaysia's East Coast Rail Line touted as a game changer, 22 December. Available at: https://www.straitstimes.com/asia/se-asia/malaysias-east-coast-rail-line-touted-as-a-game-changer.

von Richthofen, F. (1877). Über die Zentralasiatischen Seidenstrassen bis Zum 2. Jh. n. Chr. Verhandlnngen der Gesellschaft für Erdkunde zu Berlin, pp. 96–122.

Wong, E., Chi, L.K., Tsui, S. and Tiejun, W. (2017). One Belt, One Road: China's strategy for a new global financial order. *Monthly Review* 68(8), 36–45.

Wu, S. (2014). The search for coal in the Age of Empires: Ferdinand von Richthofen's odyssey in China, 1860–1920. *The American Historical Review* 119(2), 339–363.

Yee, A. (2011). Maritime territorial disputes in East Asia: A comparative analysis of the South China Sea and the East China Sea. *Journal of Current Chinese Affairs* 40(2), 165–193.

Zen, F. and Anandhika, M.R. (2016). ASEAN maritime connectivity: Overview and insights. Paper presented at the Conference on Logistics and Maritime Studies on One Belt One Road. The Hong Kong Polytechnic University, Hong Kong.

Chapter

9

China's Belt and Road Initiative and ASEAN's Maritime Clusters*

Hans-Dieter Evers and Thomas Menkhoff

1. Introduction

Since its announcement as One Belt One Road (OBOR) in 2013, China's Belt and Road Initiative (BRI) has attracted the attention of scholars and journalists, leading to the publication of thousands of scholarly papers, journal articles and books (Habib and Faulknor 2017, Hong 2015). This paper adds a new perspective on the China's BRI and the possible effects of the "Maritime Silk Road" (MSR) on Southeast Asia's maritime clusters. BRI encompasses the overland "Silk Road Economic Belt" (SREB) and the sea-based "21st century MSR". As illustrated in Figure 1, SREB's overland infrastructure network includes the "New Eurasian Land Bridge" (NELB) which consists of several rail corridors linking Yiwu in eastern China with

*This is a reprint of an article originally published in *Southeast Asian Social Science Review* (SEASSR), Vol. 3(2), July–December 2018. The editors gratefully acknowledge the permission of the SEASSR Chief Editor to reprint this article in this edition.

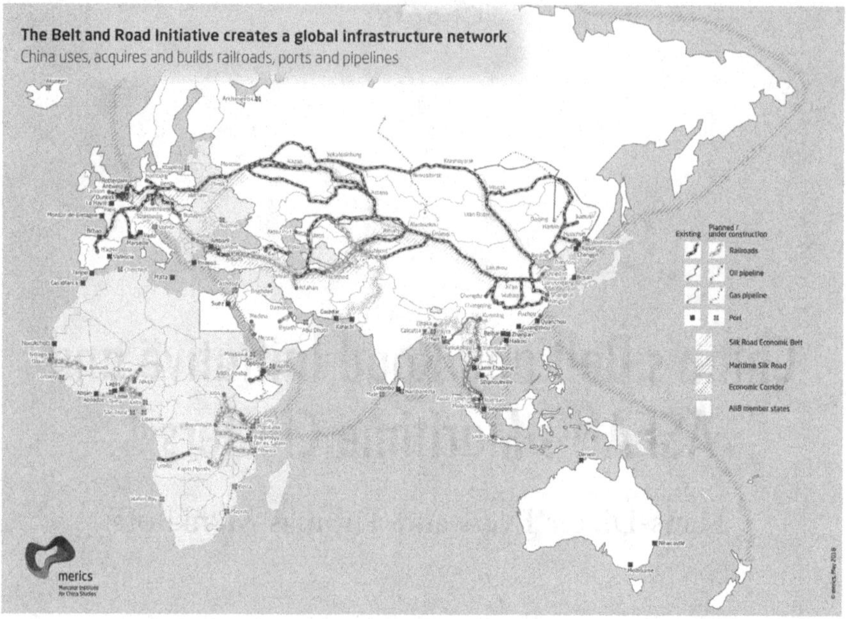

Figure 1. Reviving the Silk Road

Source: Reproduced with the kind permission from Mercator Institute for China Studies (MERICS), Berlin, Germany.

European destinations such as Duisburg (Germany), Madrid (Spain) or London (UK). SREB spans five economic corridors: China–Mongolia–Russia, China–Central Asia–West Asia, China–Pakistan, the China–Indochina peninsula and Bangladesh–China–India–Myanmar. The complimentary MSR envisages the development of key seaports along the traditional and new sea routes to Southeast Asia, Africa and the Mediterranean region with good connectivity to land-based transportation routes (Evers *et al.* 2018, Pardali 2015).

The geopolitics of Asia is changing fast. While after World War II the "Asia Pacific region" captured the attention of political analysts, the land and MSR connection from East Asia to South Asia, Europe and the Middle East gained importance and gave rise to the geopolitical concept of a continent "Eurasia" (Evers and Kaiser 2001).

The term "silk road" was "invented" by the German geographer Ferdinand Freiherr von Richthofen (1833–1905), who after travelling around China for five years started his academic career as a professor of geology at the University of Bonn, where he produced a massive five-volume work on China and outlined his idea of the *Seidenstraße* in a widely-read journal article (von Richthofen 1877). This article concludes that after the 7th century when the art of silk production became known in Europe, the silk roads stopped functioning. "Der Begriff transcontinentaler Seidenstrassen hat für die fernere Zeit seine Bedeutung verloren" (The concept of transcontinental silk roads has lost its significance for the distant future.). This "distant future", Ferdinand Freiherr von Richthofen talked about in his lecture in 1877 has arrived now though the silk road has not lost its significance, but is being revived to match its former glory.

In a departure from earlier policies of maintaining a coastal line of defence, militarily and economically, along China's long coast, the Chinese-claimed territory now extended across the South China Sea within the so-called nine-dotted line. The sea, however, is protected by the United Nations Convention of the Law of the Sea (UNCLOS), which grants free passage to all shipping and air traffic beyond a narrow 12 miles strip from the coast. Free passage is guaranteed even within the 200 miles of the Exclusive Economic Zone (EEZ) that grants exclusive rights to a coastal state for the exploitation of maritime resources. To extend its territory, the Chinese government has turned rocks in the South China Sea into small islands, apparently treating them as extended territory, within an imaginary roughly drawn red dotted line on official maps. Extending its territorial boundaries into the South China Sea is one move, but proclaiming a new maritime policy featuring a gigantic development programme under the name MSR or "One Belt One Road" (where the "road" is the MSR) is another (Embong *et al.* 2017 and many other publications).

We look at these policy initiatives (which were proposed by Chinese President Xi Jinping in 2013) as infrastructural cluster strategies aimed at combining harbours, forwarding, railways, energy pipelines, industrial estates and condominiums. From a developmental point of view, a key goal is to enhance economic interconnectivity and cooperation across Eurasia, East Africa and more than 60 partner countries. A similar emphasis on "connectivity" is found in the Masterplan on ASEAN Connectivity 2025 (ASEAN 2016, Jetin 2017).

In Southeast Asia, BRI is regarded as a new force for regional economic integration — filling a vacuum created by the abortion of the Trans-Pacific Partnership (TPP) by the US. To foster increased investment in countries along BRI, the Chinese government set up the Silk Road Fund (US$40 billion) in 2014 (http://www.silkroadfund.com.cn/enweb/23773/index.html). In 2016, China established the Asian Infrastructure Investment Bank (AIIB), "a multilateral development bank with a mission to improve social and economic outcomes in Asia and beyond" (https://www.aiib.org/en/about-aiib/index.html). Its headquarters is located in Beijing. AIIB has 80 approved members from various parts of the world: "By investing in sustainable infrastructure and other productive sectors today, we will better connect people, services and markets that over time will impact the lives of billions and build a better future" (https://www.aiib.org/en/about-aiib/index.html).

An important question is how BRI will impact Sino–Southeast Asian economic ties in general and maritime clusters in particular with special reference to Singapore, Malaysia and Indonesia. As Koh (2015) has argued, "modern Singapore is a major shipping nation and port state. It is only logical that Singapore should be an important hub in the 21st Century Maritime Silk Road". According to Singaporean media reports, China's investments in Singapore "amount to about one-third of its total investments in Belt and Road countries. Singapore's investments in China accounted for 85 per cent of total inbound investments from Belt and Road countries" (Shanmugam 2017).

While there have been a lot of discussions about China's BRI threatening Singapore's maritime hub position, Singapore's Home Affairs and Law Minister K. Shanmugam had this to say at a 2017 talk at the Lee Kuan Yew School of Public Policy:

> "There will be fierce competition, certainly. We must anticipate that our neighbours will, for example, want to build big ports to challenge our port. We must be nimble, quickly adapt — modernise, expand our own container port; have the foresight to make the necessary changes today for a better tomorrow. If we do so,

> we can secure our future, and ensure we remain a key port of call in South-east Asia. And don't be easily rattled. As a Straits Times article pointed out, it is not so easy to displace our port. Don't be spooked by social media disinformation campaigns that claim we are about to be surrounded and cut off. We achieved what we have by thinking bold, and thinking big. We didn't allow anyone to bully us, or subject ourselves to the demands of other countries. Many have tried. We resisted" (http://www.straitstimes.com/opinion/how-spore-can-gain-from-one-belt-one-road-initiative).

As speakers at a BRI seminar at Beijing Foreign Studies University have pointed out, Singapore is well positioned to partner China and the OBOR initiative due to its expertise in planning, finance, logistics or project development. According to Singapore Business Federation chief executive Ho Meng Kit, "some 60 per cent of ASEAN projects are already financed mainly by Singapore-based banks" (MFA 2017). According to an interview conducted in Mandarin with news agency *Xinhuanet*, Singapore's Prime Minister Lee Hsien Loong views OBOR positively (Today 2017).

After the Malaysian election of 2018, the new government and its prime minister Mahathir Mohamad have taken a step back from implementing the Malaysian part of the Chinese MSR. According to media reports in Malaysia, China has become the largest foreign investor in Malaysia. Several projects have been stalled, and there is some uncertainty whether some of the projects will actually be implemented or whether terms with Chinese government firms will be renegotiated. Key BRI partnership projects include the RM55 billion East Coast Railway Line (ECRL), the RM32.6 billion Melaka Gateway project, the RM2.5 billion Trans Sabah Gas Pipeline, the RM4 billion Wuxi Suntech Power Co Ltd manufacturing project in the Malaysia–China Kuantan Industrial Park and the RM1.3 billion Xiamen University Malaysia. "Bandar Malaysia, a 486-acre transport-cum-property development project in the old Sungai Besi airport, which is planned to house the proposed Kuala Lumpur-Singapore High-Speed Rail terminus and become a major transport hub with connections to the MRT lines, KTM Komuter, Express Rail Link and 12 other highways, was launched earlier, but it is also categorised as a BRI project. The proposed RM70 billion Kuala Lumpur-Singapore

High-Speed Rail project, which invited bidders in late 2017, is categorised as yet another BRI project" (https://aliran.com/aliran-csi/aliran-csi-2017/bri-spike-chinese-investments-malaysia-implications-malaysias-politics-sovereignty/).

Several other new port construction projects include the Carey Island port-cum-industrial city complex in the Port Klang area, an energy port in Bagan Datoh (with a pipeline from Bagan Datoh in the West Coast running to a new port terminal in Bachok in Kelantan on the East Coast) and an international port in Kuala Linggi. It is also planned to upgrade the ports in Penang and in Kuantan (https://aliran.com/aliran-csi/aliran-csi-2017/bri-spike-chinese-investments-malaysia-implications-malaysias-politics-sovereignty/). The connection across the Malay peninsula is an important part of the MSR and its implementation will certainly be treated with urgency by the Chinese government (Gerke, Evers and Hornidge 2008).

According to media reports, Indonesia (a member of the OBOR programme since 2013) has reaped US$5 billion to US$6 billion in infrastructure investment from BRI while Pakistan has received US$62 billion and Malaysia US$32 billion (http://www.thejakartapost.com/news/2017/05/12/indonesia-plays-it-cool-in-competition-for-chinas-obor-money.html). While the OBOR programme may be highly relevant for cities along the old trade route between China and Indonesia, such as Sabang in Aceh, Medan in North Sumatra, Batam in Riau Islands or Pontianak in West Kalimantan, little is known about the "priority areas" (to be) earmarked by the Indonesian Government. Strategic areas include maritime projects with regard to transportation, telecommunications, tourism, industrial estates, energy and power.

2. Clusters and Maritime Connectivity

Conceptually, the paper focuses on China's infrastructure investments in selected Southeast Asian countries such as ports and the implications for maritime clustering (Doloreux 2017). We, therefore, intend to concentrate on a neglected aspect of the BRI by focusing on cluster theory to explain an important aspect of Chinese maritime policy. To appreciate the importance of both maritime clustering and ports for economic development, it is important to first consider *cluster theory* propagated by Harvard Professor Michael Porter (Porter 1990, Porter 1998, Porter 2003). According to Porter, the competitive advantage of nations and regions depends on the formation of industrial clusters: "Clusters are geographic concentrations of interconnected companies, specialized suppliers and service providers, firms in related industries, and associated institutions (e.g. universities, standard agencies and trade associations) in particular fields that compete but also cooperate. Such clusters are a striking feature of virtually every economy, especially those of more economically advanced areas" (Porter 2000: 253). Not only that, the degree of clustering determines the competitiveness of a nation or region. Firms located in a cluster have an enhanced chance of profitability and are more competitive in contrast to firms located outside a cluster in splendid isolation. The main argument of earlier industrial location theory of Alfred Weber is resurrected, namely, that transaction costs are lower in clusters than outside (Weber 1909, Weber 1981).

A great number of studies have been conducted to examine the cluster theory. According to the disciplinary home of the authors, there are coloured results. Geographers have emphasised location and proximity (Maskell 2013), sociologists emphasised social networks and knowledge (Menkhoff *et al.* 2011, Purwaningrum 2014) and economists tend to look at economies of scale and transaction costs. At this stage, it is extremely difficult to bring together the results of these studies and to draw final conclusions. It has, however, become clear that cluster formation and cluster competitiveness is a good deal more complex and complicated than the advocates of Porterian cluster policies would have it. So far, it is not entirely clear whether clusters make firms more productive and thus more competitive, or more productive and competitive firms come together to form a cluster. This poses a dilemma for cluster policies or cluster governance. "Natural" clusters are possibly formed by highly competitive firms, but firms induced by government subsidies or active cluster management may not turn out to be more competitive at all despite being colocated in a cluster. Furthermore, the "connectivity" between cluster firms does not automatically follow from a geographical distance but has to be actively managed (Evers 2014, Evers *et al.* 2010, Menkhoff and Evers 2013).

But one finding of Porter-type cluster analysis still holds, namely that despite increased broadband penetration and Internet connectivity, clusters still emerge. The basic hypothesis that the higher the economic development of a country or region (in terms of the usual measurements), the higher the degree of industrial clustering appears to hold as well. The big gap in our understanding of both the clustering process and the outcome of clustering still lies in a precise analysis of the inner workings of a cluster. In short, we need to know more about what makes a cluster tick, before a robust cluster policy can be designed.

2.1. *What Are Maritime Clusters?*

"Maritime clusters" represent a special type of clusters or sectors. According to a study by European Community (EC 2009), maritime (sea-related) sectors (combining offshore and coastal activities) can be divided into three different clusters or areas as follows:

1. "Traditional" maritime sectors (shipping, shipbuilding, marine equipment, maritime services, recreational boating, seaports, offshore supply, Navy, inland navigation, maritime works and marine aggregates);
2. Coastal (and marine) tourism and recreation (coastal tourism and cruise tourism);
3. Fisheries (fishing, fish processing and aquaculture).

Cluster formation is often linked with economic prosperity, i.e. economic regions with strong industrial clusters in terms of employment size often feature a higher GDP per capita: "The main benefits of (maritime) clusters are the increase in efficiency, the increased level of business formations and, the higher level of research, development and innovation. These benefits can be optimised by cluster organisations through activities and initiatives, e.g. promotion campaigns, structural cooperation between cluster organisations and knowledge institutions, specific (government) support programmes and platforms to exchange best practices" (EC 2009: 19).

Cluster metrics include the following: (i) *size* (value-added value/number of employed people), (ii) *specialisation* in a specific cluster category with potential spill-overs and strong linkages and (iii) *focus*, i.e. the extent to which the regional economy is focused upon the industries comprising the cluster category. To achieve cluster benefits, cluster management activities such as promotion campaigns, structural cooperation between cluster organisations and knowledge institutions, specific (government) support programmes or platforms to exchange best practices are required.

2.2. *BRI: A Maritime Cluster Strategy?*

What motivates the Chinese Government to promote BRI? One group of observers has argued that a key driving force is economics. As China has successfully developed its own infrastructure industry as well as rail and air networks across the country, it is keen to export this expertise (including cement and steel) to foreign markets in view of slowing domestic growth. China's GDP rate was estimated to slow from 10.6% to 6.5% in 2018.

A cluster perspective would go beyond such a rather narrow view and argue that the ultimate outcome of the BRI strategy might be the creation of strong maritime clusters for the benefit of both China and the respective foreign partner. If that holds promise, we must explain with regard to the concept of a maritime cluster why China is building so many ports across the region. To answer that question, let us first examine the interplay between ports and maritime clusters.

According to Lam and Zhang (2011), ports can contribute to the development of robust maritime clusters depending upon their functions, overall port traffic and macroeconomic influences. Port roles and functions vary "significantly from generation to generation. First- and second-generation ports, respectively, relating to ship/shore and industrial interfaces, operate bulk and breakbulk cargo in a traditional manner, with the second generation-type being reliant more on capital than labour. Third-generation ports are the product of the unitisation of sea trade and multimodal cargo packaging (mainly in the form of containers) which has led to the development of ports as logistics and intermodal centres offering value-added services, with technology and know-how being the major determining factors...." Whether port traffic has a positive effect on the local economy system depends on many factors such as the maturity of the local ecosystem in which the port is embedded. Increasingly, port-related services seem to outperform traditional port activities. The impact of port-related services on maritime cluster strength needs to be examined based on case studies.

Marine subclusters include marine insurance, financial services, ship registry, ship owners, operators and managers, ship classification society, ship agency and forwarding, ship brokers, legal services, shipbuilding and repair, marine personnel, research, education and training, information and communication technology (ICT) services, regulators such as maritime organisations and associations.

Ports and port cities are nodal points in maritime networks of differing rates of *connectivity*. The success of a maritime policy can, therefore, be assessed not only by measuring the contribution of the maritime sector to gross national product (GNP) but also by the increase of connectivity. The concept of "connectivity" requires some further explanation and definition. In general terms, "connectivity" refers to the number and strength of connections between points of a surface. In another paper, we have used an indicator on scientific cooperation to show changing connectivity between universities in the ASEAN region (Evers 2016: 22, Evers and Gerke 2012, Gerke and Evers 2018).

In the context of this chapter, "maritime connectivity" refers to the number of ports connected by shipping services. The strength of the maritime connectivity can be measured by the *amount of cargo* (in tons or TEU) transported between ports (see Figure 2) or alternatively by the *number of sailings* between ports, measured by the *number of ships* or the *combined DWT of ships.*

Container shipping is growing worldwide (see Figure 3). Malaysian and Singapore ports have become the central hubs in the ASEAN region, with an ever-increasing throughput of containers mainly filled with manufactured goods. Malaysia, in particular, has outgrown most

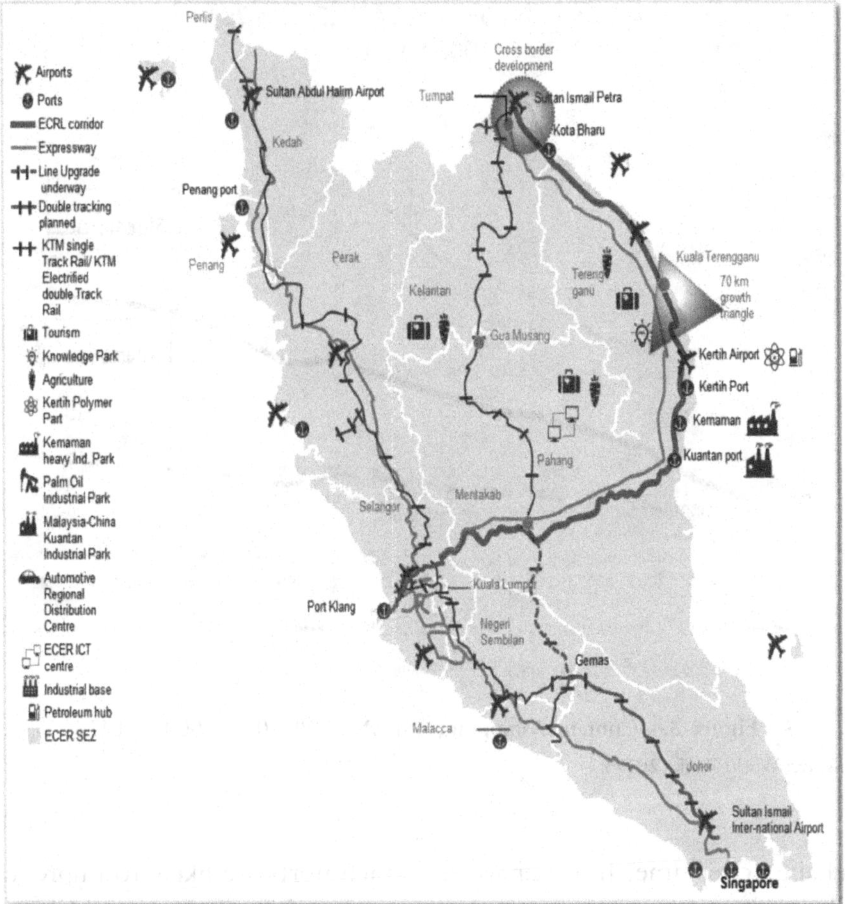

Figure 2. The East Coast railway line route

Source: http://www.spad.gov.my/land-public-transport/rail/east-coast-rail-line-ecrl-project.

other ASEAN countries and has matched Singapore's growth rates. The dynamics of container shipping is shown in Figure 1, where the dominance of Singapore and Malaysia is evident (Evers and Sezali 2012).

The position of each of Malaysia's official ports within the network of ports in ASEAN needs to be ascertained by further research, including the question of how these positions have changed or will

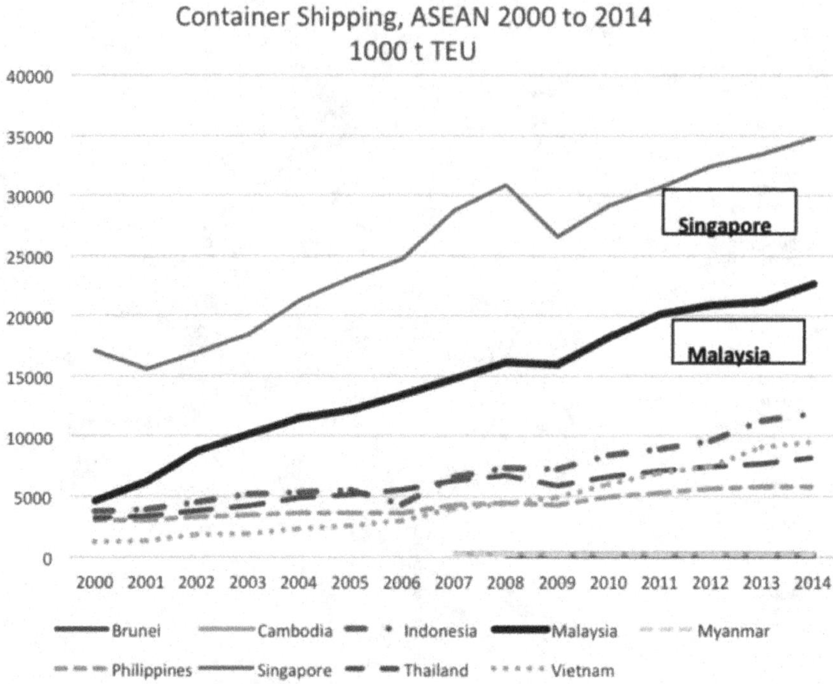

Figure 3. Container shipping, ASEAN 2000–2014, 1000 t TEU

Source: World Bank (2017).

change over time. In other words, which ports are likely to improve their relevance to their home countries as maritime nations and China as a whole? And which ports are likely to be surpassed by competitors like Singapore or Surabaya?

According to media reports, a contract has been signed in 2017 between a consortium of Chinese and Indonesian firms to build a high-speed train connection between Jakarta and Bandung: "The Engineering, Procurement and Construction (EPC) contract was signed in the premises of Indonesia's state-run construction company Wijaya Karya (Wika). The 142-km line is expected to be built in 3 years, allowing trains to run at speeds of 350 km/h. For the needed rolling stock, CRRC Sifang Co. will supply eleven 8-unit high-speed trains". To finance the mega project, China Development Bank is expected to provide a US$4.7 billion loan facility. Key partners include PT Pilar Sinergi BUMN Indonesia (PSBI), a consortium of Indonesian state-owned enterprises led by construction firm PT Wijaya Karya, and a group of Chinese firms led by the China Railway Corporation (http://www.railwaypro.com/wp/contract-jakarta-bandung-construction-signed/).

A key problem which has emerged in Indonesia is to persuade villagers to leave their land on the proposed route (Straits Times 2017: A0): "Gains for China, such as access to key markets and tackling overcapacity in domestic industries, are often more obvious than those for their partners" (refer to Table 1).

Port cities have a long history in the Nusantara. Before and after the advent of European traders and their companies, three well-documented "Malay" port cities stand out: Malacca, Aceh and Banten (Guillot 2005). They were nodal points in a widespread commercial trading network with a high degree of connectivity. "Formerly, as far as we know, old trading cities were actually made up of two distinct towns built along the same river; such was clearly the case with Pasai, Banten, and Malacca, where royal compounds and harbour settlements were located several kilometres apart, each town sometimes bearing a different name. This physical split reflected a peculiar perception of society: the harbour population on the shore was turned towards the sea and the sea activities, whereas the king faced landward, indicating that he wanted to be considered as the necessary intermediary between inland and coastal populations. A neat

Table 1. At a glance: China projects in trouble

Indonesia: Villagers have not moved out of land earmarked for Jakarta-to-Bandung high-speed rail	Kazakhstan: Free trade zone at China border seen as bringing more benefits for Chinese
Thailand: Financing and labour tussles in the rail project	Kyrgyzstan: Country opposes China-to-Uzbekistan railway line that runs through it
Laos: Questions about whether costly railway plan will help the country	Pakistan: Pipelines, trains blown up; Chinese engineers attacked

Source: Straits Times (2017).

boundary specified the different roles. The king had political power over the land and its populations. The harbour population, of foreign extraction, had the right to settle in the kingdom and to trade in exchange for taxes paid to the king. But as guests of the country, they had no say in political matters" (Guillot 2005: 44).

Modern Malaysia has many ports along its long coastline. Most are recognised as official ports, administered by a port authority or port management company. These ports differ greatly in their capacity for cargo handling and their function within the shipping networks (Jeevana *et al.* 2015, Soon and Lam 2013). Only two ports, Tanjung Pelepas in Johor and Port Klang in Selangor qualify as major nodal points of international sea traffic. Both serve as harbours for major transhipment throughout the Straits of Malacca and the South China Sea areas. How they relate or will relate to BRI remains to be seen.

Port cities also have inherited specific social characteristics from their historic past (Guillot 2005). The distinction between government offices, mainly staffed by Malay civil servants and a multitude of workers of different ethnic origin populate the port cities. As the result of their historic role and as points of entry for migrants (now largely replaced by airports) they have a greater ethnic diversity than surrounding areas. Their diasporas interact commercially and privately with other countries, thus enhancing the connectivity of port cities. An interesting side aspect is also the fact that ports tend to have a higher rate of biodiversity than surrounding areas. Biologists talk about the "invasion of foreign species" through shipping, a somewhat awkward term given to misinterpretation, if applied to human migration.

A high degree of *diversity* accounts for the high productivity of port cities and coastal areas. Not all, but most "silicon valleys" or high-tech hubs are found in coastal areas. Trying to create a Cyberjaya (Evers and Nordin 2012) far away from the coast has proven to be more difficult than locating high-tech industries and research labs in Butterworth, Penang Island or Singapore. We are not advocating geographical determinism, but rather the "value of diversity" for productivity and innovation.

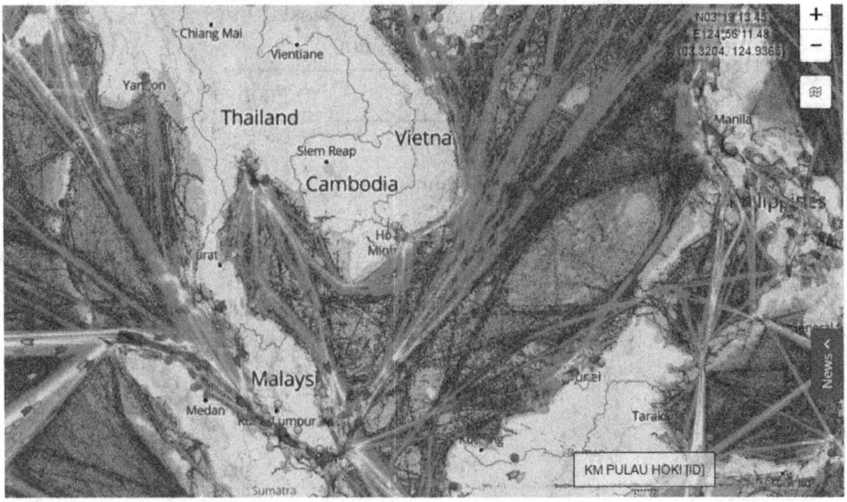

Figure 4. Density of shipping, Maritime ASEAN, April 2017

Source: Screenshot: https://www.marinetraffic.com as of 3rd April 2017.

The changing connectivity of Malaysian and Indonesian ports among themselves and ASEAN and the rest of the world will be an essential aspect of the move towards a truly maritime nation status. A glimpse of the current situation is shown in Figure 4 (screenshot) from the density of shipping in the ASEAN region as of April 2017.

This density map shows the dominance of maritime connectivity of shipping across the South China Sea from and to China and through the Straits of Malacca. Another dense connectivity is seen on an N–S axis from the Gulf of Thailand along the Eastern coast of Peninsular Malaysia towards Indonesia's Java Sea. A relatively low density of shipping is visible between Peninsular and East Malaysia and the Philippines. Overall, the maritime connectivity between ASEAN countries is not yet intense.

Data from our earlier study (Evers and Azhari 2011) show the performance of the maritime economy relative to the maritime potential. Singapore ranks highest among the ASEAN nations and Philippines the lowest (see Table 2). Malaysia occupies the middle position but has improved its rank since 2000. This means that there is still a lot of unused potential in the maritime economy of ASEAN

Table 2. ASEAN nations ranked by maritime performance, 2000

Rank	ASEAN	2000
1	Singapore	98.53
2	Myanmar	65.88
3	Indonesia	60.33
4	Cambodia	40.79
5	Vietnam	33.00
6	Thailand	28.69
7	Malaysia	28.17
8	Brunei	-0.20
9	Philippines	-3.40

Source: Evers and Azhari (2011: 120).

countries such as Malaysia or the Philippines. More recent data will show that Malaysia has moved up and has improved its relative position in ASEAN. From the year 2000 to 2005, the ranking order changed considerably, indicating the dynamics of the maritime sector in the ASEAN countries. It should be noted that we are dealing here with ranking orders rather than absolute figures.

The great potential of further enhancing maritime connectivity also points to the necessity for a stronger ASEAN maritime policy. Indonesia with its Maritime Fulcrum and China with its OBOR policies are set to consolidate their maritime connectivity.

More detailed research will be necessary to follow trends and open opportunities for a closer maritime cooperation and integration of ASEAN countries such as Indonesia. An important strategic question for Indonesia is to effectively link the maritime silk route plans to its maritime ecosystems.

According to a report by Pradhan (2016), "Jokowi aims at building 24 seaports and deep seaports that will connect the archipelago's 17,000 islands together, for this he will need as many foreign investments as he can and China's plans of the MSR gels right with it. Jokowi approximately needs about US$6 billion to expand five major ports in North Sumatra, Jakarta, East Java, South Sulawesi and Papua, and China being Indonesia's largest trading partner and an increasingly important investor can certainly take the opportunity to boost cooperation with Indonesia."

As Indonesia requires substantial foreign investments for further developing its infrastructure and to connect its archipelago, it can benefit from the Silk Road Fund and the AIIB. A stronger relationship with Indonesia can help China to develop better ties with other countries in ASEAN which in turn can help China to dispel doubts about its rise.

3. Conclusion

As argued in this chapter, cooperative ties between China and partners in Southeast Asia such as Singapore, Malaysia and Indonesia can be instrumental in further developing the region's maritime clusters. In theory, BRI can become a key enabler of greater maritime connectivity in Southeast Asia and help mitigate issues pertaining to the South China Sea. As Koh (2015) has argued, China is well advised to: (i) work harder to explain its proposal and to gain the understanding and trust of China's neighbours such as Japan, Vietnam, the Philippines and India; (ii) adopt an open and inclusive approach so that no country is excluded and (iii) solicit the views of regional countries and consider those in future iterations of BRI-related proposals: "The best outcome is for the proposal to evolve from being seen as a Chinese project to being the region's project. It is desirable for China to obtain the region's ownership of the proposal." Given the past experiences with British, Dutch or French imperialism, this may be wishful thinking in view of China's rise to an economic superpower and China's geopolitical strategy to secure its trade routes. Creating maritime clusters around ASEAN port cities may, however, satisfy Chinese geopolitical needs for secure trade routes and ASEAN states' need for vibrant port cities and effective maritime economies.

To shed light on the complementarity of BRI and regional maritime clusters, more case study-based research on Asian port ecosystems is necessary. Key research questions include the following: (i) What is the impact of Chinese capital and infrastructure investments on Sino–Southeast Asian economic relations in general and Southeast Asia's trade routes in particular? (ii) What is the role of BRI-enabled infrastructure connectivity for the region's development? (iii) What are the evolutionary dynamics of Sino-Southeast Asia port construction in the region and how does all this contribute to maritime cluster development in Southeast Asia? (iv) What constitutes a globally competitive maritime (port) cluster and how do Sino–SEA port and maritime cluster initiatives strengthen national development efforts?

Which country will emerge as the leading force in connecting oceans remains to be seen. Power gains and economic competitiveness will depend on the strength of maritime connectivity across seas and oceans. Traditional trade routes connections may gain some importance with the new railroad and road connections between China and Southeast Asia. Maritime connectivity appears to be more viable now as in the past. All participating countries, therefore, need a clear and forceful maritime policy to match those of China.

Considering China's maritime development strategy and Malaysia's current political system, the following two contrasting theses emerge: First, China's heavy investments in land and maritime infrastructure is an opportunity for the economic development of Singapore, Malaysia and Indonesia. Malaysia, for example, will make use of its geopolitical position by "connecting oceans" which presents a possible win-win situation for both China and Malaysia. Second, China's massive investments in infrastructure and ports will reduce the sovereignty of some maritime nations in Asia, strangle their own socio-economic development and lead to a sinicisation (中国化) of Malay Nusantara culture. Such a scenario would imply that the once powerful maritime position of Singapore, Malaysia and Indonesia with their capability to "connect oceans" will be reduced to just a link in China's global production chain. Both Indonesia and Malaysia have therefore raised concern over the economic and political benefits of Chinese maritime policy for their economic and political independence. This concern is justified but needs to be embedded in a comprehensive maritime policy. China's BRI could even serve as an example for designing such an action-oriented maritime policy for the ASEAN nations.

References

ASEAN (2016). Master plan on ASEAN connectivity 2025. ASEAN Secretariat, Jakarta.

Doloreux, D. (2017). What is a maritime cluster? *Marine Policy* 83, 215–220.

EC (2009). European community/directorate-general for maritime affairs and fisheries. The role of maritime clusters to enhance the strength and development in European maritime sectors. Office for Official Publications of the European Communities, Luxembourg.

Embong, A.R., Evers, H.-D. and Ramli, R. (2017). One Belt One Road (OBOR) and Malaysia: A long-term geopolitical perspective. IKMAS Working Paper No. 5. IKMAS, Universiti Kebangsaan Malaysia.

Evers, H.-D. (2014). Understanding the South China sea: An explorative cultural analysis. *International Journal of Asia Pacific Studies* 10(1), 80–95.

Evers, H.-D. (2016). Nusantara: Malaysia and the geopolitics of the South China Sea. The 11th Pok Rafeah Chair Public Lecture. Institute of Malaysian and International Studies, Penerbit Universiti Kebangsaan Malaysia, Bangi.

Evers, H.-D. and Azhari, K. (2011). The maritime potential of ASEAN economies. *Journal of Current Southeast Asian Affairs* 30(1), 117–124.

Evers, H.-D., Embong, A. R. and Ramli, R. (eds) (2018). *Connecting Oceans: Malaysia as a Nusantara Civilisation* (2 volumes), UKM Press, Bangi (in print).

Evers, H.-D. and Gerke, S. (2012). Globalisation of social science research on Southeast Asia. In Ibrahim, W.Z. (ed) *Knowledge and Social Science in a Globalising World*. Persatuan Sains Sosial Malaysia, Bangi, Selangor, pp. 103–16.

Evers, H.-D., Gerke, S. and Menkhoff, T. (2010). Knowledge clusters and knowledge hubs: Designing epistemic landscapes for development. *Journal of Knowledge Management* 14(5), 678–689.

Evers, H.-D. and Kaiser, M. (2001). Two continents, One area: Eurasia. In Preston, P. and Gilson, J. (eds), *The European Union and East Asia: Interregional Linkages in a Changing Global System*, Edward Elgar Publishing House, Cheltenham, pp. 65–90.

Evers, H.-D. and Nordin, R. (2012). The symbolic universe of Cyberjaya, Malaysia. ZEF Working Paper Series 95.

Evers, H.-D. and Sezali, M.D. (2012). Malaysian maritime potential and the straits of Malacca. *Annuals of Maritime Sociology* 20(1), 40–45.

Gerke, S. and Evers, H.-D. (2018). Globalizing local knowledge: Social science research on Southeast Asia, 1970 to 2000. *SOJOURN* 33, 242–263.

Gerke, S., Evers, H.D. and Hornidge, A.-K. (2008). *The Straits of Malacca: Knowledge and Diversity.* LIT Verlag/Straits G.T., Berlin, London, Penang.

Guillot, C. (2005). Urban patterns and polities in Malay trading cities, fifteenth through seventeenth centuries. *Indonesia* 80, 39–51.

Habib, B. and Faulknor, V. (2017). The Belt and Road Initiative: China's vision for globalisation, Beijing-style. Available at: http://theconversation.com/the-belt-and-road-initiative-chinas-vision-for-globalisation-beijing-style-77705.

Hong, Z. (2015). China's new maritime silk road: Implications and opportunities for Southeast Asia. *Trends in Southeast Asia* 3, Available at: https://www.iseas.edu.sg/images/pdf/Trends_2015_3.pdf.

Jeevan, J., Ghaderi, H., Bandara, Y.M., Saharuddin, A.H. and Othman, M.R. (2015). The implications of the growth of port throughput on the port capacity: The case of Malaysian major container seaports. *International Journal of e-Navigation and Maritime Economy* 3(Dec.): 84–98.

Jetin, B. (2017). One Belt-One Road Initiative and ASEAN connectivity: Synergy issues and potentialities. Working Paper No.30. Institute of Asian Studies, Universiti Brunei Darussalam, Gadong.

Koh, T. (2015). 21st century maritime silk road. *Straits Times*, 4 August. Available at: http://www.straitstimes.com/opinion/21st-century-maritime-silk-road.

Lam, J.S.L. and Zhang, W. (2011). Analysis on development interplay between port and maritime cluster. First International Workshop on Port Economics, December 5–6. National University of Singapore.

Maskell, P. (2013). Towards a knowledge-based theory of the geographical cluster. *Industrial and Corporate Change* 10(4), 921–943.

Menkhoff, T. and Evers, H.-D. (2013). Knowledge diffusion through good knowledge governance. In Dobson, W. (ed), *Human Capital Formation and Economic Growth in Asia and the Pacific.* Routledge, Taylor and Francis Group, London, New York.

Menkhoff, T., Evers, H.-D., Chay, Y.W. and Pang, E.F. (eds) (2011). *Beyond the Knowledge Trap: Developing Asia's Knowledge-Based Economies.* World Scientific, New Jersey, London, Singapore, Beijing.

MFA (2017). Singapore can 'partner China in One Belt One Road Initiative'. *Straits Times,* 11 May. Available at: https://www.mfa.gov.sg/content/mfa/media_centre/singapore_headlines/2017/201705/headlines_20170511_2.html.

Pardali, A. (2005). The way a third generation port can boost local employment: The case of Piraeus. *European Research Studies,* VIII (3–4), 21–44. Available at: http://www.ersj.eu/repec/ers/papers/05_p2.pdf.

Porter, M.E. (1990). *The Competitive Advantage of Nations.* The Free Press, New York.

Porter, M.E. (1998). Clusters and the new economics of competition. *Harvard Business Review* 76(6), 77–90.

Porter, M.E. (2000). Location, competition, and economic development: Local clusters in a global economy. *Economic Development Quarterly* 14(15), 15–34.

Porter, M.E. (2003). The economic performance of regions. *Regional Studies* 37, 6–7.

Pradhan, S. (2016). China's maritime silk route and Indonesia's global maritime fulcrum: Complements and contradictions. ICS (Institute of Chinese Studies) Occasional Papers No 12. Dehli.

Purwaningrum, F. (2014). *Knowledge Governance in an Industrial Cluster. The Collaboration between Academia-Industry-Government in Indonesia.* LIT Verlag, Berlin and Zürich.

Soon, C. and Lam, W.-H. (2013). The growth of seaports in Peninsular Malaysia and East Malaysia for 2007 to 2011. *Ocean and Coastal Management* 78, 70–76.

Shanmugam, K. (2017). How Singapore can gain from One Belt One Road Initiative. *Straits Times,* 30 August. Available at: http://www.straitstimes.com/opinion/how-spore-can-gain-from-one-belt-one-road-initiative.

Straits Times (2017). China's silk road revival plans hit rough patch. 13 November.

Today (2017). Several ways for Singapore to work with Beijing on one Belt, One Road. 18 September. Available at: http://www.todayonline.com/singapore/several-ways-spore-work-china-obor-pm-lee.

von Richthofen, F. (1877). Über die zentralasiatischen Seidenstrassen bis zum 2. Jh. n. Chr. *Verhandlungen der Gesellschaft für Erdkunde zu Berlin* 96–122.

Weber, A. (1909). *Reine Theorien des Standortes.* Mohr Siebeck, Tübingen.

Weber, A. (1981). *Theory of the Location of Industries.* University of Chicago Press, Chicago.

World Bank (2017). World Bank Annual Report 2017. Washington, D.C.: World Bank.

Chapter

10

Strategic Linkages: China's Belt and Road Initiative and Power Capture through Global Value Chains

Pan Zhengqi

1. Introduction

The rapid emergence of China as a global economic powerhouse in a short span of less than four decades has been both an economic anomaly and an economic marvel. With decades of breakneck double-digit growth rates, together with the lifting of more than 800 million people out of poverty since 1978 (World Bank 2018b), China constitutes one of the greatest economic success stories in human history. However, while China pursued relentless domestic economic reforms, its foreign policy has remained largely low profile for much of the past four decades. Indeed, before President Xi Jinping, previous Chinese Presidents adhered to the doctrine of *tao guang yang hui*, which means that China should conceal its capabilities, cope calmly, secure its position and bide its time (Ferdinand 2016). Although China did show signs of increasing global involvement under Hu Jintao, Xi's predecessor, in the areas of UN peacekeeping, participation and leadership in the Shanghai Cooperation Organization (SCO) and BRICS summits,[1] China still lacked "a clear, coherent and unified...approach to international relations and the world order" (Breslin 2013: 633). Hu was preoccupied with maintaining economic growth and domestic reforms and was largely averse to risks, especially in the international arena.

Xi, on the other hand, is a bold and entrepreneurial strongman whose political leadership outstrips many of his predecessors' and rivals that of Deng Xiaoping's. Xi's rise to power signalled the end of China's *tao guang yang hui* doctrine to one which is much more assertive and daring. Moreover, when Xi assumed power in 2013, China had already reached major power status as the world's second largest economy and had a staggering amount of foreign reserves worth approximately US$3.9 trillion, the highest in the world (World Bank 2018a). In addition, the Chinese military is set to become an advanced fighting force, with a military budget higher than that of all the countries in the world except the United States'. Of course, the debate on whether it is China's circumstances or the personality of Xi that made China's foreign policy more assertive is futile — it is probably a combination of these factors — the key point is that China is no longer trying to conceal its power and bide its time. The time of Great Power status has arrived for China. To many in China, who recognised China's economic and military dominance for much of human history, China has reassumed its role in the world. Importantly, political scientist Peter Ferdinand pointed out three key aspects of Xi's foreign policy: (1) configuration of a new type of Great Power relations between China and the US, (2) configuration of relations between China and its neighbours and (3) outward economic adventurism as enshrined by China's Belt and Road Initiative (BRI) or the One Belt One Road (OBOR) project (Ferdinand 2016: 949). Indeed, the BRI stands out as China's most daring and entrepreneurial foreign policy till date and will also rewrite and reconfigure Great Power

[1] BRICS represents a grouping of countries comprising Brazil, Russia, India, China and South Africa.

relations between China and the US, as well as relations between China and its neighbours.

The notion of the BRI gained prominence after President Xi made a speech at Nazarbayev University, Kazakhstan, in 2013, on reviving the ancient Silk Road and creating an "economic belt or corridor linking China with Mongolia, central Asia, Russia, Iran, Turkey, the Balkans, central and eastern Europe, and ultimately Germany and the Netherlands" (Ferdinand 2016: 949–950). Moreover, soon after President Xi's speech, Premier Li Keqiang visited Indonesia and spoke about a new "Maritime Silk Road" (MSR) that links southeast China with Southeast Asia (SEA), Bangladesh, India, the Persian Gulf, the Mediterranean, Germany and the Netherlands (*ibid*). Together, the BRI aims to enhance transnational economic cooperation and investments by linking up nearly 70 countries, many of which are developing economies. Importantly, as of 2017, the countries involved made up 65% of global population and 40% of the world's GDP (Campbell 2017). Indeed, the scope of the BRI is astounding and pushes the limits of Great Power economic grand strategy.

A significant aspect of the BRI is international relations networks — countries linked by the BRI forge both strategic economic and political ties that in turn make them increasingly dependent on one another. Moreover, given that most BRI countries are developing economies, China will serve as the strategic core in the network of geoeconomic and geopolitical relations. Importantly, in an era where global production is geographically dispersed and global value chains (GVCs) constitute a significant portion of global manufacturing (OECD 2012), the BRI is set to become the world's most critical and strategic trading bloc. Moreover, with much of global manufacturing already centred on Asia, together with high economic and population growth rates in developing Asia, the BRI is a force to be reckoned with.

This chapter examines the political economy of the BRI through strategic linkages established via global value chains. In particular, how and under what conditions is economic power captured by China through the BRI? How does geoeconomic power in turn translate into geopolitical power? This chapter investigates the strategic mechanisms by which China is able to capture both geoeconomic and geopolitical powers through the BRI. This chapter argues that dense GVC linkages formed by the BRI with China as the hub will not only result in disproportionately large trade and investment benefits for China, but also considerable financial gains through the greater use and internationalisation of the renminbi (RMB). Importantly, increasing trade and financial connections between China and the rest of the BRI countries will lead to more comprehensive diplomacy, albeit the effects of China's direct political influence being constrained by scepticism regarding debt-trap diplomacy. However, the overall geopolitical ramifications of the BRI remain salient: China's BRI can be seen as a grand strategy to decrease dependence on and influence of the American-led liberal world order. Importantly, this chapter contributes to the existing international political economy literature in three major ways: (1) The mechanisms of both geoeconomic and geopolitical power capture by China using the BRI are articulated and the link between geoeconomics and geopolitics is established. (2) The complex network dynamics within the BRI is unpacked to show how the BRI can be a win–win megaproject, but that China benefits disproportionately more than the rest of the countries involved. (3) The resulting changes in and consequences on the international landscape that will significantly affect international relations are examined.

2. Global Value Chains, China and the BRI

Given that the BRI consists of a network of interdependent economies that are likely to increase trade with one another, the GVC framework is useful to analyse BRI dynamics. GVCs, which describe the "full range of activities that firms and workers perform to bring a product from its conception to end use and beyond" (Gereffi and Fernandez-Stark 2016: 7), characterise international trade dynamics of the 21st century. With advancements in information and communications technology (ICT), logistics and services, as well as reduction in barriers to trade since the 1990s and for much of the 2000s, firms have been incentivised to outsource and offshore their production resulting in complex GVCs around the world (UNCTAD 2013).

Moreover, as Pan (2015) notes, "Given that labour and capital costs are unevenly distributed across the world, firms also find it profitable and advantageous to participate in fragmented and dispersed production or supply chains" (p. 1). Indeed, OECD trade statistics in 2013 show that over 50% of global manufacturing are in the form of intermediate goods and over 70% of global service imports are in the form of intermediate services, which are all required to produce final products (OECD 2012). If the BRI is successful, trade and GVC linkages among the countries involved are likely to be enhanced: BRI countries will experience lower trade barriers and costs of doing business via trade and investment agreements, as well as improved transnational infrastructure connections.

Asia, especially East and SEA, will form the core of the BRI. Already, the East and SEA regions constitute the centre of gravity of global manufacturing in what is popularly known as the Factory Asia phenomenon (Choi and Rhee 2014, Ferrarini and Hummels 2014). As Choi and Rhee (2014) wrote, Factory Asia describes a set of production networks connecting "factories in different Asian economies; producing parts and components that are then assembled, with the final product shipped mainly to advanced economies" (p. 5). Ferrarini and Hummels (2014) aptly sum up this phenomenon: supply in the East, consume in the West. Traditionally, the structure of Factory Asia is such that the following hold:

1. The advanced East Asian economies of Japan and South Korea supply intermediate products to China and other developing (or labour-intensive) countries in SEA.
2. China and developing SEA assemble these intermediate products into finished goods.
3. Final goods are then exported to the large consumer-driven economies of the US and the European Union (EU).

Notably, the aforementioned illustration of Factory Asia is somewhat simplistic and increasingly outdated as China progresses up the GVC and is less likely to be considered as a mere assembler of goods. Nonetheless, the structure of Factory Asia underscores the tight interdependence that exists among the East and SEA economies, and the strong network connections are likely to endure in the near future as international trade becomes increasingly regionalised. Consequently, the BRI will further strengthen the existing economic connections between the network of Asian economies and will no doubt promote China as the main trading and investment hub.

2.1. *Evolution of World Trade and China's Position*

International trade has undergone dramatic transformations since the 1990s. Making sense of the interdependence and evolution of world trade would shed light on how China is able to capture economic power via complex trade linkages of the BRI. Importantly, China's evolution within the network of world trade will also provide us with the geoeconomic context in which the BRI is based on. Consequently, by investigating the world trade network, we can answer the following questions: how has the world trade network evolved since the 1990s? Which countries are the major hubs of world trade? Have the core trading countries in the world remained the same across time? How has China's position in world trade evolved?

Related to the discussion on GVCs, two sets of trade networks are of interest: (1) Domestic Value-Added (DVA) trade network and (2) Foreign Value-Added (FVA) trade network. DVA refers to the exporting country's domestic contribution to the exported good, used by the importing country either for intermediate or final goods production. As such, the DVA network represents the "close [web of] relationships of domestic value-added absorbed abroad between the export country and import country" (Xiao *et al.* 2017: 5). On the other hand, FVA refers to inputs that were imported from abroad to produce intermediate or final goods to be exported. Thus, the FVA network maps out the complexity of GVC trade relations, depicting how inputs imported from abroad are ultimately exported to third countries.

Figure 1 shows the evolution of the DVA network from 1995 to 2011. The connections between the countries represent bilateral DVA trade flows in the equipment manufacturing industry and the

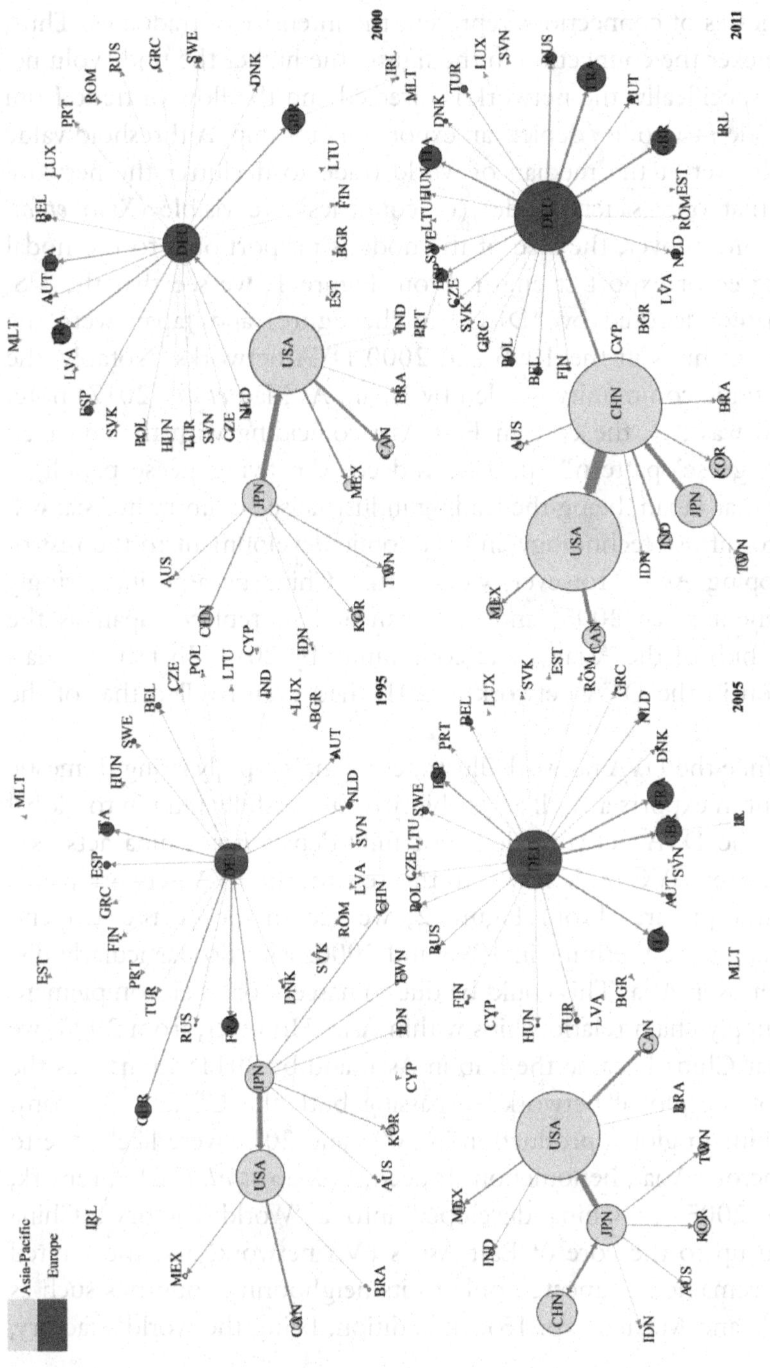

Figure 1. DVA network from 1995 to 2011

Source: Xiao *et al.* (2017).

thicknesses of connections represent the intensity of trade ties. Thus, the thicker the connection in the figure, the higher the trade volume. More specifically, the network is directed and the flow of trade from any node i to node j depicts an export relationship. A threshold value was also set at the median of world trade to declutter the network such that only salient nodes (or countries) are visible (Xiao *et al.* 2017). Moreover, the size of the node is proportional to the nodal outdegree or export strength. From Figure 1, we see that the US, Germany (denoted by "DEU" in the figure) and Japan were the dominant hubs in the 1995 and 2000 DVA networks. Notably, the Asian trade community was led by Japan. As Xiao *et al.* (2017) note, "Japan was . . . the core in East Asia coinciding with the so-called 'flying geese' pattern" (p. 13). Indeed, the flying geese paradigm posits that Japan, being the leading industrialised country in Asia, will help to diffuse technology and economic development to the rest of developing Asia. However, we see that China became increasingly prominent since 2005, and had managed to replace Japan as the major hub of the Asian trade community by 2011. In fact, China's position in the DVA network in 2011 had even rivalled that of the US.

While the DVA network illustrates China's rapidly rising domestic content in exports as well as its ability to successfully plug in to global trade, the DVA network does not fully depict *how* China acts as a conduit for GVC trade flows. In this regard, the FVA network paints a clearer picture. From Figure 2, we see that only the US and Germany were the hubs in 1995 and 2000, with no particularly distinct hubs in Asia. This could be due to nascent or weak complementary supply chain relationships within Asia. However, from 2005, we see that China became the hub in Asia, and by 2011, China was the core of the global network, surpassing both the US and Germany. The shifts in global production in 2005 and 2011 were likely due to the Factory Asia phenomenon. Indeed, as Xiao *et al.* (2017) remark, "After 2005, as China developed into a 'World Factory', China moved up to the core of East Asia's FVA network, and the United States remained connected only to its neighboring countries such as Canada and Mexico" (p. 15). In addition, being the world's factory,

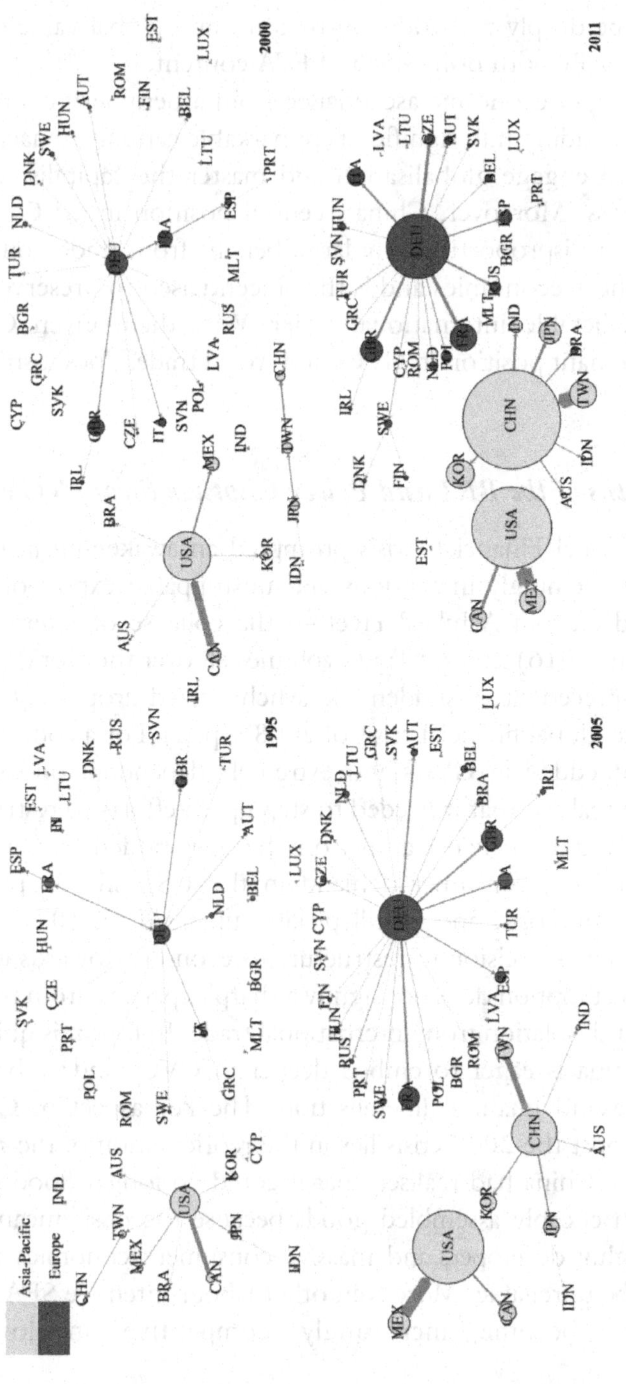

Figure 2. FVA network from 1995 to 2011

Source: Xiao *et al.* (2017).

China became deeply embedded in regional and global value chains, exporting heavily both domestic and FVA content.

China's rapid economic ascendance from a periphery country to a core global trading hub signifies its remarkable capacity, tenacity and willingness to engage globalisation and master the capitalist way of doing business. Moreover, China's central position in GVCs means that it reaps a disproportionately large benefit from trade compared to the periphery economies and is thus incentivised to preserve a stable and predictable international order. Why then, given China's existing dominant position in GVCs and world trade, does it still need the BRI?

2.2. *Impetus of the BRI and Power Capture through GVCs*

The 2008 Global Financial Crisis prompted an awakening in China: that China's seemingly impervious and unstoppable export-oriented model could face an Achilles' Heel — the collapse of international trade. As Pan (2016) notes, "Trade volumes all over the world experienced an unprecedented, sudden and synchronized drop immediately following the global financial crisis of 2008" (p. 2). For a country that is deeply embedded in GVCs and extremely dependent on external trade, China realised that it needed to step up on efforts to restructure its economy and diversify risk away from the crisis-ridden economies of the West. Indeed, consumer demand in the US and EU plunged shortly after the crisis, and is still picking up till date, 10 years on. However, China's decision to restructure its economy towards greater domestic consumption does not signify a sharp departure from reliance on exports and isolation from international trade. In fact, it is quite the opposite: China is eager to embed deeper in GVCs and embark on greater trade and financial liberalisation. The key aspect of China's trade policy post the 2008 crisis lies in the reorientation of the *nature* of its exports. China had realised that it could no longer flood global markets with cheaply assembled goods because the crisis meant that even the highly developed and massive consumer economies in the West could be unreliable. Moreover, other labour-intensive SEA economies have become increasingly competitive in low-cost manufacturing. In other words, as China turns more consumer-based, its exports have also started to shift from low value-added products to higher value-added ones. Regional economic integration as well as stability in the global multilateral framework via a strong World Trade Organization (WTO) will continue to be imperative to China's growth. Indeed, China seeks to *sustain* its dominance in GVCs and as the global trading hub, which will enhance its economic dominance in Asia and beyond.

Consequently, the BRI is a strategic plan that serves to greatly enhance China's economic interests. In lieu with the discussion on GVCs, the BRI allows China to (1) enhance economic integration with the rest of the world, (2) offload excess capacity, (3) create new consumer and investment markets for its businesses, (4) enhance intra-China trade and embed China's inland provinces to GVCs and (5) further internationalise the RMB. These factors, together with China's standing as a major global power, its overall sense of nationalism and Xi's assertive personality and leadership, create the motivations for the BRI. Consequently, although this section focuses on the economic motivations of the BRI, the BRI is a multidimensional strategic project that spans economic, political and socio-cultural realms. Importantly, the BRI is a long-term project and can be viewed in the lens of China's grand strategy to enhance dominance in international affairs.

One of the core objectives of China's foreign policy is to maintain cooperative and friendly relations with its neighbours (Yu 2017). At least through official speeches and texts, China's foreign policy stresses on amicable, cooperative and mutually beneficial reciprocal relationships with other countries, especially its neighbours, based on inclusiveness and trust.[2] Importantly, on international trade, China strongly advocates an "open and nondiscriminatory multilateral trading system across the world" (Swaine 2015: 8). Indeed, China has emerged as an ardent proponent of globalisation, voicing its preference on the world stage. Consequently, it was the Chinese president who was the vanguard of globalisation in the 2017 World Economic

[2] See for instance Xi (2014) for a compilation of President Xi's speeches and writings. Also see Swaine (2015) for a review and analysis of Xi's book.

Forum meeting in Davos, instead of the US president. The BRI would no doubt enhance the trade, investment and diplomatic linkages between China and the countries involved. Moreover, given that most of the BRI countries are developing economies that are rich in natural resources, China will be able to ease its voracious appetite for energy through the BRI. The BRI would thus create a complex network of countries with China as the core. As such, although the developing BRI economies are also likely to benefit from enhanced economic integration, China would reap the most benefits due to its size and economic clout. Mutually beneficial scenarios still exist and are likely to play out as the BRI progresses, but the relative gains will be uneven. Nonetheless, the BRI offers other countries an enticing opportunity to plug into GVCs and the Chinese market. With a vast network of developing economies supplying raw materials and energy, the BRI is likely to further cement China's position as the global trading hub.

The 2008 Global Financial Crisis resulted in large-scale excess capacity in China, especially in the steel, aluminium and cement industries. To elaborate, one of China's solutions to the crisis was to have a surge in investment spending and infrastructure building, resulting in overinvestment. Consequently, weak global markets and domestic overinvestment resulted in excess capacity. Given that the BRI comprises mostly developing economies in need of infrastructure, China aims to offload its excess capacity to the BRI countries, such that it will be a win–win mutually beneficial outcome. Indeed, an Asian Development Bank report estimates that just developing Asia would require US$1.7 trillion per year in infrastructure until 2030 "to maintain its growth momentum, eradicate poverty, and respond to climate change" (Asian Development Bank 2017: xi). Moreover, infrastructure provides the bedrock for industrial development, economic upgrading and economic prosperity for developing countries. Cross-border roads, railways, airports and seaports also help to connect economies more efficiently via more direct trade routes, reducing distribution costs.

Infrastructure helps to enhance China's connectivity with the rest of the BRI countries and facilitates the import and export of goods and services. As a major exporting country deeply embedded in GVCs, China needs to create and facilitate efficient trade routes to not only sell its products overseas but also import intermediate inputs and raw materials to manufacture its products. Consequently, both the overland economic belt and the maritime road will help to reduce transaction costs and enhance reliability in international trade and GVCs. The resulting growth and prosperity of developing BRI economies from increased trade will likely lead to a corresponding surge in middle class within these economies, which will in turn drive more demand for goods and services. New and lucrative consumer markets are created as a result. For China, the BRI economies are essential markets for "Made in China" products. The prospering and upgrading of developing BRI economies will greatly benefit China, which serves as both the BRI and global trading hubs.

Indeed, infrastructure investments form a natural part of the BRI. Moreover, as Hillman (2018) notes, Chinese contractors are awarded the vast majority of BRI infrastructure projects, capturing the lion's share of overall BRI investments. The BRI economies thus constitute lucrative investment hinterlands for Chinese private and state-owned enterprises that seek to venture out or *zou chu qu*. Besides infrastructure investments, the BRI presents a huge market for energy-related investments, be it traditional forms of energy like oil and gas, or renewable energy such as wind, solar or hydro power. Importantly, China is already the global leader in renewable energy, and the BRI presents even more opportunities for Chinese firms to spearhead alternative energy development. China's International Coalition for Green Development on the Belt and Road and the Green Investment Principles for the Belt and Road provide the roadmap for green development of the BRI, bringing multiple private and public stakeholders together and leveraging green investment opportunities.

Importantly, the BRI also enhances intra-China trade and helps to develop the impoverished inland regions of China. China's inland regions will be developed in two major ways: (1) more robust integration with the industrialised coastal regions; and (2) creative transformation of China's western inland provinces such as Yunnan into major gateways that serve China, SEA and South Asia. BRI railroads connecting China's periphery western regions with its core industrialised hubs in the east will no doubt promote greater interdependence and synergy between the local economies. The periphery economic regions will thus be more deeply embedded in China's overall supply chain network, and intra-China trade will be poised for greater growth. This may well lead to the successful industrial upgrading of China's western regions. In addition, some of China's western regions such as Yunnan can function as major gateways between China and its neighbouring countries. Indeed, as Yu (2017) notes, "Yunnan borders three ASEAN countries, Myanmar, Laos and Vietnam, and is a short distance from India and Bangladesh in South Asia, Thailand, and Cambodia in Southeast Asia . . . [the] geographical advantage enables Yunnan to serve as the international gateway or connector for China, Southeast Asia and South Asia" (p. 358). Indeed, China's land-locked western regions would also benefit from the harbour access of neighbouring economies through the BRI, facilitating economic transactions and accelerating overall economic development.

Besides trade and investment considerations, China's BRI will expand the internationalisation of its RMB. Already, China has currency swap agreements with Malaysia, Indonesia, Thailand, Singapore, New Zealand, United Arab Emirates, Russia and Uzbekistan, to name a few. As Huang and Lynch (2013) note, "These agreements are in part politically symbolic, but several agreements signed with major trading partners have the goal of bypassing the US dollar as a medium of exchange" (p. 577). Intuitively, the use of RMB in the BRI will facilitate trading relations, given that a significant portion of China's external trade is on intermediate goods circulating within the Asian region, comprising parts and components used to manufacture final goods. As discussed previously, tight interdependence exists between China and the other Asian economies, within the "Factory Asia" framework, and China is one of the major international hubs for both the DVA and FVA networks. Thus, RMB-denominated trade will help to reduce transaction costs and also "insulate China and its regional production partners from exchange rate risks of multiple cross-border movements of processing related components that are currently denominated in a variety of foreign currencies but principally in dollars" (*ibid*, p. 574). Moreover, the expected increase in China's financial power, at least in Asia, is also salient. RMB-denominated trade and investments through the BRI will not only help to accelerate the RMB internationalisation efforts but also increase the dependency that BRI countries have on China, especially for developing economies that require substantial trade and investment linkages with China. This will in turn reinforce and sustain China's role as the major hub of trade and finance in the BRI. In other words, the BRI network is likely to have a core and periphery structure, with China as the most central economy and the developing economies in the periphery. However, this is not to say that China will exploit the other periphery countries in the traditional dependency theory sense — the underlying relationship is more likely to be interdependent, through the workings of GVCs, than exploitative. Mutually beneficial outcomes are likely to occur, but the relative gains will be uneven.

3. Political Economy of the BRI

How does China's economic power get translated into (geo)political power? This section will elucidate some of the political consequences of the BRI and argue that as countries become increasingly embedded in the BRI network, they will not only become economically interdependent, but will also be more sensitive to the political interests of China, which constitutes the core of the BRI. However, China's direct political influence on the other BRI economies remains limited, given the increasing scepticism of participating countries over issues of debt-trap diplomacy. Taken together, greater economic interdependence does have some spillover effects on China's political influence, but that influence is constrained. Nonetheless, in terms of geopolitics, China's BRI is poised to reshape the American-led liberal world order. This is especially so in the current era of increasing American isolationism.

Economics is inextricably linked to politics. Economic cooperation through the BRI is likely to lead to more diplomatic negotiations among the participating economies. No doubt, participating economies would need to engage in more intensive and frequent diplomacy with China to better bargain trade and investment opportunities. Moreover, given that the BRI is a state-led strategic project, any economic negotiation is necessarily also political in nature. With more bilateral and multilateral interactions among the BRI economies, greater diplomacy might decrease information asymmetries and commitment problems that are rife in international relations. Scepticism towards the consequences of the BRI projects aside, BRI economies are involved in a long shadow of the future, with multiple opportunities for repeated interactions to escape classic prisoners' dilemma scenarios. Together, BRI economies especially the developing ones, which rely heavily on Chinese investments, are likely to be more attuned to China's geopolitical interests in Asia and beyond. Indeed, given the high economic stakes involved and the frequency of interactions, China does not need to overtly alter the political preferences of BRI economies — these economies are likely to gravitate towards China's political orbit in time to come. Notably, BRI economies might also be increasingly drawn to China's model of governance as an alternative to the Western model of liberal democracy.

Nonetheless, China's political influence in the BRI is constrained by a major factor: increasing scepticism of BRI economies over issues of debt-trap diplomacy. Many developing BRI economies had initially embraced the BRI enthusiastically, given that lenders from China require far fewer conditions and less stringent regulations such as project transparency and viability, compared to the International Monetary Fund (IMF) or the World Bank (WB). Indeed, many developing BRI economies such as Pakistan, Bangladesh, Laos and Sri Lanka are high risk economies that are likely to default in loans. The ease of Chinese investments and loans thus presents an attractive and lucrative opportunity that these economies cannot resist. However, many of these economies have fallen prey to the vicious cycle of debt and have become increasingly dependent on Chinese cash. The consequences are severe: in 2017, Sri Lanka became so indebted to China that it was forced to lease a Hambantota port to a Chinese company for 99 years. In another example, Pakistan has been overly dependent on Chinese loans that external debt has soared exponentially in recent years, reaching unsustainable levels, and the country is mired in a fiscal crisis.[3] In addition, the Balkan state of Montenegro has been building a grand highway using Chinese loans but debt has mounted to such a great extent that the government has been forced to raise taxes and partially freeze public sector wages (Barkin and Vasovic 2018). Consequently, BRI economies from Africa to Eastern Europe to Asia have been increasingly reluctant to chalk up Chinese loans for fear that they will fall into the vicious cycle of debt and Chinese control. In this case, the BRI has backfired on China's influence.

On the other hand, given its vast geographical scope, the BRI has clear geopolitical consequences. As discussed, the BRI involves nearly 70 countries spanning a few continents, and includes both developed and developing economies. The interdependent trading and financial networks emerging from the BRI with China as the hub will not only enhance China's international standing but also its geopolitical and geoeconomic centrality. The absence of the US and many of its allies in the BRI makes it clearer that the BRI has great geopolitical significance. In an era where the US is retreating from multilateralism and globalism, China's geopolitical influence is set to expand beyond Asia to Africa, the Middle East and even Europe.[4] Indeed, with the US withdrawal from the Trans-Pacific Partnership (TPP), which originally covers 40% of the global economy, as well as US criticisms of longstanding economic and security agreements such as North American Free Trade Agreement (NAFTA),[5] North Atlantic Treaty Organization (NATO), US–South Korea and US–Japan security arrangements, China faces less obstacles to extend its global reach, given the increasing tensions and schisms between the US and its allies. In short, while the US is building walls, China is building bridges.

The whole network of diverse BRI economies constitutes a powerful geoeconomic and geopolitical force, and China stands to gain the most from this megaproject. Notably, while some BRI economies might be sceptical of China's intentions, fearing debt-trap diplomacy,

[3] As of October 2018.

[4] Latin America is not mentioned because the region is not part of the BRI.

[5] NAFTA here refers to the old NAFTA deal, prior to Trump's 2018 negotiations.

they are nonetheless still willing to remain as members of the BRI, albeit with greater scrutiny of the trade and investment agreements. For instance, although Malaysia's Prime Minister Dr. Mahathir Mohamad has been doubtful of BRI projects, shelving some major Beijing-led projects, such as the East Coast Rail Link in 2018, he has nonetheless expressed general support for inbound Chinese investments. Indeed, existing and aspiring BRI economies may question China's economic and political motives, but they would rather join the BRI bandwagon than to stand excluded. After all, the BRI opens up multiple windows of trade and financial opportunities with the likelihood of capital influx and infrastructure development. On the other hand, rejecting the BRI might be seen as outright animosity towards China, which is already a major power with tremendous economic and political clout. Moreover, with increasing US isolationism and antipathy towards the multilateral international system, countries are likely to gravitate towards China and the BRI, despite the BRI's drawbacks.

China's BRI is one of the most ambitious projects in human history. In its nascent form, the BRI has already captured the attention of countries all around the world. If successful, the BRI will undoubtedly lead to fundamental changes in the international system: one in which China, the Middle Kingdom, takes centre stage. The BRI will restructure how international business operates, how international institutions are organised and how geopolitics is being played out. In other words, the American-led liberal world order will be reshaped to accommodate, in large part, China's interests. The degree of systemic change then will depend on the speed and extent in which China establishes the BRI, and the corresponding US response to the BRI and China's rise. The complex geopolitical interactions between China and the US will reshape the international order. One thing is certain — moving forward, the US will not be the sole hegemon in the international system. The current world order needs to increasingly account for China's economic and political interests, and evolve accordingly, rather than seeking to contain China or convert it in America's image. Otherwise, China, which is already a major power, is likely to embark on radical changes to the international system and recreate a global order that best advances its interests.

4. Conclusion: The BRI and the Thucydides Trap

China's power capture through the BRI will be facilitated and accelerated via GVCs and the complex network of transnational economic relations. Greater geoeconomic power also translates into greater geopolitical power, and the American-led world order will be increasingly shaped by China. A pertinent question thus lingers in the minds of international relations scholars: will China rise peacefully? This question has been systematically explored by Professor Graham Allison from Harvard University, who found that in the past 500 years, 12 out of 16 cases where a rising major power threatened the ruling power ended in war. Drawing from the works of Athenian historian Thucydides, the intuition of Allison's *Thucydides Trap* is that war is sometimes made inevitable due to the threat of the rising major power and the fear of being displaced by the incumbent ruling power (Allison 2017). The fractious dynamics and psychology between the rising and incumbent powers will lead to war. Of course, Allison's book is not meant to be pessimistic, but rather instructive, in that he lays out the conditions that make war more or less likely between the US and China.[6] Space for bargaining and cooperation still exists between the US and China, even in the face of China's growing power and US isolationism (and increasing paranoia towards China). As already alluded, the international order, whether it will be at peace or at war, will be determined by the complex geopolitical interactions between the US and China.

A related but less discussed question is: will the US allow China to rise peacefully? After all, to sound cliche, it takes two hands to clap. Current US withdrawal from globalism and the multilateral international system, together with its paranoia of China at almost every turn, does little to abate the increasing fractious dynamics in Sino–American relations. If the US is bent on containing China's rise because China is an authoritarian regime — in a simplistic dichotomous categorisation — or otherwise, then the world would surely become a more dangerous place. China, with its long history and culture, as well as painful memories of a "century of humiliation", will

[6] For more details, see Allison (2017).

chart its own path of political and economic governance, shaped by its own national interests and exigencies.

References

Allison, G. (2017). *Destined for War: Can America and China Escape Thucydides's Trap?* Houghton Mifflin Harcourt Publishing Company, New York, US.

Asian Development Bank (2017). Meeting Asia's infrastructure needs. Available at: https://www.adb.org/sites/default/files/publication/227496/special-report-infrastructure.pdf (Last accessed: 4 October 2018).

Barkin, N. and Vasovic, A. (2018). Chinese 'highway to nowhere' haunts Montenegro. *Reuters* (*World News*), 16 July. Available at: https://www.reuters.com/article/us-china-silkroad-europe-montenegro-insi/chinese-highway-to-nowhere-haunts-montenegro-idUSKBN1K60QX (Last accessed: 4 October 2018).

Breslin, S. (2013). China and the global order: Signaling threat or friendship?" *International Affairs* 89(3), 615–634.

Campbell, C. (2017). China says it's building the new silk road. Here are five things to know ahead of a key summit. *Time Magazine Online*. Available at: http://time.com/4776845/china-xi-jinping-belt-road-initiative-obor/ (Last accessed: 4 October 2018).

Choi, B.-i. and Rhee, C. (2014). *Future of Factory Asia*, Asian Developmental Bank and Korea Economic Research Institute, Manila, Philippines and Seoul, Republic of Korea.

Ferdinand, P. (2016). Westward ho — The China dream and 'One Belt, One Road': Chinese foreign policy under Xi Jinping. *International Affairs* 92(4), 941–957.

Ferrarini, B. and Hummels, D. (2014). Asia and global production networks: Implications for trade incomes and economic vulnerability. In Ferrarini, B. and Hummels, D. (eds), *Asia and Global Production Networks: Implications for Trade Incomes and Economic Vulnerability*, Edward Elgar Publishing Limited, Cheltenham, UK.

Gereffi, G. and Fernandez-Stark, K. (2016). Global value chain analysis: A primer. Center on Globalization, Governance & Competitiveness (CGGC), Duke University.

Hillman, J. (2018). China's Belt and Road Initiative: Five years later. Statement Before the U.S.–China Economic and Security Review Commission, Center for Strategic and International Studies.

Huang, Y. and Lynch, C. (2013). Does internationalizing the RMB make sense for China? *Cato Journal* 33(3), 571–585.

OECD (2012). Interconnected economies: Benefitting from global value chains. OECD Synthesis Report. Available at: https://www.oecd.org/sti/ind/interconnected-economies-GVCs-synthesis.pdf (Last accessed: 4 October 2018).

Pan, Z. (2015). Global value chains and production networks: State-business relations and complexity in economic crises. Ph.D. Dissertation, University of North Carolina, Chapel Hill.

Pan, Z. (2016). The great trade collapse: Shock amplifiers and absorbers in global value chains. The National University of Singapore Global Production Networks Center Working Paper Series, GPN2016-008.

Swaine, M. (2015). Xi Jinping on Chinese foreign relations: The governance of China and Chinese commentary. *China Leadership Monitor* 48, 1–14.

UNCTAD (2013). World investment report 2013: Global value chains: Investment and trade for development.

World Bank (2018a). World Bank Development Indicators. Available at: http://data.worldbank.org/data-catalog/world-development-indicator (Last accessed: 1 August 2018).

World Bank (2018b). The world bank in China. Available at: http://www.worldbank.org/en/country/china/overview (Last accessed: 4 October 2018).

Xi, J. (2014). *The Governance of China*. Foreign Languages Press, Beijing, China.

Xiao, H., Sun, T., Meng, B. and Cheng, L. (2017). Complex network analysis for characterizing global value chains in equipment manufacturing. *PLOS ONE* 12(1), 1–22.

Yu, H. (2017). Motivations behind China's 'One Belt, One Road' initiatives and establishment of the Asian Infrastructure and Investment Bank. *Journal of Contemporary China* 26(105), 353–368.

Chapter 11

Sustaining the Momentum of the Belt and Road Initiative

Andrew Elek

1. Introduction[1]

The unprecedented scope of the Belt and Road Initiative (BRI) has been described in the preceding chapters of this volume. Up to US$1 trillion dollars have already been earmarked for investments. Many projects are already under way to improve transport, communications and energy networks, generating an early harvest of mutual benefits.

That is a good start, but the BRI is a long-term undertaking.[2] If the pace of investment can be sustained for several decades, the world

[1] This chapter is based on the 2017 monograph by the author prepared for the Qianhai Institute for Innovative Research (QIIR): *The Future of the Belt and Road: Long-term Strategic Issues*, available on the QIIR website.

[2] Shen (2015) explains that

> "*Aspiring to build Eurasian infrastructure connectedness, especially in terms of highway, fast train and maritime transportation, the OBOR has to be a*

economy will be transformed. By the middle of the 21st century, the quality of physical, institutional and people-to-people connectivity among countries in several continents participating in the BRI could be comparable to the 2016 links between the Pearl River Delta and Hong Kong.

1.1. *Will That Happen?*

Linking many diverse economies will need to deal with many risks and uncertainties. It is impossible to anticipate all of the problems that will arise, but financing will be one of them. Tens of trillions of dollars will need to be invested in the economic infrastructure.[3] Such massive financing will not be possible without attracting massive private sector investment into economic infrastructure projects, many of which are public goods.

To meet that challenge, it will be essential to demonstrate that BRI infrastructure is being maintained and operated efficiently. Objective monitoring of early projects will need to confirm that they are generating sound economic rates of return. Moreover, once they are up and running, they will also need to have a commercial rate of return sufficient to attract interest from private investors, especially institutional investors.

Such returns are possible, but will require huge improvements in the skills, institutional capacity and policy environment of most of the countries involved. Efficient transport, communications and energy

---

very ambitious program entailing a vast amount of resources through multi-lateral collaboration. … One shall not forget about the enormous differences in the Eurasian continent that promises the completion of the OBOR would take tens of years if not centuries."

[3] Hong Kong Trade Development Council (2017) points out that

"*A crucial factor behind China's economic miracle in the late 20th century was aggressive infrastructure investment, and to create similar infrastructure improvements through Asia and Africa, annual investment of US$2 trillion to US$3 trillion will be needed. Altogether, the initiative could need public and private investments roughly 12 times the size of the Marshall Plan that helped rebuild Europe after World War II.*"

See http://beltandroad.hktdc.com/en/insights/commentary-one-belt-one-road-gaining-traction-unanswered-questions-leave-funding-uncertain.

networks will need a high and sustained level of policy coordination, but the foundations for effective coordination are yet to be laid.

With genuine commitment, all of these challenges can be overcome by governments which are committed to development and cooperate flexibly to achieve a shared vision. The success of the BRI depends on quick and creative thinking about long-term challenges, including the following:

- nurturing mutual trust and mutual respect among a very diverse group of countries;
- managing a transition to shared leadership of the process;
- reaching agreement on priorities and targets;
- sharing responsibility for efficient project design, construction, operation and maintenance;
- mobilising the massive financing that will be needed.

The *Action Plan on Belt and Road Initiative* published in March 2015[4] is an excellent document which indicates sound understanding of these challenges. However, several years later, there is little evidence, and certainly no assurance, that these difficult issues are being tackled effectively.

2. Connecting Belt and Road Economies

The BRI's on emphasis on connectivity is appropriate. A rapidly growing body of evidence from the OECD, the Asian Development Bank, the World Bank and the World Economic Forum confirms that readily achievable gains from better connectivity far exceed the potential gains that come from getting rid of all remaining traditional border barriers to trade.[5] For perspective, the cost of goods spent stuck for one day in a port or at a border is as much as a tariff of 1%. In this

---

[4] This document, a detailed official publication setting out the nature and scope of the BRI will be referred to as the 2015 Action Plan in this chapter. It is available at: http://english.gov.cn/archive/publications/2015/03/30/content_281475080249035.htm.

[5] See http://www.adbi.org/files/2009.08.31.book.infrastructure.seamless.asia.pdf; Wilson *et al.* (2003); World Bank Report, http://www.weforum.org/reports/enabling-trade-valuing-growthopportunities.

era of rapid digitisation, affordable access to high quality broadband and good transport networks are more important to businesses than the residual barriers to importing and exporting the few products which remain heavily protected.

The 2015 Action Plan explains that transport, communications and energy networks — the most visible ways to boost connectivity — are to be backed up by policy development and capacity-building to make international commerce among Belt and Road economies cheaper, easier and faster. It is relatively easy to build roads, bridges, ports or power stations. But it is hard to ensure their efficient operation and adequate maintenance, which require ongoing policy coordination among capable institutions in all of the economies being connected. It will be essential to make progress on all of the dimensions of connectivity illustrated in Figure 1.

Governments will need to work and learn together to design, then implement, the policies and the institutions needed to create enabling environments for business which can make it possible to finance, construct, then operate improved transport, communications and energy networks.

Some of the greatest gains from cooperation among governments and the private sectors of Belt and Road participants are likely to flow from improving regulatory environments, including growing respect

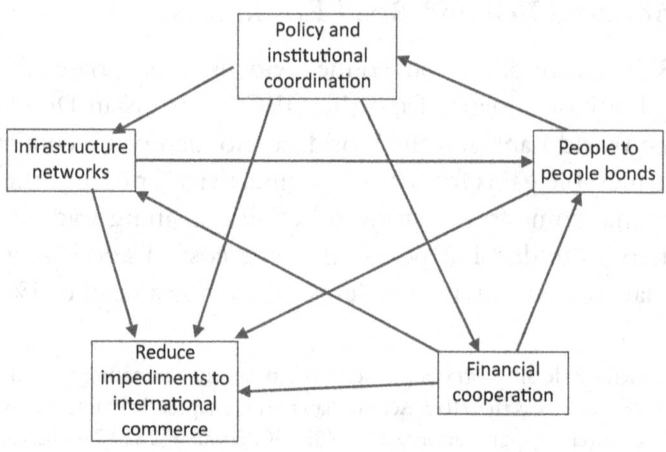

Figure 1. Mutually reinforcing dimensions of connectivity

for sound legal systems. Sharing information, experience, expertise and technology among the very diverse group of Belt and Road countries will be essential to create the human and institutional capacity for efficient project design, construction, operation and maintenance. The high levels of performance needed to ensure investments are commercially viable and will also require incentives for efficiency.

3. Foundations for Successful Cooperation

The many participants in the BRI vary greatly in the size of their populations and economies, forms of governance, institutional development and productivity. Effective coordination among them needs to be based on agreed principles. Several decades of experience of economic cooperation, inclusive of Association of Southeast Asian Nations (ASEAN) and Asia-Pacific Economic Cooperation (APEC), show that successful and sustained cooperation among such a diverse group should be voluntary, based on the principles of openness, transparency, mutual benefit, mutual trust, mutual respect and careful evolution (see Drysdale 1998).

The guiding principles set out in the 2015 Action Plan are consistent with this essentially Asian mode of international cooperation. All countries are invited to join the BRI, respecting each other's sovereignty and the paths and modes of development they have chosen. Cooperation is to be based on dialogue to ensure that the interests of all participants are accommodated. Cooperative arrangements and investments are to abide by market rules and international norms and designed to lead to mutual benefit.

The challenge for the coming years is to put these guiding principles into practice. China's decisive early leadership has been essential and welcome. Early momentum has been made possible by China's willingness to finance most of these investments through state-directed lending, by state-owned Chinese financial institutions and then by Chinese state-owned enterprises (Zhang 2016).[6]

[6] "*In late 2014, China's State Council outlined a framework for how China's financial system was to support financing and investment for the Belt and Road initiative. The*

In practice, that means that China is dominating the decision-making process within the bilateral agreements with other BRI participants.

The time has come to begin a decisive move away from a hub-and-spokes process towards a genuinely shared leadership.[7] Even if China is willing to cede more control over the BRI, it is not certain that others will be able to take more responsibility for sharing the costs as well as the benefits of cooperation.

Belt and Road governments need to begin wider and regular consultations to make well-informed decisions about the evolution of the process. Creating and strengthening mutual trust needs to ensure that even the smallest participants can help shape Belt and Road networks.

3.1. *Openness*

The global economy is now highly integrated, so openness is essential. The current participants in the BRI already account for 55% of global gross national product (GNP) and 70% of the world's population. Their links to the rest of the world are, in many cases, just as strong as their links to participants in the BRI.

Therefore, it is welcome that the initiative is not intended to be the trading bloc. To ensure that the physical, institutional and

---

China Banking Regulatory Commission has developed guidelines on how China's banking and financial institutions should be prepared to finance Belt and Road projects. Since early 2015, major Chinese policy and commercial banks have geared up to finance railway, road, airport, port and other infrastructure projects in Belt and Road countries."

[7] The need for transformation of the BRI to shared leadership has been emphasised by India's Foreign Minister, who has called for "a cooperative rather than unilateral approach and believe that creating an environment of trust and confidence is the prerequisite for a more inter-connected world": see http://www.mea.gov.in/Speeches-Statements.htm?dtl/26432/Speech_by_External_Affairs_Minister_at_the_inauguration_of_Raisina_Dialogue_in_New_Delhi_March_01_2016. Stephen Nicholas (Visiting Professor, Guangdong Institute for International Strategies) stated that the Belt and Road "... will not succeed as a 'community of common destiny' without a more collaborative approach" at a presentation to the China (Guangdong) International Think Tank Forum of the 21st-Century Maritime Silk Road Consensus-building, Guangzhou, May 2016.

people-to-people networks strengthen, not weaken, their connections to the rest of the world, it would be useful to agree that cooperation to improve connectivity of Belt and Road economies should be consistent with the following key principles of open regionalism:

- all people or firms, from all economies, should be able to use investments in the infrastructure and participate in cooperative arrangements on equal terms;
- cooperation among Belt and Road economies should seek to reduce impediments to international commerce among them, without intending to damage the interests of any others.

Openness can also guide the design of particular investments and cooperative arrangements. It is not realistic to expect all members of a large and diverse group to participate in all arrangements for cooperation. Some may not be ready for, or interested in, some specific arrangements, for example, to harmonise banking regulations or to facilitate easier international movement of people. But others can set examples for them and make sure that the arrangements they pioneer are genuinely open to others. Then, the first movers should help and encourage others to join these arrangements.

3.2. *Transparency*

Transparency is essential for mutual trust and informed decision-making. A lot of information is available about the many projects already under way, but it is neither comprehensive, nor readily available. The BRI urgently needs to be supported by a publicly available knowledge-sharing platform, readily available on a website, that sets out the following:

- what projects are under way or committed;
- how they are being financed, constructed and operated;
- whether expected targets for completion and performance are being met;
- how costs and benefits are shared among the participants.

While the aims of the BRI are shared by most governments, the perceived lack of transparency has led to decisions to propose alternatives, rather than join the initiative. Japan launched a Partnership for Quality Infrastructure (PQI)[8] in 2015 and a new joint initiative with India to create an Asia–Africa Growth Corridor (AAGC).[9] In 2018, Australia, the United States, India and Japan had begun to discuss a quadrilateral regional infrastructure scheme.[10]

All of these initiatives to accelerate investment in infrastructure are timely since the need is so great: even the US$1 trillion committed to the BRI is well short of what the Asian region should be investing in infrastructure each year.[11] They could complement each other. However, until all of them are transparent and establish effective lines of communications and coordination, there will be needless duplication and inefficiency.

3.3. *Consultations*

The first summit of BRI leaders was held in May 2017.[12] Some participants expressed concern about the lack of commitments to social and environmental sustainability, transparency and access of non-Chinese firms.[13] However, there was widespread support for President Xi Jinping's stated objective to

[8] See http://www.mofa.go.jp/files/000081298.pdf and https://www.lowyinstitute.org/the-interpreter/japan-plans-build-free-and-open-indian-ocean.

[9] See http://www.eria.org/Asia-Africa-Growth-Corridor-Document.pdf.

[10] See http://www.asahi.com/ajw/articles/AJ201802190018.html.

[11] The Asian Development Bank (ADB) estimates that US$26 trillion needs to be invested in infrastructure between 2016 and 2030 to maintain growth, cut poverty and deal with climate change. Moreover, the gap between the actual and required spending is about 2.4% of the region's gross domestic product in 2016–2020. See https://www.ft.com/content/79d9e36e-fd0b-11e6-8d8e-a5e3738f9ae4?emailId=58b4c7df473581000435df57&segmentId=22011ee7-896a-8c4c-22a0-7603348b7f22.

[12] See https://www.ft.com/content/88d584a2-385e-11e7-821a-6027b8a20f23?emailId=5918b2d27351b40004e315d4&segmentId=60a126e8-df3c-b524-c979-f90bde8a67cd.

[13] See https://www.reuters.com/article/us-china-silkroad-germany/germany-demands-more-free-trade-guarantees-on-china-silk-road-plan-minister-idUSKCN18A0AG?m

"build an open platform of cooperation and uphold and grow an open world economy".[14]

The principles of the BRI, which were first stated in the 2015 Action Plan, were reaffirmed and China pledged additional funding. This successful summit now needs to be followed up by a framework for regular communications among officials, business leaders and researchers from Belt and Road.

Ongoing policy-oriented consultations are essential foundations for the future of the initiative in order to nurture a sense of community and to identify shared interests, making it possible for participants to learn from each other, then build consensus on the design of the policy settings and institutional upgrading needed for sustained improvements in connectivity.

Policy-oriented working groups are the foundations of cooperation which can

- facilitate the sharing of information, experience, expertise and technology;
- assess what policies and institutions will work in different environments;
- help each other to develop the skills and financial capacity to participate effectively on improving all the essential dimensions of connectivity.

The organisers of the BRI are beginning to think about the long-term challenge of creating these foundations.[15] Constructing them can draw on the experience of ASEAN and APEC, whose agendas for cooperation are quite similar to the aims of the BRI.[16]

od=related&channelName=ousivMolt and https://www.theguardian.com/world/2017/may/15/eu-china-summit-bejing-xi-jinping-belt-and-road#img-1.

[14] See https://www.reuters.com/article/us-china-silkroad-africa/china-pledges-124-billion-for-new-silk-road-as-champion-of-globalization-idUSKBN18A02I.

[15] See Wang (2018), who describes some early moves towards upgrading skill and networks to support the BRI.

[16] See http://asean.org/wp-content/uploads/archive/5187-10.pdf and https://www.apec.org/Publications/1995/12/Osaka-Action-Agenda-1995.

3.3.1. *Learning from Experience*

3.3.1.1. ASEAN

The scope of ASEAN cooperation has expanded cautiously since its formation in the 1960s, based on patient consensus building. Considerable progress has been made, including the removal of many policy barriers to the international movement of goods, services, investment, people and information on the way to creating an ASEAN Economic Community (AEC). It will take some time to complete the AEC agenda, but ASEAN is already the most closely linked group of economies other than the European Union (EU).[17] Its flexible model of voluntary cooperation is more likely to lead eventually to even closer cooperation, since it will be able to handle shocks far better than the rigid structure that has been imposed on members of the EU.

3.3.1.2. APEC

APEC was built on foundations which were laid in the 1960s. Annual Pacific Trade and Development (PAFTAD) conferences started to assess the changing economic environment of the Asia-Pacific. PAFTAD's work was complemented by the Pacific Basin Economic Council (PBEC), a group of senior business people seeking to forge closer economic links in the region. These groups analysed the growing, market-driven interdependence of Asia-Pacific economies with very different and often complementary resources. The Pacific Economic Cooperation Council (PECC), established in 1980, engaged government officials in discussions about international economic cooperation — at that stage in a personal capacity.

PECC's analysis identified region-wide interests in trade and investment policy, agriculture, minerals and energy, transport, telecommunications and tourism. Regular consultations throughout the 1980 identified shared interests and opportunities for mutually

[17] A mid-term review of performance by ERIA is available at: http://www.eria.org/Mid-Term%20Review%20of%20the%20Implementation%20of%20AEC%20Blue%20Print-Executive%20Summary.pdf.

beneficial economic cooperation. The most important among these is the region's overriding interest in a rules-based, open and non-discriminatory system for international commerce. By 1989, sufficient mutual trust was created to allow the successful launch of the APEC process.[18]

3.3.2. *Creating New Networks*

The BRI will also need several decades to build these foundations, so it is urgent to create, then strengthen a new consultative network, covering a wide range of issues in order to identify shared interests and opportunities for cooperative arrangements.

It will be hard to bring all participants together. Meetings of people from up to 100 countries are unlikely to prove productive. A practical option may be inviting all participants to all meetings of the BRI consultative network, but not requiring them to attend. People from participating countries can then decide if the agenda is of sufficient interest to them; whether they can expect to learn from the discussions, and/or whether they can expect to influence decisions. Another option would be to set up consultative networks among the countries along some of the Belt and Road corridors.

3.4. *Sharing Leadership*

In principle, all of the governments involved in the BRI will have the right to influence its scope and priorities. In practice, the right to influence decisions will have to be earned through a combination of the following:

- demonstrating constructive contributions to practical cooperative arrangements to boost connectivity: for example, to adopt

[18]The creation of PECC, the APEC are described in Chapters 2 and 5 of *The Evolution of APEC: The First 25 Years*, Pacific Economic Cooperation Council, Singapore, 2015.

interoperable systems to reduce the time and cost of moving people or products across borders;
- contributing to the cost of Belt and Road investments in, or through, their countries, in line with their financial capacity;
- commitment to the efficient operation and maintenance of these investments.

These are difficult criteria. But it is quite unrealistic to expect mutual respect among groups where only one, or just a few, participants take responsibility for implementing the BRI.

At present, many of the relatively small, or weak, economies involved will not be able to meet these requirements which can earn the right to shape the future of the BRI. However, if they demonstrate a commitment to improve their capacity to do so, others should be ready to help. China has already set up the Asian Infrastructure Investment Bank (AIIB) — that new institution, alongside other multilateral development banks, can make a valuable contribution to a massive capacity-building effort needed for a gradual transition to the genuinely shared leadership of the BRI.

4. Implementing the BRI

The BRI depends on cooperative policy development, leading to agreed strategies for the following measures:

- planning and constructing efficient transport, communications and energy networks;
- reducing policy impediments to using them efficiently;
- encouraging institutional innovations.

4.1. *Planning to Improve Networks*

Investments in transport, communications and energy links should fit into coherent networks. But it is hard to plan how thousands of investments in hardware and software are to be sequenced, financed, constructed and operated. The many uncertainties about the future of the BRI include the following:

- the future priorities and capabilities of many governments;
- the technology, especially new transport and information technology, that may become available;
- the expected cost of financing;
- whether related investments are completed.

These unavoidable uncertainties mean that it is not realistic to expect a grand *Master Plan for the Belt and Road*. However, scoping studies, similar to the Master Plan on ASEAN Connectivity (MPAC) can provide an idea of the expected costs and achievements, at least in broad terms, for the next few decades.[19] The Chinese Government's State Council's guidance for the Pearl River Delta provides another useful precedent.[20]

Decisions on future investments in all the dimensions of connectivity should be based on information about the projects already under way, comparing their actual to expected costs and benefits. That feedback, relying on transparency and objective monitoring, can then influence decisions on the sequence and timing of subsequent investments.

4.2. *Setting Targets*

The Belt and Road will never be finished. As more economies join the initiative, there will always be opportunities to extend the existing networks and, as technology becomes available, there will always be room for improving them. Therefore, it would not be useful to set a final deadline for connecting all Belt and Road participants.

[19] See http://www.asean.org/storage/images/ASEAN_RTK_2014/4_Master_Plan_on_ASEAN_Connectivity.pdf.

[20] See http://www.gov.cn/zhengce/content/2016-03/15/content_5053647.htm.

A more effective way to provide incentives for progress is to set measurable and realistic medium-term targets for better connectivity among some economies. These targets should focus on the "outputs" of investments — their expected net benefits — rather than for "inputs" such as the miles of roads built and their costs.

Measurable targets can be set for improvements in performance, for example, the cost and time taken to move products or information. For the currently best transport and communications links, it is probably sufficient to ensure there is an incentive to take advantage of new technology to make them even better over time. For weaker links, targets can be set in terms of performance which is raised, progressively, closer to what has already been achieved for comparable links. Targets can be set for realistic improvements in widely accepted indices of performance, such as the World Bank's indicators of trade logistics and the ease of doing business.[21]

4.3. *Monitoring Progress*

A high standard of transparency will be essential to monitor progress towards agreed targets by

- measuring progress relative to initially expected targets;
- estimating the economic benefits that are generated by BRI projects and the distribution of these benefits;
- calculating the financial rates of return to investments — that is vital for sustainable financing.

Monitoring should be objective, carried out by independent institutions rather than government officials, and the results of monitoring and evaluation should be made available to the public on a Belt and Road Knowledge Sharing Platform.

---

[21] See http://www.doingbusiness.org/rankings. Targets can be set on improvements in economies expected to benefit from particular Belt and Road investments. Such improvements are worthwhile even if they do not change rankings compared to other economies.

It may be possible to use the evaluation capacity of the AIIB. The actual results of all past investments in the Belt and Road will be a vital input to the AIIB's decision-making process. Therefore, the bank has an incentive to monitor all of them, not just projects it has financed directly.

4.4. *Boosting Efficiency*

The networks to be created by the BRI should make it possible for many more economies to become successfully involved in international value chains. Their ability to do so will be improved by reducing and, where possible, getting rid of policy obstacles to economic transactions along Belt and Road networks and by taking advantage of new technology.

4.4.1. *Reducing Impediments*

Cooperation among Belt and Road governments to reduce natural and policy obstacles to the movement of products, people, finance and information along value chains should focus on

- which are the most important obstacles;
- where voluntary cooperation can expect to achieve significant mutual benefits.

Based on the stated priorities of the business people engaged in value chains and the evidence of relative gains from reducing impediments, the BRI should continue to concentrate on connectivity — investing to upgrade physical networks and the policy coordination and cooperative arrangements needed to operate them efficiently.[22]

---

[22] A recent survey of their priorities for economic integration within the emerging AEC can be summarised as follows:

- Across-the-border issues: For example, import and customs administration, efficiency and integrity including greater use of information and communications technology.

These are positive-sum, win-win opportunities which are in line with the comparative advantage of voluntary cooperation.

Business people are well aware that the gains from better connectivity are now far greater than the potential gains from further liberalisation of traditional border barriers to trade, such as tariffs and quantitative restrictions. These policy barriers are costly, but they affect only a rapidly shrinking share of international commerce. Further trade liberalisation is desirable, but not a strategic issue for the success of the BRI. Trade liberalisation needs negotiations — which are certainly not the comparative advantage of voluntary cooperation.

Most BRI economies are already part of preferential trade agreements (so-called Free Trade Areas) and/or involved in negotiations for more trade deals, so trade liberalisation should be left to trade negotiators. Progress on more rewarding opportunities to improve connectivity should not be delayed by waiting for marginal progress on trade liberalisation.

4.4.2. *Towards a Seamless Regional Economy Investment*

Deep, mutually beneficial economic integration needs far more than the massive investment in new transport, communications and energy hardware that the BRI has catalysed.[23] Some BRI economies

---

- Standards and conformance measures: Strengthening certification bodies and moving towards international standards.
- Investment facilitation: Adopting international best practices.
- Transport and communications: Better connectivity, including harmonising rules and regulations to improve ICT connectivity.
- Non-tariff barriers: Including work towards automatic import licensing and mutual recognition of professional qualifications.
- Strengthening and implementing rules: Including procompetitive regulations and effective intellectual property rights.

See ERIA (2012, p. 4), available at: http://www.eria.org/MidTerm%20Review%20of%20the%20Implementation%20of%20AEC%20Blue%20Print-Executive%20Summary.pdf.

[23] For example, the efficiency of the massive new dry port on the China–Kazakhstan border will depend on the quality of its operating software; see https://www.nytimes.com/2018/01/01/world/asia/china-kazakhstan-silk-road.html?emc=edit_mbae_20180101&nl=&nlid=30774450&te=1&_r=0.

are already using modern software and exchanging data that optimises the efficiency of transport and energy networks and allows the clearance of people and products across international borders without any need for time-consuming inspections. These pathfinding countries will benefit from sharing the information, experience, expertise and technology to help others adapt already proven systems to their operating environments, generating significant positive network effects.

Taking full advantage of technological opportunities needs effective policy coordination among institutions. Investments in physical connectivity will need to be backed by investments in institutional capacity to allow them to cooperate smoothly with the corresponding organisations of other governments, for example, by adopting compatible software and data formats and nurturing mutual trust among officials in these institutions. Some of these opportunities are summarised below.[24]

4.4.2.1. Transport Systems

The efficiency of transport networks can be raised by encouraging and helping all governments to adopt sound operating standards including safety, harmonising them towards widely accepted international norms and conventions, and then enhance the capacity of their institutions to enforce them (Bhattacharyay and De 2009).

Information technology and constantly improving software systems are already being used widely to optimise the efficiency of energy networks; they can also be used to boost the capacity of road and rail networks, including the ability to recover costs.

Adopting an up-to-date software is the key to improving the efficiency of Belt and Road ports and airports. Additional gains can be made if shipping and flight information systems can be combined with the information systems of land transport operators.

[24] These examples draw on Section 8 and Annex 2 of the Belt and Road monograph (referenced in footnote 1) which set out many other opportunities to make measurable gains in the efficiency of transport, communications and energy networks.

4.4.2.2. Authorised Exporters

All customs authorities need strategies that allow them to let most of them through and concentrating inspections on a few. This requires risk management based on information whether items are being shipped by trusted producers or agents. The Authorized Economic Operator (AEO) programme is a systematic way to define who can be trusted.[25] Several Belt and Road governments have implemented this system. Encouraging and assisting others to follow their example would lead to significant positive network effects.

4.4.2.3. Single Windows for Customs Clearance

The benefit of creating single windows to streamline customs procedures by individual governments is greatly magnified by creating a network of single windows, for example, among as many BRI participants as possible, using interoperable software systems, backed by efficient real-time exchange of information. ASEAN's progress towards their region-wide system provides a useful precedent (Luddy 2012).[26]

4.4.2.4. Belt and Road Travel Card

Making it possible for citizens of any Belt and Road country to travel freely through all others — as they did along the original Silk Road — can be a long-term objective. This will have to be approached in several stages, striking a balance between promoting the mobility of trusted travellers while avoiding the security and political risks of unrestricted international travel.

An early step would be to issue a Belt and Road Travel Card to business people who already hold an APEC Business Travel Card, then to widen its coverage to all BRI countries who are willing and

---

[25] The AEO program is described in Humphries (2014).

[26] This paper provides an excellent explanation of the actual process of, and the practical human and institutional constraints to, implementing cooperative arrangements to facilitate international economic transactions.

able to implement essential software and security protocols. A subsequent step can be to extend eligibility to all skilled workers. If these stages can be implemented successfully, then it could be widened at some time to include additional categories, for example, officials or academics.

4.4.3. *e-Commerce and Digital Connectivity*

All e-commerce depends on digital connectivity. Realising the potential benefits generated by the Belt and Road programme will depend on ensuring that data can flow smoothly among all of their economies and to connect them to the rest of the world. Full and real-time access to computing and information anywhere in Belt and Road economies can unlock the technology potential of the "Internet of things", blockchain technology and e-commerce in all regions connected to the physical and digital Belt and Road.

The technology needed for low-cost access to the Internet already exists. Access to information will also depend on policies to ensure adequate competition among service providers. Current concerns about content, privacy and where data are stored impede the flow of data. These problems can be overcome in time if mutual respect and mutual trust among Belt and Road participants is progressively improved. The benefit of the Belt and Road program will depend on ensuring that data can flow smoothly among all of their economies and connect them to the rest of the world.

5. Financing the BRI

The number of countries participating in the BRI continues to grow, so it is not possible to know how much will be needed. Current estimates indicate that the investment needs for the Belt and Road could be in the order of US$15–20 trillion up to 2030, and more is likely to be needed in later years.[27]

[27] The McKinsey Global Institute estimates a global requirement for infrastructure investment at US$57 trillion over 18 years, till 2030. The BRI estimate was derived

There is wide consensus that it will be necessary to attract private investment to finance in economic infrastructure on such a large scale.[28] The challenge of attracting more private financing for this infrastructure, much of which will be in public goods, has been studied extensively. However, there is no solution in sight to overcome the correct perceptions of the high risk of investing in economic infrastructure, especially in developing economies. Unless that problem is solved, the Belt and Road vision will not be realised.

5.1. *Limiting Risks*

Trillions of dollars have been accumulated by sovereign wealth funds and institutional investors, so global savings are available to finance investment in economic infrastructure.[29] However, only a very small proportion of these savings is being invested in economic infrastructure, due to the perceived high risks of investing in infrastructure, which include the following:

- uncertainty about the policy environment of many economies;
- long lead times;

from this figure together with the fact that the 65 participating countries account for some 40% of the global gross domestic product (GDP). *Infrastructure Productivity: How to Save $1 Trillion a Year*, January 2013.

[28] This consensus was acknowledged in the Keynote Speech by Luky Eko Wuryanto, Vice President (AIIB) to the Deepening Asian Economic and Financial Cooperation: Promoting regional integrated development seminar, International Economics and Financial Institute (IEFI), Ministry of Finance China, Beijing, 21 October 2016.

[29] The International Monetary Fund (IMF) notes that: "*Institutional investors such as pension funds, insurance companies and mutual funds, and other investors such as sovereign wealth funds hold around $100 trillion in assets under management. In 2013 CityUK estimated that pension funds, insurance companies, and mutual funds respectively held $33.9, $26.5 and $26.1 trillion in assets under management (see Figure 2). In addition, sovereign wealth funds and central banks have accumulated savings approaching $15 trillion.*" (see http://www.imf.org/external/pubs/ft/wp/2016/wp1618.pdf).

- inadequate project design;
- difficulty of predicting costs and demand.

Until these risks are reduced, it is unrealistic to expect investment in infrastructure from institutional investors, especially in developing economies with weak institutions and governance.[30]

5.1.1. *Policy Risks*

Attracting any investment, including investment in infrastructure projects will be far more likely in economies with sound macro economic management that reduces the risk of unpredictable inflation or foreign exchange crises that cut off sources of essential materials. A legal system that protects property right, enforces contracts and provides swift and fair dispute settlement procedures is certainly desirable. Efficient regulation of domestic markets to ensure safety and encourage competition will help reduce costs. Capable institutions are needed for efficient operations and for adequate cost recovery.[31]

Unfortunately, many of these essential ingredients of a sound investment environment are missing in many Belt and Road economies.[32] Government guarantees and/or subsidies can compensate for weaknesses in the policy environment to launch a few new projects.

---

[30] All of these risks have been acknowledged and discussed in official Chinese publications (including the 2015 Action Plan), as well as in researches on the prospects for investment in economic infrastructure, including Grenville (2013). Extensive work by the OECD (see http://www.oecd.org/dataoecd/61/27/40953164.pdf and http://www.oecd.org/dataoecd/59/33/48634596.pdf) and by multilateral development banks (see MDBs Joint Declaration of Aspirations on Actions to Support Infrastructure Investment, Annex to the G20 2016 communique).

[31] The 2015 Action Plan and a Chinese State Council document (available at http://www.gov.cn/zhengce/content/2016-03/15/content_5053647.htm, p. 8) stress the importance of a sound policy environment for BRI investments.

[32] See http://www.chinausfocus.com/finance-economy/one-belt-one-road-a-new-source-of-rent-for-ruling-elites-in-central-asia and http://www.chinausfocus.com/finance-economy/one-belt-one-road-a-new-source-of-rent-for-ruling-elites-in-central-asia.

But they will not be sufficient to attract sustained investment in any economy.

5.1.2. *Financial Risks*

Early investments in developing Belt and Road economies are being financed by generous lending from Chinese sources. The lack of transparency about the design and implementation of these projects, combined with lack of assurance about their consistency with the stated market principles of the BRI, has raised widespread concerns about their economic viability.[33] If many projects fail to generate expected benefits, they will lead to significant debt servicing problems for China's Belt and Road partners.[34]

Some have argued[35] that this is a means of providing Chinese leverage, but that would destroy the prospects for the stated objective of a long-term partnership based on mutual respect and mutual benefit. It is far more likely that China would need to write off loans for non-performing projects.[36] Even China's pockets are not deep enough to accept such risks for long.[37] It is essential to create a well-documented

---

[33] See https://www.nytimes.com/2017/06/10/world/asia/china-bridges-infrastructure.html?_r=0, http://www.eastasiaforum.org/2017/05/24/setback-in-sri-lanka-for-chinas-silk-road/ and Huang (2015).

[34] https://www.ft.com/content/8c59e674-e746-11e4-8e3f-00144feab7de#axzz4874hO4s3 cites fears, expressed in private, of Chinese officials of significant potential losses on loans to some poorly governed Asian economies.

[35] See https://www.project-syndicate.org/commentary/china-one-belt-one-road-loans-debt-by-brahma-chellaney-2017-01?utm_source=Project%20Syndicate%20Newsletter&utm_campaign=ebb6631dad-sunday_newsletter_31_12_2017&utm_medium=email&utm_term=0_73bad5b7d8-ebb6631dad-93521953.

[36] The Hambantota port in Sri Lanka is widely cited as an unviable investment that imposed an impossible debt burden, leading to China accepting the financial loss and taking ownership of a loss-making operation. See for example, http://www.eria.org/Mid-Term%20Review%20of%20the%20Implementation%20of%20AEC%20Blue%20Print-Executive%20Summary.pdf, which also discusses potential debt problems for Pakistan.

[37] Xu (2014) questions about investing in the infrastructure and technology in some developing countries: "*can bring China sufficient return on investment, especially since the political and economic environment in the countries involved is uncertain at best.*

track record of economically sound early investments in Belt and Road projects to reduce the current high perceptions of financial risk.

5.1.3. *Political Risks*

The political, strategic and commercial concerns about the BRI by several significant economies, including India and Japan, can be eased. A determination to be more transparent would help to ensure that the BRI is designed to benefit all, not just its participants. Placing the Belt and Road programme on progressively more commercial footing will ease concerns that it is designed mainly to create opportunities for China's state-owned enterprises. A demonstrated willingness to help improve the capacity of developing economies to manage investment and, in due course, the capacity to mobilise financing for investment, can foster mutual trust.

A decisive move towards shared leadership is vital. If it can be achieved, then there will be shared support for the initiative and China will no longer be alone in reassuring the rest of the world that it aims to benefit everyone. Once the Belt and Road is seen to be a multilateral, rather than just a Chinese initiative, it will become easier to reach out to governments and encourage more of them to become constructive participants.

5.2. *Sharing Costs and Benefits*

Many Belt and Road projects will provide domestic or international public goods, so governments will need to contribute a significant share of the financing. Except for China, most participating governments have a limited capacity to invest in infrastructure.

Early investments in developing Belt and Road economies are being financed by generous lending from Chinese financial institutions which have accepted the repayment risks. This approach has generated the much-needed momentum by delivering rapid

Investing in these countries might risk increasing China's debt burden for the sake of limited returns."

and visible economic benefits. However, as already noted, China cannot be expected to continue to carry this financing burden indefinitely.

To facilitate cooperation based on mutual respect and a right to shared leadership (as distinct from donor–recipient relations), all Belt and Road participants will need to take responsibility for a gradually greater share of financing. Project risks are also more likely to be lower if governments have a substantial financial stake in the success of projects located in their countries.

This points to an urgent need to improve the capacity of all Belt and Road economies, including many developing economies, to find ways to mobilise resources for investment in their economic infrastructure. Unless more participants can begin to share the costs of investments, rather than just the benefits, the BRI will be no more than a large Chinese aid programme — that would not be consistent with the intention that long-term relations among BRI economies should be based on mutual respect rather than one-way dependence.[38]

5.3. *Mobilizing Private Investment for Economic Infrastructure*

Most public–private–partnerships (so-called PPPs) to encourage private sector investment have proven to be disappointing. The risks to investors are not reduced, and the additional costs resulting from this are either passed on to governments or lead to inflated financing

[38] Chinese officials and researchers have made it clear that the Belt and Road is not Marshall Plan. The Belt and Road is open to all, while the Marshall Plan was designed to reward America's friends and exclude its enemies after World War II. In a 2016 speech in Shenzhen, Li Xiangyang explained that the

> "*Marshall Plan after World War II was a US economic aid program to assist its European allies for a short time, actually it lasted less than four years.*"

In contrast, the Belt and Road is expected to be long-term investment over several decades and much larger in scope — many trillions are expected to be invested compared to the Marshall Plan spending of 130 billion in current dollars.

costs and unaffordable user charges (Arezki *et al.* 2016).[39] Governments cannot expect cost-effective private investment in economic infrastructure until existing projects are running efficiently and project risks are lowered.

A sound strategy for attracting private sector investment in economic infrastructure needs to balance and satisfy both public policy and commercial objectives — so that private capital can be attracted at a reasonable cost (measured in both user charges and debt-servicing terms). Such a strategy will need to build on a sound understanding of the nature of public goods and project development cycles.[40]

5.3.1. *Financing Public Goods*

All investments in connectivity will need to be paid for from a combination of direct cost recovery or by taxpayers. For most investments in the public goods needed for better connectivity, including those to improve skills and upgrade institutions, some subsidy will be required, especially in their early years. Massive investments in public goods will need to be sustained for many years. That will not be possible unless the following conditions are met.

First, while investments may not be commercially viable, they will need to have an adequate economic rate of return. Governments will then be able to recover a significant share of their investments through a combination of direct user charges and additional revenue from the increased economic activity generated by these projects. The subsidy required will then be limited to the difference between the economic rate of return and the rate of return which would have been needed for private sector financing.

Second, all the subsidy should be a capital subsidy, injected during the early stages of the project cycle. Once the project is up and running, it should be possible to recover the full financial cost of

---

[39] This paper provides an excellent overview of the issues and options for private sector financing of economic infrastructure.

[40] This financing strategy is set out in detail in Annex 1 of the monograph references in footnote 1.

operations and maintenance through direct, or indirect, cost recovery.[41] It will then be realistic to expect private investors to invest in a fully operational project. They could be expected to invest an amount which is a significant share of the costs incurred to design and construct the project, releasing funds for future public investment in public goods. That is essential for sustaining improvements in connectivity.[42]

5.3.2. *An Innovative Strategy to Mobilise Private Investment*

It will not be easy to strike a balance between affordability and financial sustainability. However, there are precedents for success where governments have been willing to engage teams of highly qualified professionals to take good ideas through each phase of the project development cycle.

Motivated by well-designed incentives, these teams can work with public authorities during the low-cost, but high-risk, origination and structuring phases and then partner with other stakeholders to finance and execute the construction phases. These teams can then exit after projects are up and running with the option to refinance projects using private capital (at an affordable cost) once the risks have been reduced.

Such a project catalysis strategy has been implemented successfully by Infraco in both Asia and Africa.[43] Infraco is an independent private-sector enterprise funded by the Private Infrastructure

---

[41] Direct cost recovery is technically feasible for many investments in physical connectivity. For example, tolls can be imposed on roads or bridges, and freight and energy transmission charges can be set on rail and energy links. However, micro economic theory and experience indicate that it is not easy to design pricing policies that will meet cost recovery expectations and generate expected demand for the use of these links. Moreover, it can be very hard to impose charges for some investments. The alternative is indirect cost recovery, using some of the revenue from the additional economic generated by new infrastructure assets.

[42] The need for private sector investment in economic infrastructure and the stages of project cycles are discussed in detail in the monograph cited in footnote 1.

[43] See www.infracoasia.com and www.infracoafrica.com.

Development Group (PIDG) — a multi-donor organisation with members from seven countries and the World Bank Group.[44] Infraco operations have leveraged US$1.2 billion of PIDG capital to attract US$21 billion of both private and international financial institutions capital into infrastructure projects. Governments involved in the BRI should support initiatives along these lines to raise private sector investment. Starting from a small base, the volume of private investment in economic infrastructure could then be scaled up, gradually, to finance a growing share of investment in the Belt and Road networks.

6. Conclusion

China has provided welcome early leadership of the BRI and almost all of the financing for early investments. China is, therefore, the clear leader and decision maker for the direction of the initiative set out in many bilateral agreements.

China is also accepting the risks of investments. These risks are very high in some of the participating countries with weak governments, sometimes pervasive corruption and ineffective institutions. China may be willing and able to sustain its generosity for some time. However, that will not lead to cooperation which is consistent with the agreed principles of mutual trust and mutual respect as well as mutual benefit. A system with one dominant leader — China — will be a massive aid programme rather than any new model of cooperation.

Many years will be needed for a transition from a hub-and-spokes pattern of cooperation towards collective leadership. Shared decision-making, based on mutual respect, will not happen until a critical mass of participants in the BRI are able to finance a meaningful share of investments and acquire the skills and institutions needed to operate new assets in coordination with other governments. The capacity for policy coordination relies on sharing of information, experience, expertise and technology. That, in turn, requires an effective network

[44] See www.pidg.org.

for regular, policy-oriented consultations among officials, business people and researchers.

So far, there is no assurance that the political leaders of the BRI are taking adequate steps to build the consultative and financing models essential for tackling the long-term challenges of managing a transition to shared leadership of the process. Therefore, the future of the BRI remains quite uncertain.

References

Arezki, R., Bolton, P., Peters, S., Samama, F. and Stiglitz, J. (2016). From global savings glut to financing infrastructure: The advent of investment platforms. IMF Working Paper. Available at: http://www.imf.org/external/pubs/ft/wp/2016/wp1618.pdf.

Bhattacharyay, B. and De, P. (2009). Restoring Asian silk route: Towards an integrated Asia. ADBI Working Paper 140. Tokyo, Asian Development Bank Institute. Available at: http://www.adbi.org/working-paper/2009/06/17/3025.restoring.asian.silk.route/.

Drysdale, P. (1998). *International Economic Pluralism*; Allen and Unwin and the 1991 Seoul APEC Declaration. Available at: http://www.apec.org/~/media/Files/MinisterialStatements/Annual/1991/91_amm_jms.pdf.

ERIA (2012). Available at: http://www.eria.org/MidTerm%20Review%20of%20the%20Implementation%20of%20AEC%20Blue%20Print-Executive%20Summary.pdf.

Grenville, S. (2013). Financing for infrastructure: What contribution can the G-20 make? In *Tax, Infrastructure, Anti-Corruption, Energy, and the G-20*, Lowy Institute.

Hong Kong Trade Development Council (2017). One Belt One Road gaining traction: Unanswered questions leave funding uncertain. *Hong Kong Trade Development Council Commentary*. Available at: http://beltandroad.hktdc/en/commentary/one-belt-one-road-gaining-traction-unanswered-questions-leave-funding-uncertain.

Huang, Y. (2015). Don't let 'One Belt, One Road' fall into the trap of Japan's overseas investments. *Zhongguo Gaige Wang*, 10 February.

Humphries, N. (2014). Global value chains, border management and Australian trade. Lowy Institute Analysis. Available at: http://apo.org.au/node/41527.

Luddy (2012). Background Briefing Note on Institutional Connectivity. Presented to the APEC Symposium 2013, Jakarta, Indonesia, December.

Shen, D. (2015). Available at: http://www.chinausfocus.com/finance-economy/china-advances-its-one-belt-one-road-strategy/#sthash.cXLHPTfv.dpuf.

Wang, W. (2018). Belt and Road Initiative: Creating a smoother path. Chongyang Institute for Financial Studies. Available at: http://en.rdcy.org/displaynews.php?id=46318.

Wilson, J. S., Mann, C. and Otsuki, T. (2003). Trade facilitation and Economic Development: Measuring the impact. Policy Research Paper 2988.

Xu, G. (2014). Looking at the 'One Belt, One Road' strategy from a return on investment point of view. *Financial Times* (Chinese Version), 20 November.

Zhang (2016). The making and implementation of the Belt and Road (B&R) Policy. Seminar Paper, EABER, ANU.

Chapter

12

Conclusion

Linda Low

1. Introduction

Authors giving external views, mainly as non-participants in the Belt and Road Initiative (BRI) route, in the 11 preceding chapters have presented BRI as globalisation with Chinese characteristics. It is a lifelong project for leaders in China, economies in direct participation and all those involved in the evolving geopolitics and geoeconomics. This concluding chapter will not try to summarise the diverse and strategically important points already made.

Seemingly ending with more questions than answers as social sciences go, with worldwide attention, the BRI will remain a work-in-progress with ongoing research for the ongoing long and winding journey. Given the scale, magnitude and complexity of challenges and responses depending on different national perspectives, the BRI will provide economic growth as a certainty with multidisciplinary findings for debate and nuances for interpretation.

2. China's Arrival in a More Challenging Bipolar World with the US

As the US–Soviet cold war eclipsed, China has arrived with economic fundamentals to "stir the pot". Xi Jinping unveiled his OBOR-renamed-BRI (in 2013 and 2018, respectively) with OBOR as the literal translation in Chinese and BRI still a conceptual plan rather than a physical comprehensive long-term masterplan with a purpose-oriented strategy. By 2018, Xi sensibly and diplomatically adopted the ASEAN Way of consensual decision-making, and not any Sino-BRI Way.

China needs ASEAN as much for ASEAN commodities to fuel its factories as for political support. The ASEAN Way embodies the six principles of ASEAN's Treaty of Amity and Cooperation (TAC) for mutual respect for independence, sovereignty, equality, territorial integrity and national identity; right to national existence without external interference, subversion or coercion; non-interference in internal affairs; peaceful way to settle differences or disputes; no threat or use of force and effective ASEAN cooperation.

Extending these principles across all BRI participants is trickier, but ASEAN10 can be a powerful group of developing and some more developed economies for exemplary conduct of interstate behaviour and decision-making. Quintessentially, BRI progress needs consensus building, not BRI associated with China by name-cum-ownership, even with Chinese finessing its construction in the first place.

The hardware aspect of different sizes of railway tracks to necessitate transfer of passengers and goods onto different national trains is unavoidable. The software aspect of managing cross-border immigration and other cross-border control is no different from managing busy seaports and even airports and telecommunication portals to grow along the BRI. Efficient fast turnaround matters all round for cooperation, collaboration with trust and harmonious bargaining to join the dots on the BRI map.

After Deng Xiaoping's momentous opening in 1978, Xi Jinping is as astute as the globaliser, almost by default as Donald Trump's

Make America[1] Great Again seems like building walls in contrast to BRI connectivity. Xi as the globaliser is witnessed in his speeches in Davos (World Economic Forum, 16th January 2017), Boao Forum (12th April 2018) modelled on WEF-Davos and the 19th Communist Party Congress (18th October 2018), speaking only in Chinese, is just as telling.

Xi's economic understanding underpinning the BRI is as clear as Trump's "mad" trade war by tariffs to make America Great Again, seeming only retaliatory. The facts are, first the US, remaining the importer-of-the-last resort as Americans seem born to consume, has the world's largest trade deficit for about half a century. The trade deficit is more in goods than services. On the other side of the coin, the Asians (Japanese) seem born to save.

Second, as Americans buy with cheap credit (no surprise, the global financial crisis by 2007), China became the factory of the world, thanks to multinational corporations (MNCs) relocating there including a dozen of Taiwan's Foxconn factories[2] making Apple iPhones an ironical trilogy of unholy matrimony. No surprise that China overtook Japan as the second largest economy after the US by gross domestic product (GDP).

Third, Trump sees trade deficit not by the US losing its comparative and/or competitive advantages as structural fault lines *vis-à-vis* importers winning. In his business thinking of only win–lose, no win–win or all win, his trade war attacks all, allies (European Union, Mexico) and foes (China), with no self-diagnosis of any structural malaise.

Fourth, even North American Free Trade Agreement (NAFTA) is being renegotiated, forgetting that it was begun by Ronald Reagan in 1984, completed by Bill Clinton in 1994 more with Mexico in mind. Mexico then a basket case could be a competitive buffer for US MNCs and DFI instead of going to China. A more prosperous

[1] Chen (2018) pointed out that Trump's America may be the USA in his mind, and not America as a continent of North and South to make "great", be it for precise or as tongue-in-cheek.

[2] Half of the world's Apple iPhone production takes place at a sprawling Foxconn complex in Zhengzhou, an iPhone belt by any name.

Mexico, creating jobs at home, would keep out illegal Mexicans across the US's long border.

Fifth, all may have equally forgotten the 1930s Great Depression caused by the Atlantic trade war with allies in an economic war. As noted, the reality is US trade deficits by the 21st century reflect structural weakness in competitive strength not merely as price differentials. Accusations of unfair trade practices, currency manipulation, wage suppression, government subsidies for exports and such serve as comfortable political palliative as Trump simply deterring the US imports.

Equally forgotten is the 21st-century global production–consumption network where retaliation by tariff or non-tariff barriers (NTBs) may not work so simply. Simply, *buy American* may not make America Great Again as the global supply chain and criss-crossing of Apple–Foxconn–China factories have shown. Never mind that a weak US$ favours cheaper imports or a trade deficit, offset by capital inflows, related to gap-saving investment.

US simply spends more than it produces to necessitate the importing of foreign goods and services. As cheap credit fuels debt-financed consumption, increased trade deficit, coping with the total US household debt from a diverse range of mortgages and loans from students, autos to credit cards, sounds like a developing rather than a mature and developed US. The US has to attend to its structural economic and trade issues to regain its greatness.

Sixth is a military and security angle. No less worrisome is the burgeoning US government budget deficit, so the US closed-up military overseas bases with Trump demanding payment for defence from Japan to South Korea. Again, Trump forgot General Douglas MacArthur in the Pacific theatre during World War II. Japan's defeat also meant limiting its defence spending; later more of the same in the Korean War (1950–1953) to extend fighting communism beyond the Korean peninsula.

Maybe, Make America Great Again need not cover military greatness. The world is at peace, even from North Korea as the Trump–Kim Jong Un Meeting in Singapore in 2018 may prove. Taken for granted elsewhere in the world (except the Middle East), the two Koreas want peace for prosperity, especially families at peace, above all else.

On the other hand, China has claimed the status of victimhood, from the Mongol invasion to building the Great Wall and its hibernation from the world until Deng's opening. Xi has mastered a bigger and more artful opening by BRI now as the seventh aspect of China-rising as the renminbi (RMB) way *vis-à-vis* Trump making US Great Again. The BRI along over 65 states offers new allies infrastructural connectivity, jobs and income along the way has to be the better way.

Post-war US supremacy had the US$ reigning as the *de facto* international reserve currency as the US provided the world with liquidity-cum-perceived military strength. It also means the US as a safe haven for others to keep their financial assets, as the perception remains for the US supplies international liquidity by issuing global reserve currency with many economic advantages.

One is seigniorage as the difference of face value of currency note relative to the cost of note issue. With growing foreign demand for US$, the key is more US$ in circulation means more treasury bills at the Fed, so the US can run deficits almost indefinitely by creating more debt or sell assets. As the demand for $-denominated assets, such as US Treasury bonds raising their prices, that lowers interest rates to finance both consumption and investment.

As foreign investors buy low-yield, short-term US assets, US can invest abroad in higher-yielding, long-term assets. As the US usually reaps higher returns as investment than what the US pays for debt, the US earns an exorbitant privilege whereby the $'s role as a major reserve currency allows the US running chronic trade deficits.

The US thus cannot afford to give up its $ as a global reserve currency status which will have major implications for US economy, finance and living standards. Over time, with Japan, then the EU in the global game, the result is the ¥€$ trio. As China-finessed BRI reeves up as globalisation across the board, the RMB[3] is joining the trio ¥€$ as ¥€$R? *In God We Trust* is embedded in the US$, not ¥€$R?

---

[3] In 2015, RMB joined ¥€$£ as the fifth currency in the IMF basket of Special Drawing Right (SDR) as an international reserve asset to augment members' traditional official reserves.

Whether Make US Great Again by Trump will try to win the trade war remains an old Great Depression nightmare. There is enough disruption with globalisation at turbo-speed like technology such as sewbot shedding labour as all robots do or financial technology with cryptocurrencies affecting monetary policy. The BRI as the biggest venture capital project (S&P Global Ratings 2018) be disruptive too.

Ironically again, as Trump wages trade wars on both foes and friends, China gains in geopolitics–geoeconomics. China may want to be a different kind of Asian power *vis-à-vis* Japan, as the BRI attracts former Soviet "stans" as new allies and as a different brand of economic colonisation. Historically, China has always been interested in Southeast Asia. Mao Yuanyi compiled the *Mao Kun* (named for his grandfather) in 1621, which was published in 1628. Modern Chinese sources referred it to *Zheng He's Navigation Map*, all in the Ming dynasty.

Today, the BRI is as much more than trade as extending to oil and gas to renewable as energy security. The need for infrastructure is unquestionable with physical-and-people connectivity and network to achieve benefits perhaps more than free trade agreements (FTAs), regional trade agreements (RTAs) and World Trade Organization (WTO) dismantling tariffs including other NTBs. China's soft power has arrived with BRI as the hard infrastructure versus hard military as threatening the fundamentals of peace for prosperity.

From understanding what the BRI is, or at least so perceived along the way, it remains a debate for what it is not. The BRI is not Marshall Plan by scale, ambition and in peace by China. China claims it is not for China to export its excess capacity. Neither is it a shortcut to the EU versus a connectivity link as Eurasia (Millward 2007, Millward 2013) or Euroasia (combined continental landmass of Europe and Asia), with Indo-Pacific linking the two oceans and two continents rather than Asia-Pacific around the Pacific Ocean.

Whether the BRI is another way to internationalise the RMB depends on how the world would trust the currency as any reserve currency as the ¥€$ trio has. Incidentally, yen diplomacy as the currency for trade and official development assistance (ODA) in Southeast Asia is now the RMB game as well at the same time dedollarisation as in Myanmar (Kubo 2017) is promoting its local currency with more trust.

3. BRI Sharing Prosperity or Issues?

On the financial front, there is the BRI debt-trap diplomacy or BRI globalisation with Chinese characteristics. Malaysia may not be the only country laden with debt owed to the Chinese. China is as keen to put money into developing ports from even Malacca port despite piracy in the Straits of Malacca to the Kra Canal. Thai Kra Canal as not yet an idea whose time has come, but pop up on the horizon, is perhaps the longest delayed infrastructure project in history proposed in the mid-1600s[4] since the Suez Canal and Panama Canal.

China has to balance its BRI as strategically as it also is a claimant to islands from Senkaku (versus Japan) to Spratly (ASEAN claimants including Vietnam with remembrance of its wars with China). The US may worry about freedom of navigation (FON) plus Free and Open Indo-Pacific (FOIP) strategy. The US is different from Singapore also for FON as the US; the small city-state is "remanded" by China for commenting on the Spratly as a non-claimant.

A bigger, more belligerent Taiwan has its new Southbound Policy (NSP) as meeting the US FOIP Strategy.[5] The NSP aligned with FOIP has both opportunities and risks for Taiwan. The NSP aims to help Taiwan form meaningful relationships with Indo-Pacific predicated on arenas in which Taipei has a comparative advantage over Beijing. The aim to foster and preserve favourable geopolitical relationships at a time when China appears ever expanding, whether rising peacefully as per Deng, remains moot. On the other hand, the NSP creates more ire in China for obvious historic reasons.

---

[4] Thailand was then as small trading empire as the Kingdom of Ayutthaya. King of Ayutthaya possessed neither finance nor technology to turn ideas into reality. Japan offered as China did, but North Thailand as Buddhist and the South as Muslim with threat of secession remain to be the problem.

[5] See https://thediplomat.com/2018/06/taiwans-new-southbound-policy-meets-the-us-free-and-open-indo-pacific-strategy/Diplomat, 28 June 2018.

How public–private–partnerships (PPPs) may work for BRI may seem to be attempts to associate government-inspired projects with private sector investors to pay upfront for the construction of infrastructure. The PPP experience has been quite disappointing as explained in one IMF paper.[6] It is far more realistic to expect private sector interest after a project is operating successfully. It will take time for them to be willing to invest (*ex-post*) a large share of the initial costs (including construction) in the BRI and its running.

The BRI remains without a masterplan (not even any hint of work-in-progress), overall lack of transparency and any apparent interest in sharing leadership with partners along the BRI route, the grading for BRIs may be dropping and sinking over time. The good ideas for connectivity, if properly implemented in line with the principles that the BRI/China have expressed, would be the best, but it is finding it hard to follow without some action.

Many BRI conferences, summits and such by as many varied and diverse parties seem to be on the road more than real bricks and mortar. The various chapters bear evidence from near and far. While China claims and wants the Asian Infrastructure Investment Bank (AIIB)[7] as separate from its BRI, the pair is related. History again bears out how China has been wary of the US-dominated World Bank,[8] EU-dominated IMF[9] and leadership in WTO[10] and Japan clearly in charge in the Asian Development Bank (ADB).

---

[6] See Andrew Elek's chapter which cited Arezki *et al.* (2016).

[7] Interestingly, AIIB recruited three Singaporeans: Tony Wan, 73, Senior Adviser on Human Resources (HR) to AIIB president; Mr Pang Yee Ean, 47, Director-General of Investment Operations and former civil servant Thia Jang Ping, 41, to set up AIIB's Economics Unit.

[8] Until Jim Yong Kim an American–Korean from South Korea took the helm in 2012.

[9] Christine Lagarde French lawyer and politician is Managing Director of IMF since 2011; still Europeans are in charge.

[10] Leadership in WTO seems more balanced with Mike Moore, the former prime minister, foreign minister, trade minister and deputy finance minister from New Zealand as head in 1999, Supachai Panitchapakdy as Director-General in 2005 and currently Roberto Azevêdo of Brazil.

The pun seems to be all roads lead back to the Sino–US rivalry. The US needs its own reckoning as seemingly withdrawn to Make America Great Again.[11] Does the US see it as political or geopolitical rivalry more daunting than Vladimir Putin or Putin–Xi as a pair? The US has neither the money nor the people to spare as China has in terms of its largesse in balance of payments (BoP) surpluses and near 1.4 trillion population to even have Chinese populating parts of Spratly as territorial claim by habitation.

Any BRI shadows in Central Asia or Indian proximity may be as unfamiliar to the West, as EU and US, but physically as Asian is nearer if not quite dearer to China. With infrastructure as the prize, barring any BRI-fuelled illiberalism, there are good reasons and logic not to heed BRI. While pledges do not always equal projects to materialise and whether, as in Africa, Chinese villages populated by Chinese labour will happen is yet undetermined, as the Bandung-to-Jakarta railway line has proven with a $5.5 billion deal Indonesia signed with China in 2015, land rights is one problem.

The infamous and enormous Chinese debt trap on small, cash-strapped countries such as Sri Lanka's inability to pay off massive loan of $1.5 billion for the construction of Port Hambantota ended up with an uncomfortable debt-for-equity swap for China in securing a 99-year lease over the port. The theory of a string of pearls strung up by China as a threat to India and its neighbourhood may be a conspiracy theory, but it is there. In the past, Japan was the dominant player in infrastructure projects with the ADB as geoeconomics.

For Malaysia, with the reincarnated Prime Minister Mahathir Mohamad cancelling/postponing the Chinese-backed high-speed rail (HSR) in Kuala Lumpur–Singapore route, there are implications for BRI connectivity to the rest of the way south to Indonesia. High-flyers in budget airlines may do rather than the HSR, but goods and cargoes on the BRI are more economical. As petty as politics can get, Mahathir's comeback means the death of all

---

[11] See https://thediplomat.com/2018/05/the-us-needs-a-reality-check-on-chinas-belt-and-road/.

deposed Prime Minister Najib Razak's future projects as planned. The HSR may be the first to go.[12]

For all, careful reflection of threat and opportunity remains paramount as all relook at the evolving geoeconomics as well. Subregional conflicts come into play as land grabs in Myanmar connected to the BRI with ethnic minorities, providing fodder to armed insurgencies raging inside the country.

The Koh Kong Port is part of the Tianjin Union Development Group's Cambodia–China Comprehensive Investment and Development Pilot Port Zone as an illegal 45,100-hectare land concession. The company has owned the land free-of-charge for the last decade by a secretly negotiated lease. Construction of tourist destinations and industrial infrastructure has led to accusations of environmental degradation and human rights abuses.

The BRI will have much to ruminate on sustainable ecological aspects, as much as the orangutan seems a threatened species as it is already.[13] How Chinese colonies are taking shape from Africa at the other one end of the BRI, Gwadar Port in Pakistan, Cambodia to Sri Lanka, all have long-term implications for all to be aware of.

Withdrawn as the US is, it should understand what makes BRI funds attractive to cash-strapped developing economies with weak infrastructure and massive needs. The US may also recognise the flaws of the Chinese development model exported via the BRI compared to the inherent advantages that US investors can offer. Coupling all with private sector knowledge and expertise to transfer, and experience of governments for making comprehensive strategy, the US and its corporate sector can help build the BRI as competitive, peaceful

---

[12] See, *Transportation Research Part D: Transport and Environment* 17(1), pp. 1–7 (2012) that analyses the climate implications of investments in high-speed railway lines given uncertainty in future transport demand, technology and power production. Available at: https://www.sciencedirect.com/science/article/pii/S1361920911001155.

[13] See Laurance, W.F. Director of the Centre for Tropical Environmental and Sustainability Science (TESS); https://cleantechnica.com/2018/05/31/the-dangers-of-chinas-belt-road-initiative/ and https://www.chinadialogue.net/blog/10726-Why-scientists-fear-the-AIIB/en.

and prosperous for 21st-century Indo-Pacific, Euroasia or Eurasia or other economic-centric routes.

How BRI is changing dynamics within China, as well as outside in the US, Australia, New Zealand, ASEAN and the rest, needs scrutiny. China and its BRI as building roads is its form of leadership in Asia in contrast to the relative abdication by US and Japan in Asia just as how geopolitics may change with the two Koreas possibly getting closer are scenarios beyond the scope and time for this volume. Similar to the Sino–US rivalry going in the global sphere, would the China–Japan infrastructure nexus turn into competition or collaboration?

Can cooperation build ASEAN and Asia the much-needed infrastructure? China and Japan have intensified efforts to build infrastructure. Both have placed infrastructure at the heart of regional strategies in the new era of infrastructure diplomacy. China's flagship was BRI in 2013, and Japan initiated Partnership for Quality Infrastructure in 2015. At the same time, ASEAN also reoriented its growth strategies to prioritise infrastructure. China and Japan facilitate the shift via offering big financing and by increasing infrastructure exports. Across the big ticket infrastructure contracts were fought over almost exclusively by firms from China and Japan.

Some illustrations offer glimpses for the BRI: ASEAN's most heavily populated Indonesia is a good case in point illustrated by trends, all spoilt for choice. In the period 2015–2019, the Indonesian government estimated that it needs some $360 billion in infrastructure investment. This expenditure on transport infrastructure is more than Singapore, Malaysia, Thailand, Vietnam and the Philippines combined. Of particular interest to Japan and China as financiers and contractors is Indonesia's desire to build HSR.

President Joko Widodo has unveiled his global maritime strategy with five objectives for security, stability and economic prosperity in the region[14] in synchrony with the BRI. It involves the following: (a) rebuild Indonesia's maritime culture, (b) maintain and manage

[14] *Jakarta Post*, 13 November 2014 at the East Asia summit, President Jokowi Widodo announced his signature maritime-axis doctrine spanning the Pacific and Indian Ocean region (PACINDO).

marine resources, (c) provide priority to the development of maritime infrastructure and connectivity, (d) through maritime diplomacy, Indonesia to invite other nations to cooperate in the marine field and eliminate the source of conflicts at sea and (e) develop its maritime defence forces. As "big brother", Indonesia's leadership is a huge fillip to BRI.

Jokowi's ideas about Indonesia as a global maritime fulcrum includes the first major HSR project opened for bidding as 150-kilometre HSR link from Jakarta to the fourth largest city, Bandung. After due diligence and feasibility studies, Japanese officials were close to securing the project in 2015 as the window for bidding drew to close. The Chinese offer sought to undercut Japanese and change specifications of HSR. The Chinese side did not require full Indonesia government guarantee in contrast to Japan's offer.

The race to the bottom ensued, as both China and Japan finessed with money and reduced the timeframe for project completion and such. As the Chinese consortium won the project, Japan was accusing the Chinese consortium of offering unrealistic timescales, underestimating project costs and others. Such start hiccups will bug construction along a longer BRI route involving many more nationalities and terrains. More than firms from China and Japan, the BRI will attract other global companies and parties, including non-governmental organisations (NGOs).

In particular, Prime Minister Shinzo Abe's stance on China's BRI evolved from reticence to acknowledge that potential synergies exist. In May 2018, the Japan Bank for International Cooperation proposed joint Japan–China consortium to build the HSR system in Thailand. If the project goes forward, it will be the first time for contractors from both countries to work together in an infrastructure project in a third country. As both governments plan to establish a public–private council to discuss common infrastructure projects, the early signs of cooperation built may be meaningful, depending on both sides' ability to compromise.

Japan's largest BRI concern centres on BRI's opacity, governance and debt risks among other concerns. These concerns have not disappeared. Realistically, China should seek a more moderate stance with

Japan. Can geopolitics be temporarily put aside for the geoeconomics? With Trump losing interest except to make America Great Again, some joint Asian–ASEAN leadership may not be bad? Can the BRI rouse India to some opening too?

Be it BRI, Japan's FOIP Strategy or Asia–Africa Growth Corridor conceived in collaboration with India, all negotiations mean compromises. It is a long, winding way to go, with as many obstacles to overcome as gains to make. Whether the changes in North–South Korea dynamics will add more tracks to the BRI is another unknown area. Peace as a rare commodity in the Korean peninsula is the most sought-after ingredient to build prosperity.

In the final analysis, the BRI further shifts global strategic landscape in China's favour with infrastructure lending as the primary lever for global influence. Planned network infrastructure projects financed by China's bilateral lenders, China Development Bank (CDB), Export–Import Bank of China (CEXIM), new multilateral AIIB are historically unprecedented in scope.

The BRI seems as the only natural progression of the global sea change (literally and figuratively) to develop all economies along its way with infrastructure and finance. Perhaps, the West has long ceded leadership to China with the phenomenon largely driven not by foreign policy but by domestic infrastructure policy. Trump may have joined the EU late with its EuroStar and EuroPort projects. The BRI spanning billion-plus populous China and India is only part of the arithmetic. Whether Asia rising as a whole in the new century is linked to the BRI as the hip is another paradigm.

The Great Wall old mindset to keep out barbarians and victimhood has changed to the diametrically opposite, as China and BRI open new frontiers. China is yet to reveal its ambition, with its interest extending to the Arctic for routes and even outer space for resources. China joins the US and the USSR, both started since the 1950s and 1960s in exploring space assets, enabling and weaponising space and command. The difference is with both money and people, China may prove to be more powerful in a different strategic game.

China has established two of its own courts for dealing with BRI maritime and overland disputes, respectively, with many outstanding worrisome questions. Construction projects inevitably create disputes, no less along the BRI. Such monopoly[15] with China as the BRI owner-cum-operator and Chinese courts as the judge-cum-jury may render futile other courts, including the London Court of International Arbitration or international courts in Hong Kong or Singapore, which follow the international New York Convention of the 1950s.

4. BRI at Home and BRI Abroad

One conclusion tendered is for more thoughts and views for the BRI to include a domestic section to complement and supplement the external BRI to become a reality. It spans across some 70 economies over two continents and two oceans from Asia to Europe as intended, starting from Xi'an. It is possibly the biggest construction and investment project on earth for all in general and for China in particular to catch up with the US even faster. It is another matter whether it means peaceful coprosperity or otherwise.

History has seen the rise and fall from the Roman Empire to many of China's own empires. Japan imploded on its own accord to its lost decades, with China taking its place as the second largest economy by GDP in 2011. China may be even overtaking the US between 2020 and 2030. The scenario is beyond this book, neither is there another book providing any roadmap and literary journey to follow that of the BRI.

Three arguments for a domestic branch of the BRI are offered. The first is for economic growth attained, overtaking Japan as noted, for economic development should to for China. Deemed simply as quality of life per capita GDP, economic development is

[15] In 2018, the Republic of Djibouti terminated its partnership with DP World to operate its Doraleh Container Terminal (DCT) to augment the capacity of the International Autonomous Port of Djibouti. The joint venture for DP World to operate DCT in a 30-year concession agreement in 2006 came into effect in 2008. The unilateral termination followed an unsuccessful suit in 2014 by Djibouti to exit, claiming improper payments and illegal control. China may exploit the situation to gain control of ports as in Djibouti and more along the BRI way. See https://www.ft.com/content/b64d7f2e-8f4d-11e8-b639-7680cedcc421, *Financial Times*, 25 July 2018.

another matter as China pays attention to pollution as the detritus of fast growth, with income distribution and inequality just as nagging. Technology has enabled China to grow its own food baskets, including growing rice in salt water without land grabs as in Bangladesh.

Various models of other developed countries in America (US and Canada), the EU and other Scandinavian and Australasian economies may bear some lessons for China. As clear as the BRI is the external foreign policy arm of China's peaceful rising, it cannot forget to keep happy its domestic arm of 1.4 trillion people. In plain sight, China needs its own domestic BRI as infrastructure is as needful and lacking in its central and western parts compared to the much developed and prosperous coastal side.

The second reason is the crucial balancing act for China to develop its domestic BRI arising from the challenge of rural–urban migration. This leaves as much deficit in its agricultural sector and farms. Plainly, the question about who feeds 1.4 trillion people is an uneasy situation to invite turmoil all round. One strategy, as the flying geese model goes,[16] has China moving its factories inland to the countryside lured from the coast as Xi Jinping focuses on rural revival.

A case in point is a factory in Henan run by the Jintai Garment Company making clothes for foreign brands such as American Eagle and Uniqlo. Instead of exporting labour to various coastal Special Economic Zones (SEZs), Henan is bringing them back as authorities are building factories in its villages to counter migration. The rural–urban migration has thinned its population as well as agriculture, with crops untended. Brought up by grandparents, many children have other social issues over time.

The Communist Party of China (CCP) needs domestic stability not social unrest as much by seeking to revitalise the countryside. The need to address income inequality is as imperative as ensuring food baskets to feed 1.4 trillion people. Rural wages and standards of living

[16] Among Japanese scholars writing on the rise of Japan as the technological leader in the development of Southeast Asia in the 1930s, the flying geese model gained traction in the 1960s as branded by Akamatsu (1962).

have stagnated to result in the rural–urban shift. Creating rural agricultural jobs has become as urgent and vital as jobs in big cities for manufacturing, finance among others. Long-term, continued economic growth and development is a pincer strategy with an external and internal BRI complementing and supplementing each other.

From first-tier cities such as Beijing and Shanghai to fourth-tier cities, county towns and villages joining the consumer class constitute the real aim of the rural revitalisation strategy. The case study[17] of the shift is in Henan where its Hua county houses the first satellite factories, as garment factories relocated wholesale from the wealthier coastal regions. Jintai Garment has satellite factories rebuilt in rural villages with funding from poverty alleviation initiatives. If it draws a circle on a map and finds enough villagers to employ, it will build a factory. Jintai Garment based in the affluent coastal province of Zhejiang is operating small textile factories in Hua county since 2015.

Finally, the third argument for a domestic BRI is to twin with the external BRI to avoid the critique of China merely exporting its excess capacity. The external BRI cannot totally absorb all excess capacity as exported. China like continental US and Europe needs infrastructure direly. Faced with SOEs as zombies as China has the largest SOE sector in the world, the domestic BRI may help ease layoff fears for struggling SOEs with some 20 million jobs as potential redundancies. A 2017 report compiled by the OECD showed 51,000 SOEs in China valued at US$29.2 trillion, which puts the challenge into perspective as by the end of 2017, China had a corporate debt amounting to 159% of GDP or about 60% of the total corporate debt.[18]

A two-pronged BRI at home and abroad would also assuage the rest of the world that China has both internal and external responses to its challenges. The domestic and external branches of BRI will together lend greater weight to ensure that China does not export its excess capacity as well as its potential financial debt crisis. The debt

[17] *Financial Times*, 3 April 2018; Available at: https://www.ft.com/content/fe86f76c-1215-11e8-8cb6-b9ccc4c4dbbb.

[18] See OECD Economic Surveys China March 2017 in http://www.oecd.org/eco/surveys/economic-survey-china.htm and McMahon (2018).

crisis is as real within China as it is abroad. Whether the world can withstand and suffer another global financial crisis like the one that occurred in the Wall Street, US in 2007–2008 is a question that should worry all humanity, this time it could occur in China.

On top of this debt crisis, an implosion in China from social unrest and domestic instability is not just President Xi's nightmare. It should be worrisome to everyone as it would affect the socio-economics of the world jointly and severally. There may be some political cheer in the Western democratic world like the fall of the USSR with *glasnost* and *perestroika*. The Chinese version may be less disruptive and somewhat peaceful, but again, it is another matter for another book on how China may avoid a breakup as suffered by the USSR.

The domestic BRI is the *raison d'etre* for Xi Jinping to follow up Deng Xiaoping's version of no *glasnost* with the CCP as supreme, but economic opening as successful *perestroika*. Democracy, however defined, may be a luxury good and with prosperity and higher quality of life, will follow in logical sequence.[19] The time is ripe for China's own version of economic freedom or democracy, rather than following the Western democracy as a political choice as suited to its political economy.

In fact, a communist China has enabled its "strongman-politics" for growth first as a young economy needs. With maturity, China's BRI may become an extension of its continued growth and development enabling it to continue to rise peacefully at home and abroad. The BRI is not just about China's globalisation with Chinese characteristics but also concerns China as a global player with its characteristics, with the world accepting American, European, Asian and other versions as emerging.

Any perceived neglect of regional development within China *vis-à-vis* the BRI outside of China will have its backlash on Xi and China's own economic growth and development. Tying the domestic

[19] Extensively debated are many issues like whether democracy as a political system is distinguished from the conditions for its stability and longevity, or democracy is normally good in itself or is election necessary, but there is no sufficient condition for democracy among many others. See a review by Trevor Munroe of Huntington (1994).

and external components is simply a win–win as it is a balanced strategy from all perspectives. As Japan has shown, its own self-implosion from within halted its position as second in global GDP and lost to China which has to be as mindful of its own potential implosion. Inequality across a vast expanse is as inevitable as it is a recipe for implosion and with no peaceful rising within China itself. The domestic BRI may be one valve.

5. Conclusion as China Is Seeking Consensus Globally and Holding Together Domestically

In his first term, President Xi Jinping opened China further with the BRI enunciated in 2013. In his second term in 2018, he made rural revitalisation his priority as a policy challenge to achieve balance and for spreading the rising of China inland. The lack of success to attend to the countryside by his predecessors dating back to Hu Jintao has China's State Council devoting its first official policy document to agriculture. The 2018 Document No. 1 laid out a strategy and expanded party control over rural economic development. Logically, for infrastructure, the likes of BRI domestically have to come about.

Henan's satellite factories to lure young workers back home is the model for many counties in the western region of Xinjiang and Shandong province. Small factories manufacturing garments by employing low-skilled workers need connectivity for the products to be easily shipped from anywhere. In short, the room and capacity to grow is at home and abroad. The BRI in both dimensions is the formulaic secret to China rising, peacefully and attending to environmental, ecological and sustainability concerns.

Making a BRI masterplan across some 70 economies is one challenge more formidable than finessing the construction in money and labour for China. Implementing the masterplan is quite the hardest part. What China can learn at home may not be as easy or simple to replicate abroad as geoeconomics and geopolitics multiply in magnitude and different hues. For a start, delaying, temporalising or even ignoring issues at home such as pollution or human rights may be possible for a while compared to situations abroad in the long BRI.

Yet, keeping domestic stability has become harder with the rising affluence in the country.

To offer any palliative for any negative or pessimistic views on the BRI, it can be said that China led by Xi Jinping is as aware of these challenges and responses as the volume has noted. Having made himself the lifelong president, he is all game to see the BRI through, at home and abroad. What needs attention now is how China can convince the rest of the world, participating and non-participating economies in the BRI, to make up their minds to travel alongside Xi's BRI.

President Xi himself is travelling as extensively with a highly symbolic state visit to Germany as Angela Merkel herself had been to Beijing in May 2018 following Theresa May in January 2018. Both the UK and Germany have recognised there is a lot of business to do in China and with China elsewhere. Bilateral relationships have become more strategic meetings as the Group of 20 or Group of 7 are not as good opportunities for closer relations, with or without Trump. Whether the UK and Germany can work together with China to calm the world's unrest is another consideration.

For the BRI link to the Middle East, during the China–Arab States Cooperation Forum (CASCF) in July 2018 in Beijing,[20] China announced loans to Arab countries to the tune of some US$20 billion, in addition to aid packages of over US$100 million to Palestine, Yemen, Lebanon, Jordan and Syria. President Xi's opening remarks to the Forum offered few details, but heralded financing for economic reconstruction in transportation infrastructure, oil and gas, finance, high-tech fields, digital economy and artificial intelligence (AI) projects to hint at BRI projects across the region.

With an overall lack of BRI as a masterplan from China, concerns and questions are as clear as mud but revolved at least on three key areas in the Middle East. First is the debt sustainability among poor countries, also with China's debt-trap diplomacy as seen in 2017, Sri Lanka's handover of majority control of its Hambantota port. Jordan

[20] Reported in *The Diplomat*, 18 July 2018; https://thediplomat.com/2018/07/chinas-bri-bet-in-the-middle-east/.

seems to be another target by China in its latest round of aid packages.[21]

Second is the lack of transparency of BRI projects, both from China and debtor nations. Such opaque information flows are entirely in keeping with China's character, but not in keeping with international norms of transparency, accountability and verifiability of sovereign nation financial practices around the world. In turn, this begs the question: if the BRI projects are so good for the recipients and China itself, isn't China being not more specific about the details a puzzle? Such reticence worsens, as many of the recipients and China itself are already high on Transparency International's Corruption Index.[22]

Third is the viability of BRI's success in Middle East, a hotchpotch of ongoing conflicts, no less terrorism and extremism. At the simplest level for the BRI, China needs to maintain equilibrium within the hostile Saudi Arabia–Iran relationship in the Middle East. Again, in sum, China may be embroiled in the politics and sustainability in the Middle East from Riyadh to Tehran, with respect to relations with Yemen, Iraq, Syria, Qatar and the UAE, which are all in the Arab equation.

In the end, it is equally debatable whether economics or politics comes first. If it is for economics to provide the wherewithal for political understanding, then the BRI is one way to build upon for jobs, income, GDP and other needs. Logically, peace for greater prosperity follows until elections and politics as time of some turmoil. If German and British leaders seem to be shying away from the Trump

---

[21] The Centre for Global Development, a Washington think tank, March 2018 paper entitled, "Examining the Debt Implications of the Belt and Road Initiative from a Policy Perspective," notes that outside of the China–Pakistan Economic Corridor (CPEC) projects, China does not report cross-border project lending in a systematic or transparent manner. Debtor nations also tend to be less than forthcoming. Therefore, information on BRI projects comes from a variety of publicly available sources.

[22] The vast majority of BRI countries fall below 50 on a scale of 0 to 100 in their citizens' perception of the cleanliness of their nations' public sectors; the Baltic states, Poland and the UAE are notable exceptions.

brand of Make America Great Again, some balancing or calming would be as welcome and supportive for China and BRI at home and abroad to create more jobs and income all round.

India may be the next to win over with Kashmir and Nepal on one side of some turmoil, and India itself may want to open up some from the domestic side. For all appearances, this is barring Mahathir postponing if not cancelling the HSR between Kuala Lumpur and Singapore. China may ruminate over this as well as affecting BRI to Indonesia and further south. By all appearances, ASEAN is as solidly with the BRI as can be perceived and it is as geopolitically and geoeconomically a lynchpin for China.

Indeed, not many elsewhere can easily ignore the BRI as geographically widespread or China as it stands today. This is one positive conclusion to work on for peace and coprosperity. In particular, small city-state can play its usual role as a hub for connectivity physically and in all services especially on software transfer in managing, training, R&D and among others for smart liveable BRI cities along the way.

In conclusion, on a simplistic scale of 1 to 5, how would we rank the BRI remains to be a question, depending on who one asks and how the answer matters in a holistic integrated and systemic way? Alek Andrew offered one view: "It is not easy to grade the BRI. The 2015 action plan is excellent…So top grade 5 at the outset. But, since then, the lack of transparency and no apparent interest in sharing leadership, my grade is dropping — maybe to 3 and sinking."

It takes two hands to clap, from China as well as from others including ASEAN as a whole or individual members and other tripartite groups of government, business and academia like the APEC and PECC with environmental issues in mind. The hardest part of any project, no less cross-border projects, is implementation. Funding of infrastructure involves the World Bank, ADB and AIIB among others. Naïve as it sounds, politics aside, infrastructure by any name should be beneficial to humanity. The BRI is massively a cross-border project, and no other man-made object is visible like this as confirmed by Apollo 12.[23]

---

[23] See https://www.nasa.gov/vision/space/workinginspace/great_wall.html.

The BRI can equally double for all manners of illegal transactions, as cryptocurrencies[24] are neither legal tenders issued by central banks nor controlled by any institution. Both the scale and dynamics of financial technology (Lee and Low 2018) have immense bearings. The one and only denominator in all forms of BRI, from physical infrastructure to connectivity via finance, technology and people among the others, is trust as the quintessential ingredient for success.

This volume on China's BRI is only one of many, with more to follow. The BRI will take time as it is progressively built and managed with implementation of cross-border efforts. The assumption that China gains and benefits in geoeconomics and geopolitics is an assumption that needs rumination from external partners as well as from stakeholders within its domestic socio-economic politics. Xi Jinping needs to ensure stability at home.

There is just one worrisome aspect after Xi's sweeping crackdown on corruption. The campaign snared over 1.5 million cadres including some highest ranks of those in the party and military. It seems to have resulted in a bureaucracy paralysed by fear with inaction rather than action as in the heady double-digit fast growth to a mature economy naturally slowing down to single digit. If the BRI is to export excess capacity to continue China's growth path, Xi's balancing act at home and abroad is unenviable.

References

Akamatsu, K. (1962). A historical pattern of economic growth in developing countries. *Journal of Developing Economies* 1(1), 3–25.

Arezki, R., Bolton, P., Peters, S., Samama, F. and Stiglitz, J. (2016). From global savings glut to financing infrastructure: The advent of investment plat-

[24] BTC-E was a Russian cryptocurrency exchange which became the platform of choice for criminals because it did not collect identification documents from customers, leading to the infamous 2013 Silk Road widely used online marketplace for drug transactions, other illegal purchases, until it was shut down by US law enforcement agencies in 2017.

forms. IMF Working Paper. Available at: http://www.imf.org/external/pubs/ft/wp/2016/wp1618.pdf.

Chen, E. K. Y. (2018). Economic cooperation and integration in China and the Region. SUSS Talk Series, 4 May 2018.

Huntington, S. P. (1994). The third wave: Democratization in the late twentieth century. *Social and Economic Studies* 43(3), 206–221.

Kubo, K. (ed) (2017). *Dollarization and De-Dollarization in Transitional Economies of Southeast Asia*, IDE-JETRO Series, Palgrave Macmillan.

Lee, D. and Low, L. (2018). *Inclusive FinTech*, World Scientific Publishing Company, Singapore.

McMahon, D. (2018). *China's Great Wall of Debt: Shadow Banks, Ghost Cities, Massive Loans, and the End of the Chinese Miracle*, Houghton Mifflin.

Millward, J. A. (2007). *Eurasian Crossroads: A History of Xinjiang*, Columbia University Press.

Millward, J. A. (2013). *The Silk Road: A Very Short Introduction*, Oxford University Press.

S&P Global Ratings (2018). China's Belt and Road Initiative: Is this the world's largest venture capital project? A report by the China Senior Analyst Group. spglobal.com/ratingsdirect.

Printed in the United States
By Bookmasters